Copyright © 2025 Larry Blake.

All rights reserved.

ISBN
978-1-327-00449-0

Table of Contents

Chapter 1. A Spring Start 1
Chapter 2. Destiny In Disguise 11
Chapter 3. Building Forever 17
Chapter 4. A Home For Our Hearts 30
Chapter 5. The Gift Of Sacrifice 49
Chapter 6. Grace Despite Hard Race 78
Chapter 7. Angels And Fathers 108
Chapter 8. Light In The Storm 123
Chapter 9. Legacy Of Love 135
Chapter 10. To Infinity And Beyond 147
Chapter 11. More Than A Mom 154
Chapter 12. The Silent Strength 162
Chapter 13. Faith Without Limits 169
Chapter 14. When Time Stood Still 178
Chapter 15. Moments That Mattered 201
Chapter 16. The Power Of Presence 213
Chapter 17. Fighting For Forever 225
Chapter 18. Sacred Promises 249
Chapter 19. Endings And Eternity 261
Chapter 20. Through It All 271
Chapter 21. A Mother's Way 287
Chapter 22. Hope In Her Eyes 314
Chapter 23. Tiffany's Touch 332
Chapter 24. Forever Starts Now 371

To my eternal partner,
my soulmate — Tiffany.

To our children: Patrick, Rylee, and Brennan
— the greatest gifts of our love.

To Vicki, Pat, and Julie, thank you for sharing her with me.

And to all those lucky enough to have had her in your life
— she truly loved you.

I will love you forever, Tiff.

CHAPTER 1.
A Spring Start

Tiffany was born on a warm spring morning, May 17, 1980, in a quiet suburban town nestled along the shimmering shores of Lake Michigan, just a short drive south of Chicago. The town, modest in size and rich with charm, had tree-lined streets and a certain stillness to it, the kind of place where neighbors waved from their porches and children rode bikes until dusk. It was here, in that peaceful stretch between the lake and the city, that Tiffany first opened her eyes to the world—a world that, though it didn't yet know it, had just been given something incredibly special.

From the moment she arrived, there was something different about Tiffany. Her mother, Vicki, a schoolteacher with a gentle but determined spirit, swore she could see the spark in her newborn daughter's eyes before she even took her first breath. Her father, Pat, a firefighter, believed she had inherited his courage and her mother's wisdom. Together, they raised her in a home filled with warmth, purpose, and unshakable love.

She grew up under a roof where values weren't just taught; they were lived. Sunday mornings meant pancakes and cartoons, followed by long drives to the lake. Holidays were loud and joyous, often filled with extended family crammed into small rooms with big hearts. Her older sister, Amanda, was her first role model—four years her senior and already a master of grace and confidence. Tiffany admired her in the way only a little sister can—part admiration, part mimicry, all love.

It was during those early years that Tiffany's story began to take shape—not in the dramatic sense, not yet. Rather, in the subtle ways that most great lives begin. In the way she cared for others with sincerity far beyond her years. In the stories she would write late at night with a pencil and a spiral notebook. In the way she lit up any room she walked into, not because she tried to, but because she simply couldn't help it.

Many of her most treasured childhood memories were made at her Aunt Sandy and Uncle Scott's lake house—a place of magic where laughter echoed off the water and cousins ran wild through the sand and sunshine. It was there, with the wind in her hair and her feet in the water, that Tiffany fell in love with the beach. The waves didn't just calm her; they connected with something inside her, something deep and spiritual. The rhythm of the water became a rhythm of her life: constant, cleansing, and eternal.

When she was just nine years old, Tiffany sat down to write her first book. She titled it "When Sandy and Tiff Went to Florida." It was a simple tale of a trip filled with sunshine and smiles, but what it represented was much more—a glimpse into the heart of a young girl whose imagination was limitless and whose love for her family spilled over onto every page. Only one copy was ever made. Today, it sits on a bookshelf in her husband's office, aged and fragile but treasured above all else. He calls it his favorite book, not because of its prose, but because of the girl who wrote it.

Even then, Tiffany was already dreaming of motherhood. She used to cradle her younger cousins—Scotty, Ryan, Christian, Nathan—as if they were her own children. She played house, not to pretend but to prepare. Her nurturing spirit wasn't a skill she developed later in life; it was woven into her DNA from the start. Her love for others, her instinct to care, her ability to lift people up—it wasn't taught. It was born into her.

Tiffany loved with a kind of fearlessness rarely seen in this world. She gave her heart freely, never guarding it, never hesitating. She didn't love halfway. She dove in headfirst, arms wide open. And if that love was ever returned, even a fraction of what she gave, she would hold on forever. It wasn't in her nature to give up on people.

On the outside, Tiffany could seem quiet, even reserved. She was never the loudest in the room, rarely the center of attention. But those who knew her—really knew—understood that beneath that calm exterior was a roaring fire. A light that glowed bright and warm, illuminating everyone lucky enough to stand in its path. She didn't need to demand attention to be remembered. Her kindness, her presence, and her very soul was unforgettable.

She had a way of making people feel seen. Not just noticed—but truly seen. It was as if she looked directly into people's hearts, bypassing the noise and getting to the truth of who they were. She made you feel special. Like you mattered. And she did it effortlessly.

Tiffany was, simply put, a rare soul. The kind you meet once in a lifetime—if you're lucky. The kind of person who leaves fingerprints on every heart she touches, whose memory lingers in a room long after she's left it. Her spirit, full of grace and strength, lit a path for others to follow. And once you met her, you were never quite the same.

This is where Tiffany's story begins. In the small town by the lake, in the arms of a loving family, in the laughter of beach days and the pages of a homemade book. It is a story of light, of imagination, of kindness—and, above all, of love. And though it started quietly, it would become a life that echoed in the hearts of everyone she met.

A life that mattered. A life that inspired. A life that, even now, continues to shine.

It was the fall of 1992 when Tiffany met the girl who would forever change her life. They were just twelve years old, sitting across from one another in a middle school classroom filled with the chaotic energy of first-day jitters, whispers of summer now past, and the shuffling of paper and pencils. There was something magnetic about Holly from the very beginning—her confidence, her smile, the way she seemed completely comfortable in her own skin. Tiffany, ever observant, ever quietly intuitive, noticed it immediately. Within minutes, the two exchanged glances, a spark of recognition passed between them, and in that quiet, effortless way that only happens in childhood, they became inseparable.

From that day forward, Tiffany and Holly built a friendship that would not only stand the test of time—it would shape their lives. They became each other's mirrors, sounding boards, co-conspirators, and confidantes. Wherever one was, the other was not far behind. They shared sleepovers, secrets, hairbrushes, and heartbreaks. They whispered dreams into the darkness during late-night phone calls and pinky-promised their way through the trials of adolescence.

But even the truest friendships are not without their stumbles, and their first real adventure together nearly ended in disaster. Tiffany had walked to Holly's house after school, and the two hatched a plan to walk four miles to the local Burger King. Tiffany knew—without a doubt—that her mother, Vicki, would have never agreed to it. The plan was reckless, exciting, and absolutely typical for twelve-year-olds longing to taste a sliver of freedom.

Holly's mother, Diana, either missed the finer details or trusted the girls a bit too much that day. But the truth was, burgers were never really the goal. Their actual destination was a nearby park where, rumor had it, a boy they both liked—Dan—might be hanging out. It was innocent in its intent but daring in its execution. And as the sun dipped low and the dinner hour came and went, panic set in back home.

Holly's older brother, Larry—twenty-two at the time—got into his car and drove through the neighborhood, scanning the streets, worried and determined. Vicki and Diana were doing the same, their motherly instincts laced with growing fear. The girls were eventually found, safe but wide-eyed, and Tiffany was immediately grounded. She didn't argue; she knew she'd crossed a line. But what she didn't realize then, what no one realized, is that the day had unfolded exactly the way it was supposed to. Not because of Dan, the boy they had risked it all to see. But because of Larry, the quiet, watchful older brother who was out driving around that day, worried, protective… and completely unaware that he had just crossed paths with the girl who would one day become his wife.

FOREVER TIFFANY

Dan faded into memory. Larry, unknowingly, became destiny.

In those early years, Tiffany already showed a remarkable sense of self-awareness. She knew how to step back so others could shine, even if it meant dimming her own light. When Holly liked Dan, Tiffany didn't compete. She chose friendship over flirtation, loyalty over desire. That moment would define the kind of person she was—a girl who loved with her whole heart and who believed deeply in the people around her. She never needed to be the loudest in the room to be heard or the brightest star to feel important. She found joy in cheering for others.

In middle school, Tiffany was a cheerleader—not for the title or the uniform, but for the simple joy of lifting others up. She had a full circle of friends who adored her, but she never craved attention. Popular, yes. But never flashy. She was that rare kind of girl who could sit quietly in the back of the room and somehow still make it feel like she was the center of everything good.

She maintained a solid B average through school, not because she couldn't do more, but because she was never chasing accolades. Her parents encouraged her, gently nudging her to go further, to reach for the heights they knew she was capable of. And Tiffany believed she could, too. But she also believed that sometimes, the beauty of life wasn't found in pushing to outshine others—it was in learning to love the life you lived exactly as you lived it.

She didn't chase trophies or titles. She didn't need to outdo anyone, least of all her sister.

Amanda was the golden child in many ways. She had the brain of a valedictorian, the grace of an athlete, and the drive of a champion. She was crowned an Indiana State Champion in gymnastics and graduated at the top of her class, just like their mother had before her. And Tiffany admired her with a heart so big, it couldn't possibly compete. Instead of jealousy, she felt pride. Instead of rivalry, she chose reverence.

She had the same path available to her, paved by her parents' love and support, but Tiffany's footsteps wandered in softer ways. She stayed in the shadows—not because she had to, but because it's where she could see everyone else more clearly. Her love for her sister was absolute. There may have been moments—quiet ones, unspoken ones—where Tiffany wondered if she could ever outshine Amanda. But the truth was, she never wanted to. She wasn't built to climb over others to get to the top. She was built to build bridges.

That selflessness, that humble grace—it became her superpower.

She learned to lead without shouting, to guide without pushing, and to love without limits. And as she and Holly grew into young women, their friendship deepened with those same values. Through school, through heartbreak, through loss and laughter—they never left each other's side.

Tiffany didn't just believe in love. She was love. The kind you don't see coming. The kind you don't forget. The kind that shapes your world and changes the way you see people forever.

And that, too, began in a middle school classroom. With a glance. A shared smile. A walk to Burger King. And a friendship that would grow into something sacred. Something rare. Something eternal.

This is how Tiffany's story unfolded—not in grand entrances or loud declarations, but in the quiet moments. In the choice to put others first. In the courage to love without fear. And in the grace of a friendship that would carry her through the most beautiful and the most difficult seasons of her life.

The summer of 1998 settled in with the kind of golden warmth that wraps itself around memory. Tiffany stood on the edge of everything—freshly eighteen, with a high school diploma in hand, her future a wide open road of possibility and promise. The world seemed both inviting and overwhelming, as it does for all young women standing at that peculiar intersection between childhood and adulthood. She could go anywhere and do anything. But with all the options spread out before her like stars in the night sky, Tiffany—ever thoughtful, ever cautious—didn't rush her decision.

Thankfully, she didn't have to face it alone. She had Holly.

Holly had always been her compass, the best friend who had walked beside her since the age of twelve. While Tiffany tended to move quietly through life, Holly charged forward with a determined light in her eyes. They were different, but they complemented each other in a way only best friends could. Holly had earned her way into prestigious universities and Ivy League schools that practically begged her to attend, but she turned down those offers in favor of something closer to home—a school filled with sentimental ties and generational memories.

The state university Holly chose was more than just a campus. It was where her brother, Larry, had once been a college baseball standout. It was where her father now coached the men's basketball team. The place was woven into her family's story like a thread through the fabric. Tiffany, inspired by Holly's grounded decision, followed suit. Not because she lacked her own direction but because sometimes home isn't a place—it's a person. And Holly was home.

Meanwhile, Larry's world was shifting beneath his feet. Having married young in November of 1995, he was now quietly navigating the unraveling of a marriage that had arrived too soon, too fast. By the summer of 1998, Larry found himself in limbo—between what was and what might be. He spent his evenings back on familiar turf, helping out with the university's baseball team, walking the same diamond he'd once dominated. When he wasn't on the field, he was courtside, supporting his father's basketball team, sometimes joining them for road games. It gave him purpose. It gave him peace.

In December, the team traveled to Indianapolis for a holiday tournament, a trip that set the stage for fate to pull a few strings.

Holly and her boyfriend, Steve, were planning to drive down and cheer on her father's team. But when Steve had to leave early, she needed a ride home. She asked Larry if he could drive her back, but Tiffany had another idea.

Tiffany had just been gifted a new car by her parents—a bright red, two-door Ford Escort, gleaming and proud like a symbol of her newly minted adulthood. She offered to take Larry instead, a simple offer made without fanfare, just kindness. What neither of them knew was that this ride would become a turning point.

Larry slid into the passenger seat, expecting a quiet drive. What he got instead was a magnetic pull, the kind that only happens once or twice in a lifetime. The car might've been moving forward, but time stood still. For three hours, the road beneath them disappeared, and in its place was easy conversation, shared laughter, and a connection so natural it felt like catching up with someone he had known forever.

It was the second time their lives had truly intersected. And yet, in those few hours, Larry knew something had shifted. He felt it. And quietly, he hoped their paths would cross again.

Once in Indianapolis, the girls dove into the excitement of the tournament—laughing with players, cheering from the stands, soaking in every moment of college life. During one of those nights, Tiffany met a young freshman guard. He was tall, athletic, and charming in that fresh-faced way that only 18-year-old athletes can be. He swept her off her feet with ease.

It wasn't a fling. It wasn't a crush. It was young love—the kind that makes your heart race and your world narrow to the space between two people. Tiffany was spellbound. She gave herself to it completely, believing this boy was her forever.

And while Tiffany's heart chased love, Larry—now single—was living his own version of young adulthood. He dove headfirst into the freedom he'd never really known. His weekends were filled with road trips, laughter, and late-night memories made with his closest friends. It wasn't aimless—it was healing. It was joy. He was building a type that was not defined by mistakes or missed chances.

FOREVER TIFFANY

Then came the fall of 1999.

Tiffany was still in love with the basketball player, dreaming of their futures and talking about someday. But life had other plans. When she discovered she was pregnant, she didn't panic. She didn't cry. She smiled. This, she thought, was what she was made for. Tiffany had always known she wanted to be a mother. She embraced the news with a calm, radiant strength that belied her age. But the boy she loved didn't feel the same. He left.

It was heartbreaking. But Tiffany, true to her spirit, didn't break. She lifted herself, her dreams, and her baby forward, step by steady step. She chose love over regret. Hope over shame. On July 14, 2000, she gave birth to Patrick, a baby boy with wide eyes and a heart full of life. He became her sun, her anchor, her reason for everything.

Larry hadn't seen Tiffany since that drive to Indianapolis eighteen months earlier. But on the night of Patrick's birth, something stirred inside him—a whisper in the wind, a pull on the heart he couldn't ignore. As he drove home from work, the name "Tiffany" echoed in his mind. So he called.

The timing stunned her.

She picked up the phone, her arms wrapped around a newborn, and her voice soft with surprise. She hadn't heard from Larry in over a year. He didn't know about the breakup. He didn't know she had just become a mother. But he knew something had led him to call.

The conversation wasn't long, but it didn't need to be. The connection was there again, steady and unshakable. As Larry hung up, he felt compelled to do something—something bigger than a phone call. He drove to a local baby store and wandered the aisles aimlessly, letting instinct guide him. He filled a cart with blankets, shoes, baby clothes, and tiny socks. Things he didn't know much about but knew she might need. It wasn't logical. It wasn't planned. It was just... right.

He didn't know it yet, but this was his first act of love. Not the fireworks kind, not the movie kind—but the real kind. The quiet kind that builds over time, that sees people as they are and embraces them fully.

This was the beginning of something bigger than either of them understood at the time. It was the moment the threads of their separate stories began to weave together. A story of resilience. A story of love. A story that was only just beginning.

CHAPTER 2.
Destiny in Disguise

After filling his shopping cart with baby clothes, Larry didn't think much about Tiffany or Patrick in the days that followed. Life carried on as usual—weekends spent with friends, late nights, and more partying than he probably should have been doing. He was living in the moment, not realizing that his life was on the brink of something profound.

Then came the night of August 12, 2000. It was a warm summer evening, and Larry had been out with friends. When he pulled into his driveway, he sat in his new Corvette, overwhelmed with a sudden wave of emotion. Without warning, tears came, and he found himself praying. He pleaded with God to help him change—to introduce him to someone who would be his best friend, his wife, his partner in life, and someone his family would love as much as he did.

Larry had grown up in a home filled with love. His parents shared a deep, unshakable bond, the kind of love that lasts a lifetime. It was the kind of love he wanted for himself. In that moment, with his heart laid bare, he spoke aloud, "God, I know you answer prayers in your time, but if you could put a rush on this one, I'd really appreciate it."

With that, he went inside and passed out around 4:30 a.m.

Larry was raised in the Church of Jesus Christ of Latter-day Saints (Mormon), but he hadn't attended services in years. So, when, at 6:30 a.m., just a few hours after his desperate prayer, he heard a clear voice—just as real as if someone were speaking through a television or radio—say, "Go see your mother at church today," he was stunned.

Without questioning it, without even connecting it to the prayer he had just spoken hours earlier, Larry slowly got out of bed. He didn't need to call his mom to ask if she would be there; he already knew where she and his father would be sitting. He made the fifty-minute drive, arriving about fifteen minutes late.

When he walked in, something felt different. His father, usually seated next to his mother, was sitting along the wall side of the pew—a rare sight. His mother sat in the center. But it was the woman sitting on the aisle that stopped him in his tracks.

There, holding a tiny four-week-old baby boy, was Tiffany—the same beautiful blonde he had shared a car ride with to Indianapolis eighteen months earlier. She wasn't Mormon; she had grown up Southern Baptist. Holly wasn't with her, so why was she there?

After the service, they all went back to Larry's parents' home, where they spent the afternoon together, enjoying Sunday lunch and watching sports on TV.

At one point, Tiffany changed into a pair of Tommy Hilfiger jeans and an orange top. She moved across the room, stepping over Larry, who was lying on the floor watching TV. When he looked up at her, something clicked deep inside him.

Tiffany stood just 5 feet 4 inches tall, her petite frame barely tipping the scales at 100 pounds. But what she lacked in size, she more than made up for in presence. She had flowing blonde hair that cascaded softly over her shoulders and the most captivating blue eyes—eyes that sparkled with mischief, kindness, and wisdom far beyond her years.

She was delicate, almost ethereal, but Tiffany was mighty. There was a strength within her, a quiet power that didn't need to be announced. It was just there, in her every word, every gesture, every smile. She was fierce in her love, unyielding in her loyalty, and steadfast in her faith.

From the moment Larry first laid eyes on her, she had his full attention. And she knew it. Tiffany was smart and perceptive. She understood the effect she had on him, how his heart raced whenever she was near, and how his eyes followed her every move.

FOREVER TIFFANY

She would claim for years that the moment she stepped over him at his parents' house was unintentional—that she didn't even realize he was lying there watching TV. But deep down, she knew. She had felt his gaze, felt the connection that sparked between them.

The truth was, she saw in Larry what he saw in her—a forever love. From the very beginning, she knew that he was her soulmate, her partner, her everything. They were drawn to each other by something bigger than themselves, something unexplainable yet undeniable.

Tiffany's beauty went beyond her delicate features and captivating eyes. It radiated from within, shining through her laughter, her kindness, and her love. She was breathtaking, not just because of how she looked but because of who she was.

She was Larry's light, his angel, his heart. And from the moment she stepped over him that day, she was his forever, and, in that moment, he knew he had to ask her out.

Friday, August 17, 2000—the day Larry had been anticipating all week and, if he were honest, his entire life. He picked Tiffany up and took her to a Mexican restaurant in Merrillville, Indiana. From the moment they sat down, time seemed to fly by. Hours felt like seconds. Conversation flowed effortlessly, laughter echoed, and Larry found himself wishing the night would never end.

Before their date, Larry's mom, Diana, had pulled him aside and given him a warning that stuck with him. "If you think you're going to just take her out and try to sleep with her, think again. She's not that way. She's only been with one other person. And if you do sleep with her and break her heart, don't come back here. You won't be welcome."

Even now, Larry isn't sure if his mom was serious about that last part, but the message was clear—Tiffany meant a great deal to his family. She was already one of them. With his mom's words in mind, Larry didn't even consider trying to kiss Tiffany at the end of the date.

He respected her too much, and the last thing he wanted was to hurt her or face his mother's wrath.

Their second date took them to New Buffalo, Michigan, where they enjoyed a beautiful Italian dinner followed by ice cream at Oinks. It was one of those perfect nights that you wish you could bottle up and keep forever. It was also the night they shared a memory that would make them laugh for years to come.

After dinner, Larry's stomach started to feel uncomfortable, and he realized he needed to, well... take that trapped wind out. He tried to ignore it, but it was getting worse. As they left Oinks, Larry opened the car door for Tiffany, ran around the back of the car, jumped in the driver's seat, and, forgetting she was even there, let out the loudest fart imaginable.

Mortified, Larry's face turned bright red. He couldn't believe it. How could he let that happen? But before he could even apologize, he looked over and saw Tiffany laughing, really laughing. Her shoulders shook, her face lit up, and she was laughing so hard she could barely breathe.

At that moment, Larry realized something incredible. It was as if they had known each other their entire lives. She wasn't just laughing at his embarrassing moment; she was laughing with him, making it one of the most memorable and elated moments of his life.

It was only their second date, but Larry already knew he never wanted to let her go.

Their relationship was in full swing, moving at a pace neither of them had anticipated. By October of 2000, Larry and Tiffany had made the decision to move in together, renting a new apartment and beginning a life that neither of them could have foreseen.

Moving day was emotional, especially for Tiffany's mom, Vicki. As Larry and his friends helped pack up Tiffany's things, Vicki couldn't hold back her tears. Her twenty-year-old daughter was moving in with a man ten years her senior, and baby Patrick was just three months old. It was a lot to take in, and her heart was understandably heavy.

Larry could see her pain, but he knew that no words would ease her worries. Instead, he quietly made a promise to himself that he would prove to both Vicki and Tiffany's father, Pat, just how deeply he cared for Tiffany and Patrick. He knew it would take time, but he was determined to earn their trust and love.

Soon after moving in, Larry decided to surprise Tiffany with a home-cooked meal. He called her at work and proudly announced that dinner would be ready, and he was waiting for her when she got home. When Tiffany walked through the door, she was greeted by the delicious aroma of roasted chicken. Larry was pulling the beautifully browned bird out of the oven; the table was set perfectly, and all the sides were arranged just right. Tiffany was genuinely impressed.

They sat down together and shared stories about their day, laughing and connecting over the meal. As dinner wound down, Tiffany offered to clean up. As she opened the trash can, she found the evidence—a pile of empty containers from the local grocery store. She turned to Larry, who instantly knew he was busted.

A grin broke across her face, followed by that infectious laugh that Larry loved so much. She walked over, wrapped her arms around him, and said, "It's the thought that counts." She wasn't upset; she was touched. Larry hadn't lied—he had genuinely wanted to make her happy, and she saw his intentions behind the pre-made meal.

That was Tiffany. She never expected grand gestures, just love and respect. It was her kindness and understanding that made Larry fall even more in love with her. In that small, humorous moment, they took another step closer to the life they were building together.

Their apartment was cozy and comfortable, but Patrick was growing fast, already babbling his first words. Larry knew that before long, "Dad" would be among them, and when that day came, he wanted to be ready. He wanted to raise Patrick the right way—the way his own father had raised him. With that in mind, Larry dreamed of giving Patrick the best life he and Tiffany could provide.

He shared his thoughts with Tiffany, and together, they began the search for a new home. They visited countless houses, exploring neighborhoods and envisioning their future. After weeks of searching, they found it—the perfect place to grow their relationship and family.

It was a newly constructed brick ranch with charm and character. The backyard was spacious and inviting, anchored by a majestic, sprawling tree that offered shade on warm summer days. The patio stretched the entire length of the house, creating a beautiful outdoor space for family gatherings and peaceful evenings.

The location was ideal, nestled near the local high school, close to shopping, and just a few short miles from the sandy shores of Lake Michigan—a place that held so many special memories for both of them. It was the perfect blend of convenience and tranquility, a place where they could build a life filled with love, laughter, and endless possibilities.

Standing in the backyard, watching the sunlight filter through the branches of that old tree, Larry knew they had found more than just a house. They had found a home—a place where Patrick would take his first steps, where their family would grow, and where their love story would continue and endure.

CHAPTER 3.
Building Forever

Their new home was everything they had dreamed of. The kitchen was spacious and bright, perfect for cooking meals together and gathering around the table. The family room was vast, with vaulted ceilings that stretched high above, adorned with dual ceiling fans that kept the air cool and comfortable. Patrick's room was cozy yet grand, highlighted by a large half-moon window that flooded the space with sunlight. The master bedroom was a sanctuary of its own, complete with French doors that opened onto the patio, where they had installed a brand-new hot tub.

Life was perfect.

It was June of 2001. By now, their little family had settled into the rhythm of their new home, and things were falling beautifully into place. But one thing was about to change.

Larry still had his Corvette—the same car he had prayed in on that warm summer night when he asked God to bring Tiffany into his life. He cherished that car, a symbol of freedom and success. It was the car he had worked hard for, the car he loved. But Tiffany brought up an idea that he never saw coming.

"Why don't we trade in my two-door sports car and your Corvette for a new minivan?" she suggested one evening, her blue eyes sparkling with excitement.

Larry's jaw dropped. A minivan? He could hardly believe what he was hearing. More than that, he couldn't believe he was even considering it. This was the Corvette he had dreamed of, the car he adored. But when he looked at Tiffany—at the woman who had made his heart feel more alive than that car ever could; he knew what he had to do.

They went to the dealership together, holding hands as they walked the lot. After browsing the rows of vehicles, they chose a brand-new minivan, perfect for their growing family. When the time came to turn over the keys to the Corvette, Larry felt a pang in his chest. He stood there for a moment, running his fingers over the steering wheel one last time, and felt a tear slip from his eye. Was it a tear of sadness or joy? Perhaps it was a bit of both.

Sacrifice is never easy, but love has a way of making it worthwhile. As they drove away in the minivan, Tiffany's smile was radiant, her joy contagious. Larry looked at her, his heart swelling with happiness. He realized that giving up the car didn't feel like a loss at all. In fact, it felt like a gain, another step forward in their love story.

They were building a life together, a family, a future. And while Larry had let go of his prized Corvette, he knew he had gained so much more. With Tiffany beside him and Patrick in the backseat, the road ahead looked brighter than ever.

September 8, 2001. Larry decided to spend the evening with his good friend, Esteban. They started the night at a local high school football game and eventually made their way to a nearby bar to throw darts and have a drink. After one beer, they decided to check out another spot. There, they ran into their friend Eric L., who joined them as the night moved forward.

As the hours slipped by, Larry didn't think much about the fact that he was out late while everything that truly mattered—Tiffany and one-year-old Patrick—were at home. Maybe he was trying to relive the freedom he had willingly given up a year earlier. Maybe he wasn't thinking at all.

They wrapped up the bar, agreeing to one more drink at Esteban's before calling it quits. Eric offered to drive Esteban's Mustang, with Esteban in the passenger seat and Larry crammed into the tiny back seat behind him. It was just a short drive, and Larry had left his car at Esteban's house, so he didn't see the harm. What he didn't realize was that Eric had been drinking more than he let on.

FOREVER TIFFANY

As they sped down the dark streets, Esteban dozed off in the front seat. Larry watched from the back as Eric's head started to nod, his eyes growing heavy. In a horrifying instant, Eric fell asleep behind the wheel. Larry yelled, shaking Eric desperately, but… it was too late.

The Mustang flew through a three-way stop, barreled up a driveway, crossed the yard of a quiet suburban home, and crashed head-on into an enormous oak tree, easily sixty feet tall. The force of the impact shattered the car, and for a moment, everything went silent.

Dust hung in the air as Larry tried to move, but his body wouldn't respond. He instinctively tried to push himself out of the back seat using his left arm, but it wouldn't work. Looking down, he realized his humerus was completely snapped, broken clean through. His arm dangled uselessly, unattached.

He tucked his injured arm into his pants and used his right arm to crawl out of the wreckage. Outside, he saw Eric slumped against the base of the massive tree, dazed but conscious. The car was destroyed, crumpled like a tin can, and Esteban was nowhere to be seen.

The flashing lights of an ambulance illuminated the scene as Larry was rushed to the hospital. In the emergency room, while doctors ran tests and set his broken arm, they handed him a phone and told him to call Tiffany. It was 2:30 a.m.

"I'm okay," he told her, trying to sound calm. "I'm at the ER, but I'm alive. I'll be home soon." He hadn't even thought about how he would get home. He hadn't thought about much at all.

Less than twenty minutes later, Tiffany was standing by his hospital bed, holding Patrick in her arms. Her face was calm, her eyes full of love and relief. At that moment, Larry broke down. He looked at Patrick, at his son who needed him, and he realized just how close he had come to losing it all.

Why had he left them at home to stay out so late? What was he trying to prove? A few beers and a couple of laughs—sure, but until 2:30 in the morning? The guilt rushed over him. He knew he had been selfish, putting his own desires before the family he had vowed to protect.

Was Tiffany angry? Maybe. But she never showed it. Instead, she wrapped her arms around him, kissed him softly, and whispered, "I'm just glad you're okay."

In that moment, Larry realized how lucky he truly was. Not just to be alive but to have someone like Tiffany by his side—someone whose love was unconditional, whose heart was big enough to forgive, and whose faith in him never wavered.

Larry returned home early on Saturday morning, September 9th, after spending a long, exhausting night in the emergency room. He was tired, weak, and convinced that everything was fine.

But as the day went on, Tiffany watched him closely, her heart growing heavy, her fears growing stronger.

He was struggling to breathe, his chest rising and falling unevenly, his breaths shallow and labored. His face was pale, his body weak, his eyes weary.

By nightfall, his temperature was rising, his skin burning hot, and his strength fading fast.

Tiffany knew something was seriously wrong.

She pleaded with him to go back to the hospital, her voice trembling, her eyes wide with worry.

But Larry was stubborn, his pride refusing to admit defeat, his fear refusing to face the truth. He insisted he was fine, insisted it was just exhaustion, and insisted he just needed rest.

But Tiffany knew better. She always did.

She didn't argue, didn't push, didn't fight. She just picked up the phone and called Larry's mother.

FOREVER TIFFANY

If Larry hadn't listened to her, maybe he would have listened to the one woman he respected more than anyone in the world—his mom.

She explained the situation, her voice steady, her heart racing. She told her everything—the fever, the labored breathing, the way he was fading right in front of her eyes.

Larry's mother didn't hesitate. She was out the door before Tiffany even hung up the phone.

When she arrived, she looked at her son, her face heavy with worry, her eyes full of love.

She didn't raise her voice, didn't argue, didn't beg. She just looked at him, her hand on his shoulder, her voice soft but firm. "Please," she whispered, her eyes misting, her love overwhelming. "For me. Just go back and let them check you. Please."

Larry looked into his mother's eyes, his heart breaking, his fear rising. He couldn't say no to her. He never could.

He reluctantly agreed, his pride crumbling, his fear winning. He let Tiffany help him to the car, let his mom sit by his side, and let them take him back to the hospital.

Tests were carried out, scans were taken, and doctors moved quickly, urgently, cautiously.

The news was worse than they could have imagined.

Larry had a partially collapsed lung, his body struggling to get enough oxygen, his breaths short and labored. His heart was swollen, working overtime, fighting to keep him alive.

It was serious, dangerous, life-threatening.

Larry was admitted to the hospital, hooked up to machines, wires, and monitors. He was weak, exhausted, defeated.

But Tiffany never left his side.

She was right there, by his bed, holding his hand, rubbing his forehead, whispering words of encouragement.

She never said, "I told you so." She never scolded him, never reminded him that he was wrong. She didn't have to. He could see it in her eyes, in the way she looked at him, in the way her tears fell.

She loved him fiercely, beautifully, completely. She was terrified of losing him, heartbroken by his suffering, shattered by his pain.

And he knew he had made a mistake. He knew he should have listened to her, trusted her, believed her. He knew she was right. She was always right.

But Tiffany didn't care about being right. She cared about him, about his life, about his heart. She spent every day by his side, bringing him food, fluffing his pillows, and adjusting his blankets. She read to him, laughed with him, and kept his spirits high.

She was his light, his hope, his love. When he was scared, she held his hand. When he was sad, she wiped his tears. When he was in pain, she stayed strong. She was his angel, his guide, his rock.

Larry watched her, his heart swelling, his eyes tearful. He was in awe of her strength, her love, her devotion.

He was grateful, humbled, blessed. He loved her more than words could say, more than his heart could hold, more than life itself.

She never left his side, never stopped loving him, never gave up hope. She was the reason he kept fighting, the reason he kept breathing, the reason he kept living. She was his everything.

And as he looked into her eyes, his heart full of love, his soul full of gratitude, he made a promise to himself.

He would never take her for granted again.

He would never ignore her again.

He would never make that mistake again.

Because he needed her.

He always did.

He always would.

It was the fall of 2002, and Larry and Tiffany had just completed their first year in their new home. Life was good—Tiffany was thriving in her career, and Larry was doing well in his. Everything seemed perfect.

One evening, as they were relaxing at home, Larry overheard Tiffany talking on the phone with her mom. He could hear her laugh softly before she turned to him and asked, "My mom wants to know when you're going to marry me."

Without missing a beat, Larry replied, "As soon as you can book a venue and have it planned."

He already knew the answer. He had known from the moment he saw her in church, holding baby Patrick. From that first day, it was as if they had known each other for a thousand lifetimes. It felt familiar, destined even, like they had been together long before this life. Getting married wasn't just the next step; it was inevitable.

They chose February 15, 2003, as their wedding day—a date that seemed perfect, just one day after Valentine's Day. They were excited, but even more than that, they were at peace. It just felt right.

But the night before the wedding, things took an unexpected turn. On Friday, February 14th, Patrick fell ill. Concerned, Larry and Tiffany rushed him to the emergency room, where they spent most of the night at his bedside. Their minds were consumed with worry for their little boy, and thoughts of the wedding seemed distant and unimportant. It wasn't until 3:00 a.m. on the morning of the 15th that they finally left the hospital.

Tiffany caught a few hours of sleep before racing over to the wedding venue to get ready. A heavy snowstorm had blanketed the ground, and several guests were unable to attend. Even so, around 125 friends and family gathered to celebrate their union.

Larry dressed in his suit, with Patrick by his side. The little boy still didn't feel well and clung to his father, refusing to leave him. Larry held him close, his heart full as they made their way to the altar.

Standing there with his best man, Esteban, and his brothers-in-law, Steve and Bob, Larry felt his emotions rising as he saw Tiffany step into view.

She was walking down the aisle, arm in arm with her father, looking every bit like an angel sent from heaven. Her dress flowed around her, her blonde hair perfectly curled, her eyes sparkling with joy and love. Larry's vision blurred as tears filled his eyes.

How was it possible that this beautiful, incredible woman loved him? How could she be real? She looked so perfect, so radiant, that for a moment, he wondered if she really was an angel, sent just for him.

As Tiffany reached him at the altar, Larry held Patrick close, feeling the warmth and love radiate between them. They exchanged their vows with raw emotion, their voices trembling as they promised forever. It wasn't just words—it was a sacred bond, a promise that went beyond this life.

After the ceremony, they danced the night away, surrounded by loved ones. They laughed, they cried, and they celebrated the love that had brought them together.

The next day, exhausted but blissfully happy, they headed to Chicago for a long weekend honeymoon. They stayed in a beautiful hotel, spending most of their time curled up in bed, just holding each other, talking about their dreams and their future. They dined at elegant restaurants, visited the museum, and walked through the bustling city streets, hand in hand.

FOREVER TIFFANY

But mostly, they cherished the quiet moments, the stolen kisses, the whispered "I love yous." It was the start of their forever, the beginning of a life that they would build side by side.

In those first few days as husband and wife, Larry felt a sense of peace he had never known before. Looking into Tiffany's eyes, he believed—truly believed—that she was his angel. And for the rest of his life, he would never stop feeling that way.

June 10, 2003—a day that would forever be stamped in Larry's heart. It was the day he legally became Patrick's father.

They arrived at the courthouse in Valparaiso, Indiana, surrounded by family who had come to witness this special moment. As they walked through the doors, Larry's heart raced with excitement. His mind was flooded with memories of Patrick's first steps, his first words, and all the quiet moments they had shared—moments that made him feel like a father long before this day.

Larry's birthday was just two weeks away, and Patrick's was a month after that. But nothing could top this. This was the best gift he could have ever received.

They walked into the courtroom, hands clasped tightly together. Tiffany was by his side, her eyes shining with love and pride. Patrick held Larry's hand, looking up at him with those big, trusting eyes. In that gaze, Larry saw his entire world.

The judge spoke the words that made it official, words that Larry had longed to hear. But in his heart, Larry didn't need a legal document to tell him what he already knew—he was Patrick's father. He always had been.

Water filled his eyes as he looked around the courtroom. There wasn't a dry eye in the room. Their family stood in quiet reverence, emotion radiating from every corner. Tiffany wiped a tear from her cheek, her smile as bright as the sun.

This wasn't just a legal process; it was a moment of truth, a confirmation of the love that had already bonded them. It was the final step that made their family whole, the moment that locked it all into place.

As they walked out of the courthouse, the sun shining brightly above, Larry lifted Patrick into his arms, holding him close. "I love you, son," he whispered, his voice trembling with emotion. Patrick wrapped his little arms around Larry's neck and held on tight.

At that moment, Larry knew that life had given him a gift more precious than anything he could have ever imagined. The title of "Dad."

For the rest of his days, he would carry that title with honor, with pride, and with a love that could never be broken.

Larry and Tiffany had taken their first vacation together in the fall of 2000, attending the Bridge Day Festival in West Virginia. They rented a cozy cabin nestled in a state park, surrounded by the beauty of the mountains. Patrick was just an infant then, but it was a peaceful, joyful trip—a quiet beginning to the many adventures they would have as a family.

Now it was the summer of 2003 – September, and it was time for their first big family vacation, one filled with excitement and magic. They packed their bags, loaded up the minivan, and headed for the airport to set off for Disney World in Orlando, Florida. Patrick, now an energetic toddler, was beyond thrilled, and Larry and Tiffany couldn't wait to see the joy on his face as he met his favorite characters and explored the parks.

But to fully understand the significance of this trip, it's important to back up a few weeks.

Larry was on his way home from a work conference in St. Louis, driving along the interstate, thinking about getting home to his family. His phone rang, and Tiffany's voice came through the line, cheerful and sweet. "When are you going to be home, Dad?" she asked playfully.

The word caught Larry off guard. "Dad?" he repeated, confused. It wasn't like Tiffany to call him that. But there was something in her voice—a ring of excitement, a playful tone he hadn't heard before.

"What's with the 'Dad' stuff?" he asked, laughing.

There was a brief pause before Tiffany blurted out, "We're having a baby!"

Larry's heart stopped. For a split second, the world seemed to stand still. His hands gripped the steering wheel as his mind raced. "We're having a baby?" he repeated, almost in disbelief.

"We're having a baby!" Tiffany said again, her voice bursting with joy.

Larry felt a wave of emotions—excitement, shock, joy, and a touch of panic. Was he ready? Could they do this again? But then he thought about Tiffany, about Patrick, and about the growing family he loved so much. The fear melted away, replaced by a sense of happiness and gratitude.

That's when it hit him—their Disney World vacation was even more special than he had realized. It wasn't just a fun trip for the three of them. Patrick's future sibling was there too, even if they didn't know yet if it was a boy or a girl. Their family was growing, and this would be their first adventure as a family of four.

They arrived in Orlando with hearts full of excitement and anticipation. Wanting to make the trip truly special, Larry booked a beautiful suite at the newly constructed Animal Kingdom Lodge. From the moment they walked through the grand entrance, it was as if they had stepped straight into the African savannah. The architecture, the décor, and the atmosphere were breathtaking, but the real magic lay just beyond their window.

Each morning, they would wake to the sight of giraffes gracefully strolling by, gazelles leaping across the plains, and antelopes grazing peacefully. It was a living postcard, a paradise that brought wonder and awe not just to Patrick but to Larry and Tiffany as well. They watched Patrick's eyes widen in amazement, his little face pressed against the glass as he pointed excitedly at the animals below.

The real highlight for Patrick, however, was meeting his hero—Buzz Lightyear. From the moment they began planning the trip, Patrick talked endlessly about Buzz. To infinity and beyond became his favorite phrase, and he practiced his space ranger salute with determination. Larry and Tiffany made sure every detail was perfect, booking character dinners throughout the week so Patrick could get up close to all his other favorite Disney characters.

His joy was contagious as he hugged Mickey Mouse, danced with Goofy, and laughed with Donald Duck. But meeting Buzz was the ultimate dream come true. When Buzz Lightyear walked over to him, Patrick's mouth dropped open, his eyes wide with pure delight. Buzz bent down, gave him a high-five, and posed for pictures. Patrick's face lit up like never before, and he didn't stop smiling for the rest of the day.

Of all the rides and attractions, Test Track quickly became his favorite. The speed, the twists and turns, the excitement of being in a race car—it was everything he loved. Each time they rode it, Patrick's laughter echoed through the car, his hands in the air, pure joy radiating from his little body.

This vacation was all about him. Every moment, every detail was planned with Patrick in mind, from the rides to the meals to the special experiences. Larry and Tiffany watched him with love and pride, knowing that these were the moments that would shape his childhood.

Looking back now, it feels like a time of innocence. A time when everything was perfect, and the world seemed to be full of limitless possibilities. In those days, the small family seemed to have the world by the tail, their future bright and boundless. They had no idea that hard times were just around the corner and that life would test them in ways they could never have imagined.

But in that moment, they were happy. Truly, deeply happy. And that's what made it a memory worth holding onto forever.

CHAPTER 4.
A Home for Our Hearts

It was June 2005. Rylee had just turned one, and Patrick was about to celebrate his sixth birthday. Their family was growing, and so were their dreams.

Back in the fall of 2003, Tiffany had casually mentioned how they might need a larger home as their family expanded. It wasn't that their current house was too small, but she dreamed of more space—a game room where the kids could play, a movie room for family nights, and a room for Patrick and Rylee to grow up with plenty of space to explore.

Larry couldn't get her words out of his mind. He wanted to give her everything she ever dreamed of, to create a home where they could build memories that would last a lifetime. So, they began their search, exploring the nicest neighborhood in their quiet suburban town.

The neighborhood was beautiful, filled with custom homes built by renowned builders. They could picture themselves there, raising their children in a place that was safe, elegant, and perfect for family life. But when they saw the prices, their hearts sank. How could they afford this?

But Larry, being Larry, wouldn't let that stop him. Determined to make Tiffany's vision a reality, he contacted a builder and began the process of turning their dream into a blueprint. They selected a floor plan that matched their vision and then customized it to perfectly fit their family's needs.

Five bedrooms, three bathrooms, a game room for the kids, an office for Larry, and a spacious laundry room to make Tiffany's life a little easier. It was everything they wanted and more. Larry used his negotiating skills to work out a price that fits their budget, making the seemingly impossible suddenly possible.

FOREVER TIFFANY

They purchased a beautiful lot near the park, within walking distance of Patrick's school, and just a few miles from the beach they loved so much. It was the perfect location—a place where they could watch their children grow, where they could build a life filled with laughter, joy, and endless possibilities.

Tiffany's face lit up the first time they stood on the lot, imagining the walls that would one day surround them, the backyard where Patrick and Rylee would play, and the cozy movie room where they would share countless family nights.

Standing there, hand in hand, they felt like they were on top of the world. They were building not just a house but a home—a sanctuary where their dreams would take root and flourish.

Larry looked over at Tiffany, her blonde hair blowing softly in the breeze, her eyes sparkling with excitement. In that moment, he knew that every sacrifice, every negotiation, and every hour of hard work was worth it. He would have moved mountains to give her this.

Just before Rylee was born, Tiffany made a decision that would define her legacy of love and selflessness—she chose to pause her career to become a stay-at-home mother. In doing so, she gave her children the most precious gift she could offer: her time, her attention, and her untiring presence.

It was a decision not made lightly. Tiffany was thriving in her career, with opportunities for financial gain and professional success right within her reach. But she didn't hesitate. She knew that the moments she would share with her children—their first steps, their first words, the laughter and the tears—were priceless. No job title or paycheck could ever compare.

This is who Tiffany was. She sacrificed personal ambition without hesitation, choosing instead to pour her energy and heart into her family. It wasn't about giving up her dreams; it was about living her greatest dream—being the best mother she could be.

She did it with grace and joy, as beautifully as any woman ever has. Every day, she was there to cheer them on, to wipe away tears, to encourage their dreams, and to celebrate their victories. Her children were never in doubt about how deeply they were loved.

I've known many mothers who have made this sacrifice, and it's not an easy choice. It takes courage to put oneself second and prioritize the needs of others above one's own. But Tiffany did it without question, without complaint. She did it because her love was limitless, her heart selfless.

Tiffany lived her entire life this way. She was a woman who served others before herself and whose generosity of spirit touched everyone she met. She understood that by giving love, she was changing the world—one small act of kindness at a time.

In her quiet, powerful way, Tiffany showed that true greatness is found not in titles or accolades but in the love we give and the lives we touch.

In 2005, Tiffany decided it was time to add to the family. But it wasn't what Larry was expecting.

Tiffany had grown up with dogs, and her childhood was filled with memories of wagging tails and wet noses. She wanted her children to experience the same joy and unconditional love. It was an idea she had been thinking about for a while, and she knew just how to spring it on Larry.

One evening, with her signature smile and a mischievous sparkle in her eye, Tiffany approached him. "I think it's time we add to the family," she said sweetly. Larry's eyes widened in surprise before she finished, "I want to get a pug."

Larry was speechless for a moment. He loved Tiffany and the kids more than anything, and he knew he could never say no to her or those big, pleading eyes from Patrick and Rylee. With a reluctant smile, he agreed, knowing that his love for Tiffany outweighed any hesitation he felt about having a dog.

FOREVER TIFFANY

And that's how Max came into their lives—a tiny, adorable black pug who quickly wiggled his way into their hearts. From the moment they brought him home, Max was more than just a pet; he was a member of the family.

Max was a ball of energy, a little mischief-maker with a heart of gold. He loved summer days spent lounging on the pool stairs at Tiffany's mom's house, soaking up the sun and cooling off in the water. He would race around the yard, chasing Patrick and Rylee, his short little legs moving as fast as they could go, his tongue hanging out in pure joy.

He was a kid himself, trapped in the body of a chubby little pug. The kids adored him, and Tiffany's heart melted every time she saw them all playing together. Max was a source of laughter, love, and countless memories.

For Larry, it became a love-hate relationship. Max had a way of getting into trouble, chewing on that he shouldn't, and causing his fair share of chaos. But every time Larry looked at Max's big, round eyes and his wiggly little body, he couldn't help but smile.

Tiffany knew Larry would never say no to her, and she was right. Max was her idea, her vision of a family filled with love and laughter. And like everything she touched, she made it perfect.

Their house and neighborhood became more than just a place to live—it became the heartbeat of their lives, a gathering spot filled with laughter, love, and unforgettable memories.

Holly and Steve were growing their family, too. Just one year after Patrick was born, they welcomed their son, Tyler, and a year after Rylee arrived, they had their daughter, Dylan. It was as if their lives were moving in perfect harmony, their families growing together step by step. Maybe Tiffany was inspiring others to have babies—who knows? Her love and joy were contagious.

Holly and Steve decided to build their dream home just around the corner. They purchased a lot in the same beautiful neighborhood, and their vision came to life with an amazing outdoor kitchen and a stunning pool that backed up to a sprawling wooded area. It was perfect—a sanctuary surrounded by nature, a place made for gatherings and celebrations.

Their homes became the foundation of their community. The cousins grew up side by side, riding bicycles and scooters back and forth between the two houses, their laughter echoing down the streets. They attended the same schools, rode the same bus, and played in the same yards. They weren't just family—they were best friends.

Weekends were filled with BBQs, pool parties, and late nights under the stars. Larry and Steve would fire up the grill while Tiffany and Holly prepared delicious sides, laughing and reminiscing about their own childhood adventures. It was a rhythm of life, a shared journey that started in a middle school classroom and blossomed into a lifetime of memories.

They were more than friends—they were family. That bond they formed back in middle school was stronger than ever, woven into the fabric of their lives. It was a rare and beautiful connection, one that few people are lucky enough to find.

Together, they created a world filled with love and laughter, a place where their children grew up not just as cousins but as brothers and sisters at heart. It was a time of innocence, joy, and pure happiness.

And it all began with two little girls who became best friends and decided to share their lives forever.

Tiffany's parents, Pat and Vicki, lived a life balanced between two states—Florida and Indiana. Pat ran a business with his brother Dan in Florida, while Vicki worked as a dedicated school teacher. The plan was for the entire family to move to Florida permanently, but everything changed when Tiffany became pregnant with Patrick.

Vicki's love for her daughter and her selfless nature led her to make a decision that would shape all of their lives. Knowing that

Tiffany would need her, Vicki chose to stay in Indiana to be close to her daughter and her growing family. Pat, in turn, began splitting his time between Florida and Indiana, maintaining the family's commitments in both places.

Pat was born in 1951, surrounded by love and laughter. He grew up in a close-knit family with three brothers and a sister. From a young age, he learned the values of loyalty, hard work, and devotion to family.

Pat and Vicki's love story began in high school. They were young and full of dreams, drawn to each other with an undeniable connection. Shortly after graduation, they married and began building a life together. Pat took a job with the city, dedicating himself to public service. He joined the fire department and quickly rose through the ranks, becoming a captain and later serving as the department's arson investigator.

His career was marked by courage and integrity, a legacy of nearly 30 years of service to his community. But even after retiring from the fire department, Pat continued to work for the city, always committed to making a difference.

In the fall of 2005, Pat moved back to Indiana. His health had become a concern, and he needed surgery to replace a valve in his heart. The procedure was to be performed at Northwestern University in Chicago by one of the best doctors, Dr. Patrick McCarthy, a renowned heart specialist.

Tiffany was worried. She trusted the skilled hands of Dr. McCarthy, but this was a major surgery. The thought of her father undergoing such a serious procedure weighed heavily on her heart.

Pat was the rock of their family, the man who had always been there with a reassuring smile and a hug that could make any problem feel smaller. Tiffany couldn't imagine life without him.

She stayed by his side, offering her strength and love, just as he had always done for her. It was her turn to be strong, to give back the support he had always shown her.

Through tears and prayers, through worry and hope, Tiffany held on to her faith. She believed that everything would be okay. She had to—for herself, for her children, and for the father who meant everything to her.

Pat's surgery went well, but his recovery was a struggle. His body was weak, and he faced complication after complication. He spent weeks in the ICU, his lungs unable to function on their own. Coming off the ventilator was proving to be an enormous challenge.

Tiffany watched helplessly as her father, the man who had always been her hero, battled for his life. It was a familiar pain. Loss was not unfamiliar to her. She had already said goodbye to her grandmother Fran, Pat's mother, and then on April 9, 2003, her grandfather Randy, Vicki's father, passed away from cancer. Less than a year later, her grandmother June, Vicki's mother, also passed.

It seemed that every year, just as her young family was growing and thriving, she was forced to face another heartbreaking goodbye. Each loss was a reminder of the fragility of life. Yet, through it all, Tiffany's faith remained strong. She believed deeply in God, in heaven, and in the promise that she would one day see her loved ones again.

But the thought of losing her father was different. It was a pain she couldn't imagine, a loss she wasn't ready to bear.

The thing about Tiffany was that she rarely showed emotion during the hardest times. She was a rock, the stronghold everyone leaned on. She was the shoulder to cry on, the calm voice of reason, the glue holding everything together. She inherited this strength from her mother, Vicki, who had always led by example, facing every storm with unwavering courage.

FOREVER TIFFANY

As the months dragged on, it became painfully clear that Pat was not getting better. The doctors spoke in somber tones, explaining that he would likely never return home, that his future was uncertain, and that long-term care was his only option.

On September 7, 2006, Tiffany and Larry drove to the hospital to visit Pat. They spent hours with him, talking, laughing, and simply watching TV together. Larry could see the love between father and daughter, the unspoken bond that hung in the air. He knew Tiffany needed a moment alone with her dad, so he quietly left the room, giving them that precious time together.

Later that evening, when they returned home, Tiffany shared the conversation she had with her father. Her eyes were heavy with emotion as she recounted his words.

"He told me how much he loves me," she whispered, her voice trembling. "But he said he's tired… that he's ready to go."

Larry watched as tears welled up in her eyes, slowly rolling down her cheeks. Tiffany tried to smile and be strong, but he could see the pain fixed on her face.

She explained how she had held his hand, how she had told him she understood, that she loved him, and that she would be praying for him. She didn't want to lose him, but she knew he couldn't bear to see his wife and daughters in constant worry. She knew his pain was overwhelming and that he was suffering more than he could bear.

That night, Tiffany prayed with all her heart. She prayed for peace, for comfort, and for God's will to be done. It was the hardest prayer she had ever spoken, but she did it out of love, out of selflessness, just as her father had taught her.

The very next day, on September 8, 2006, Pat passed away.

It was as if he had been waiting for that conversation, for Tiffany's reassurance that it was okay to let go. He found his peace, and his pain was finally over.

Once again, Tiffany became the rock her family needed. She comforted her mother, held her sister close, and did her best to stay strong. Her pain was real, her grief immeasurable, but she knew her role. She knew she had to be the steady hand that guided them through the storm.

She didn't cry in front of others. She didn't break down. Instead, she quietly carried her pain, finding strength in her faith, believing that her father was now in heaven, watching over her.

In the face of loss, Tiffany showed what it truly meant to love selflessly. She gave her father the peace he needed, even when it shattered her heart. She showed her family what strength looked like, even when she felt like falling apart.

Tiffany was more than just a daughter that day. She was a light in the darkness, a pillar of strength, and a reminder that love is stronger than death.

The day of Pat's funeral arrived, heavy with sorrow and the weight of final goodbyes. Tiffany held herself together as best as she could, showing strength in the face of unimaginable pain.

Larry watched her closely, seeing the anguish in her eyes and the way she held herself rigid to keep from falling apart. He longed to reach out, to hold her, to offer the comfort of his embrace. But he knew better. He knew Tiffany.

She always felt safest in his arms, and in a moment like this, if she allowed herself to collapse into him, she would break completely and irreparably. So, Larry kept his distance, giving her the space she needed to grieve in her own way. He watched as she dressed Patrick and Rylee, her movements mechanical, her voice soft and steady.

They arrived at the funeral home, the air heavy with grief. Tiffany sat beside her sister, Amanda, waiting for their turn to go up to the podium to read the chosen Bible verses. They sat in silence, shoulders almost touching, a sisterly bond that was unspoken yet unbreakable.

FOREVER TIFFANY

As they waited, Tiffany glanced over and saw Larry crying. She gave him "the look," the one that told him to pull it together. She didn't want to see him break because she knew it would be her undoing. She needed to stay strong, to keep her composure.

But as she walked up to the podium, her body stiff, her face set with determination, Larry saw the cracks in her armor. She opened her mouth to speak, but the words caught in her throat. Her voice wavered, her shoulders shook, and the tears finally came.

Larry's heart shattered. He wanted to leap up, to hold her, to protect her from the devastating pain. But he stayed seated, his arms around Patrick and Rylee, knowing that Tiffany needed to do this.

Amanda was there in an instant, wrapping her arms around her sister, holding her up when she felt like falling apart. They stood together, leaning on each other, drawing strength from the bond they had always shared.

It was a moment of raw emotion, of love and loss tangled together. Larry looked at his children, their little faces confused and frightened, watching their mother cry in a way they had never seen before. It broke him.

After the service, they made the solemn drive from the funeral home to the cemetery. As they approached the fire station, the street was lined with fire trucks, their ladders fully extended in honor of Pat's service. Police officers stood at attention, their car lights flashing in silent tribute.

First responders lined the road, standing in uniform, saluting the hearse as it came to a stop. It was a powerful sight—a community coming together to honor one of their own, a man who had given so much to his city and passed at the young age of 56.

Tiffany and Larry were in the car directly behind the hearse. Larry watched the tribute unfold, his heart heavy, his eyes filling with tears. He dropped his head, unable to hold back the sobs that shook his shoulders.

LARRY BLAKE

Tiffany turned to him, her voice firm but gentle. "Stop crying like a big baby," she said, trying to inject a touch of humor to ease the pain.

But Larry couldn't stop. He looked at her, his eyes red and swollen. "The city won't stop when I die," he whispered, his voice breaking. "This is a great honor to your father, a man who gave so much to the city he loved."

Tiffany's eyes softened; the tears she had been holding back shimmered in her eyes. She looked at the procession, at the men and women standing in salute, at the fire trucks and police cars lining the street. She knew he was right. Her father had dedicated his life to this city, to its people, to its safety.

The city truly did stop that day. It stopped to remember a hero, to honor a man who had served with courage, integrity, and love. It was a tribute to a life well lived, a legacy that would never be forgotten.

Tiffany watched through the window, her heart breaking yet filled with pride. Her father was gone, but his memory, his impact, his love—that would live on forever.

Tiffany's heart was infinite. She opened it to the world, always looking for ways to make life better for those around her. It was never about recognition or praise; it was about love, about sharing the blessings she had been given.

In November of 2006, she approached Larry and his sister, Holly, with an idea that was pure Tiffany. She wanted to sponsor an entire family for Christmas. But this wasn't just about buying a few gifts or donating a holiday meal. Tiffany envisioned something much bigger.

She wanted to provide everything—the food for Christmas dinner, toys for the children, gifts for the parents, and anything else the family might need to make their holiday special. She wanted to give them a Christmas they would never forget, one filled with joy, laughter, and love.

It was classic Tiffany—selfless, giving, and full of compassion. She saw a need and didn't just want to fill it; she wanted to overflow it. She wanted to lift an entire family's spirits, to show them that even in the hardest times, there was still hope, there was still love.

When Tiffany decided to pause her career in late 2003 to stay home with Patrick and Rylee, it was a leap of faith. It was a scary decision, one that meant giving up her own ambitions and putting her family first. But they were blessed.

Larry's career flourished, and his income grew enough to support them comfortably. It wasn't lost on Tiffany that they were lucky, that they were blessed by God's grace. And in her heart, she knew they had to give back.

To Tiffany, it wasn't about charity; it was about gratitude. It was about paying forward the love and blessings they had received. It was about making the world just a little bit brighter, one family at a time.

Tiffany was given the address of a family living in a small, modest home tucked behind a church in town—a single mother raising three young children on her own. The house was humble, worn by time, a plain contrast to the warmth and love that shone from within.

Tiffany and Holly held a small list of gift requests in their hands. The children's wishes were simple, almost heartbreakingly so—basic toys, a few clothes, nothing extravagant. But Tiffany wasn't about to stop there. She took that list and multiplied it by twenty, determined to give these children a Christmas they would never forget.

They bought mountains of food, not just for a Christmas dinner but enough to last the family several weeks. Tiffany made sure to include all the holiday staples, imagining the joy on the children's faces as they shared a warm, festive meal together.

But as she looked over the list, one thing stood out. The young single mother hadn't listed a single item for herself. Not a single wish, not even the most basic need. Tiffany's heart ached. She knew that kind of selflessness, that kind of sacrifice. She had seen it in her own mother, and she lived it herself every day.

But Tiffany wasn't going to allow this woman to go without. She bought gift cards, carefully selecting stores where the mother could buy something special just for herself. A new outfit, a day of pampering, or even just a little extra to help make ends meet. She wanted this mother to feel loved and valued, to know that she mattered too.

On the night before Christmas Eve, Tiffany and Larry loaded up their Ford Expedition. The back was filled to the brim with gifts, food, and love. They drove across town, pulling up to the small house.

They knocked on the door, and the mother greeted them with tired eyes but a warm smile. She was gracious, kind, and full of gratitude. Tiffany and Larry didn't know her name, nor did they ask. They didn't need to. To them, she was a reflection of God's love, a reminder of the beauty of giving.

As they carried in bags of food and piles of presents, three little faces peeked out from behind a couch, eyes wide with wonder. One of the children, a little boy about seven or eight years old, looked up at Larry with curiosity and hope.

His eyes sparkled as he asked, "Are you Santa Claus?"

Larry didn't hesitate. With a serious face and a twinkle in his eye, he knelt down to the boy's level and said, "No, I'm just helping him out tonight. But he wanted me to say hello to all of you."

The boy's face lit up with joy, his smile wide and genuine. In that moment, magic filled the room. Not because of the gifts or the food, but because of the love that wrapped around them like a warm hug.

Tiffany stood back, her heart full. She didn't want praise; she didn't want recognition. She didn't even want a thank you. She simply wanted to make a difference, to let her heart shine out into the world.

FOREVER TIFFANY

They said their goodbyes and drove away, the Expedition empty but their hearts overflowing. Tiffany didn't need her name in the lights. Her light shone from within, touching everyone who was lucky enough to know her.

That night, somewhere across town, a family believed in Santa Claus, in magic, and in love. And it was all because of Tiffany, who understood that the greatest gifts are the ones we give from the heart.

Christmas of 2006 was a magical, serene holiday filled with love, laughter, and the wonder only children can bring. Patrick, now six, and Rylee, just two, were buzzing with excitement, their eyes wide with anticipation for Santa's arrival.

Tiffany had a way of making Christmas unforgettable. She transformed their home into a winter wonderland, decorating it with the meticulous touch of Martha Stewart herself. Every ornament was perfectly placed, every garland draped just right. The smell of freshly baked cookies filled the air, her creations so delicious they could have been sold in the finest bakery.

She made sure every wish the children whispered was waiting for them under the tree on Christmas morning. Larry and Tiffany wrapped all the gifts marked "From Mom and Dad" with care, choosing colorful paper and delicate bows. But the gifts from Santa—those were a different story.

Santa's gifts were left unwrapped, sprawled beneath the giant Christmas tree that stood proudly in front of a floor-to-ceiling window overlooking the front yard. Only the stocking stuffers were wrapped in special Santa paper, each stocking carefully hung by the fireplace.

On Christmas morning, Patrick and Rylee would burst from their rooms, their faces lighting up as they took in the magic that Santa had left behind. Their laughter and squeals of delight filled the house, echoing through the hallways, filling Larry and Tiffany's hearts with joy.

But the real magic happened on Christmas Eve after the kids were tucked into bed, their little faces glowing with anticipation. That was when Tiffany got to work, putting together every toy that required assembly.

Larry watched her, completely mesmerized. He would uncork a nice bottle of wine, pour himself a glass, and settle into the couch, a Christmas movie playing softly in the background. A warm fire crackled in the fireplace, the soft glow illuminating Tiffany as she worked.

He was no help at all, of course. Larry hated reading directions; his patience was worn thin by the smallest of parts. Or at least, that was his excuse. The truth was, he loved watching Tiffany in her element, her focus firm, her movements graceful and precise.

She was breathtaking. The way her golden hair fell across her face, the way her delicate hands worked with determination, the way she brought every toy to life with her touch—it was magic. And Larry never got tired of it.

With every sip of wine, his emotions grew, his heart swelling with love and gratitude. It wasn't just about the gifts or the perfect Christmas she created. It was about the life they had built together, about the love that filled every corner of their home.

He would sit there, lost in the moment, his eyes fixed on her. She was his angel, his heart, his everything. Sometimes, without even realizing it, a tear would slip down his cheek.

Tiffany knew. She would glance up from her work, a playful smile on her lips, her eyes twinkling with amusement. "Stop crying," she'd tease, her laughter warm and musical. "You big softie."

She would laugh, and Larry would smile through the tears, his love for her more powerful than words could ever express. Tiffany knew he adored her, and she loved him just as much, perhaps a little more.

FOREVER TIFFANY

Together, they were perfect. They were building a lifetime of memories, one magical Christmas at a time.

As they watched their children unwrap gifts and laugh with joy on Christmas morning, they both knew—no matter what challenges the new year would bring, they would face them together.

They needed a good 2007. They deserved it. And as long as they had each other, they could get through anything.

****

It was the spring of 2007. Patrick was playing baseball, his little face beaming with pride every time he stepped up to the plate. Rylee was full of energy, her laughter echoing through the house. Life was good, and Tiffany was content. But she was also ready for more.

Tiffany had always dreamed of a big family. She loved being a mother, and she wanted to add another little heartbeat to their home. It was something she had been thinking about, planning for, and quietly hoping Larry was ready for too.

One evening in May, Tiffany walked out of the master bathroom wearing a stunning outfit from Victoria's Secret, her golden hair flowing, her blue eyes sparkling with that "come get me" smile that Larry could never resist.

There was something different about her that night, something in her eyes, a glint of playfulness mixed with purpose. But Larry was too mesmerized by her beauty to think too hard about it. She was breathtaking, and in that moment, he was lost—lost in her touch, in her laughter, in her love.

The night was full of passion, their connection deeper and more electric than ever. Neither of them wanted it to end, and when dawn broke, Larry felt like he was walking on air.

The next day at work, he couldn't focus on anything. His mind kept drifting back to her—her smile, her touch, the way she made him feel. All he could think about was getting home to her.

LARRY BLAKE

That evening, as the kids were tucked into bed, Larry waited in the bedroom, his heart beating with anticipation. When Tiffany walked in, his jaw dropped. She was wearing another stunning outfit, even more beautiful than the night before.

It was a week of magic, of passion, of love. Five or six nights in a row, Tiffany surprised him, and every night, Larry fell deeper under her spell. He was completely mesmerized by her, by her beauty, by her love.

On the sixth night, as they lay tangled together, Larry looked at her, his curiosity finally getting the better of him. "What's gotten into you?" he asked, laughing.

Tiffany's eyes sparkled with mischief. She let out a soft laugh, her fingers tracing lazy circles on his chest. "You know what we're doing," she teased, her voice light and playful.

Larry laughed, shaking his head. "Yeah, I know," he said, his eyes still full of wonder. "But something seems up."

Tiffany just smiled, a knowing smile that told him she had a plan. She had always been the planner, the one who saw the big picture long before anyone else.

A couple of months later, Larry found out exactly what that plan was. They were having another baby.

Tiffany was ecstatic, her eyes lighting up with joy. She was over the moon, ready to welcome another little soul into their family. She hugged Larry tightly, tears of happiness in her eyes.

Larry stood there, his heart racing, his mind spinning. He felt a wave of panic, his thoughts contesting with questions and worries. But then he looked at Tiffany, her face glowing, her love for him and their growing family shining brighter than ever.

In that moment, he knew that everything was going to be okay. Their family was growing, their love was deepening, and life was about to get even more beautiful.

Tiffany had a way of seeing the future, of knowing what their family needed even before Larry did. And just like that, their next great adventure began.

On February 21, 2008, Brennan entered the world, filling their lives with new excitement and boundless joy. He was perfect—a tiny bundle of love who instantly captured their hearts.

His arrival was the perfect way to begin a new chapter, and it marked the continuation of a year filled with happiness and calm. 2007 had been good to them. It was a year without loss, without tragedy, and life seemed to be moving along perfectly.

Patrick was growing up fast, still passionate about baseball and basketball, but he had discovered a new love—BMX racing. It was thrilling and adventurous, and he was hooked from the very first race. Tiffany was always there for the local events, cheering him on with Rylee and baby Brennan by her side. For the races that required traveling, Larry and Patrick would hit the road together, creating memories they would carry forever.

Their weekends became a whirlwind of adventure, filled with road trips, cheering crowds, and the exhilaration of watching Patrick soar over jumps and race around tracks. Tiffany loved seeing the bond grow between father and son, knowing that they were making memories that would last a lifetime.

Rylee had turned four, her personality blossoming with confidence and curiosity. She loved being the big sister, helping Tiffany with Brennan, and cheering for Patrick at his races. She was sweet and playful, her laughter a constant melody in their home.

Patrick was now nine, growing taller, stronger, and more determined with every passing day. He was a natural athlete, fearless on his BMX bike, but he was also gentle and kind-hearted, always looking out for his younger siblings.

Their neighborhood had grown, nearly every lot filled with new homes and young families. They were surrounded by friends, by community, by love. It was the perfect place to raise their children, a place that felt like home.

In the backyard, they made improvements to create a space where the kids could play and laugh freely. They installed a new black iron fence, which was elegant and sturdy, keeping the children safe while still allowing them to explore. Next to the fence, they built a large wooden play set, complete with swings, slides, and a climbing wall. It was a kid's paradise, a place where imagination could run wild.

The play set sat beneath a large maple tree, one they had planted in the fall of 2006 in memory of Tiffany's father. It was more than just a tree; it was a living tribute to the man who had meant so much to her, to all of them. It was a place of reflection, of remembrance, and of love.

The tree stood tall, its branches reaching toward the sky, a symbol of growth, legacy, and family. Tiffany would often sit on the back porch, watching her children play beneath the tree, feeling her father's presence with every breeze that rustled the leaves.

Life was good. They were happy, blessed, and full of hope for the future.

As Brennan cooed and giggled in Tiffany's arms, as Patrick raced around the BMX track, and as Rylee swung high above the ground, their family was complete.

It was a time of innocence, of joy, and of peace. And Tiffany held on to every moment, knowing how precious this season of life truly was.

CHAPTER 5.
The Gift of Sacrifice

Larry met Eric J. in the mid-1990s, a couple of years before he and Tiffany's paths crossed. From the start, they bonded over their shared passion for hunting. Over the years, they had embarked on countless hunting adventures together, exploring wilderness areas and chasing the thrill of the hunt.

In 2007, they planned the ultimate trip—an elk hunting expedition to the Flat Top Wilderness area in Colorado. Larry had always joked that Eric was the luckiest hunter he'd ever met, and this trip would only reinforce that belief.

They flew to Colorado, excited for the adventure ahead. At the rental agency, they picked out the most outrageous vehicle they could find—a brand-new Hummer H2. It was massive, rugged, and perfect for the journey they were about to undertake.

The drive up the mountain was nothing short of an adrenaline rush. The road wasn't really a road at all; it was more of a rocky trail littered with giant boulders and narrow ledges. At one point, they found themselves teetering on just three wheels, the Hummer's fourth wheel dangling precariously over the edge.

They set up base camp at an elevation of 9,000 feet. The air was thin, making it hard to catch their breath. Larry could feel the altitude in his lungs; each inhale was a little shorter, a little harder. But he shook it off, chalking it up to the excitement of the hunt.

Saturday morning came early. They were up at 3:30 a.m., and by 4:00 a.m., they were on horseback, making the hour-long trek up the mountain to an elevation of about 12,000 feet. The ride was steep, the air even thinner, but the landscape was breathtaking.

At the top, they split up, each taking a different guide to increase their chances of spotting a bull elk. As Larry sat on a ridge, looking out over the vast, untouched wilderness, he couldn't help but think of Tiffany. He wished she were there to see this, to feel the beauty of this place that looked like heaven itself. It was a landscape that seemed to be crafted by God's own hand, perfect in every way.

As the day began to wind down, Larry's guide received a call over the radio. Another group had downed a large bull elk and needed help locating it. They set off, climbing a steep slope toward the kill site.

That's when it hit Larry. A wave of exhaustion washed over him, his legs weak, his chest tight. He felt lightheaded, his vision blurry. He could barely stand.

His guide looked at him, concern in his eyes. "It's the elevation," he said. "This high up, the air is thin. It happens to some people."

Larry nodded, forcing a smile. But deep down, he knew something wasn't right. This felt different. This felt serious.

They continued up the slope, finally reaching the spot where the elk lay. It was a massive bull, an impressive six-by-six rack towering above its body. But Larry could barely focus. He felt like he was going to pass out.

They made their way back to camp, Larry struggling with every step. When they finally arrived, Eric was waiting for him, a giant grin plastered across his face, his eyes wide with excitement.

"Come look at this!" Eric shouted, barely able to contain himself.

Larry followed, exhausted and unsteady on his feet. When Eric led him to his kill, Larry's jaw dropped. It was another six-by-six bull elk, just as massive as the one they had helped recover.

Eric's smile grew even wider as he explained that he had downed the elk just fifteen minutes into his hunt. "I barely got settled in before he walked right into my sights," Eric laughed. "Luckiest day of my life."

FOREVER TIFFANY

Larry couldn't help but laugh, even through his exhaustion. Eric was, without a doubt, the luckiest hunter alive.

As they packed up and headed back down the mountain, Larry felt a strange sense of relief. Something about this trip had shaken him, made him question his own health, his own strength. He brushed it off, blaming the altitude, but a part of him knew there was more to it.

He didn't know it then, but this trip would stay with him, the memory of the beauty, the excitement, and that unsettling feeling in his chest. It was a reminder that life is precious, fragile, and worth every breath, even when the air is thin.

Late in the summer of 2008, Larry started noticing a nagging cough, as if something was stuck in his throat that he just couldn't clear. It wasn't just an occasional tickle—it was constant, deep, and irritating. By fall, it had become a daily struggle.

He found himself carrying around a Dr. Pepper bottle, spitting out thick phlegm throughout the day. It was disgusting, but it was the only way he could get any relief. By the end of each day, the bottle would be nearly full. He hated it, but he kept it to himself, never mentioning it to anyone—not even Tiffany.

She noticed the cough, of course. How could she not? It was persistent, and it was getting worse. She asked him about it, her concern evident. "You should see a doctor," she would say, her blue eyes filled with worry.

But Larry was stubborn. He waved her off, saying it was just a cold or maybe allergies. He had always avoided doctors, never one for routine checkups or hospital visits. Tiffany was the same way—they both avoided doctors' offices like the plague.

Looking back, Larry would come to regret that decision. He would wish he could go back and change it, that he had listened to Tiffany's gentle urging. But in that moment, he just couldn't see the importance of something as simple as a checkup.

Determined to carry on as usual, Larry and Eric set off on another hunting adventure, this time to the trophy triangle of Kansas, Missouri, and Illinois—home to some of the largest whitetail bucks in the country. It was their favorite time of year, and they were excited to chase after these giants together.

But this trip was different. The cough was relentless. As Larry sat in his deer stand, trying to be as quiet as possible, the urge to cough grew unbearable. He tried to muffle it and hold it in, but it was no use. The deep, chest-rattling coughs echoed through the woods, alerting every deer within earshot.

It was frustrating. He couldn't concentrate, couldn't stay quiet, couldn't do what he loved. Eric sat nearby, quietly watching, his eyes filled with concern. He knew something was wrong.

Despite his best efforts, Larry's hunt was a bust. He never even got close to a deer. The cough had ruined his chances before he even had a shot.

Eric, on the other hand, managed to harvest a massive buck, and his luck once again was on full display. As they packed up to head home, Eric slapped Larry on the back, his smile wide. "Next time, buddy. Maybe try not to scare all the deer away," he teased, trying to lighten the mood.

Larry forced a laugh, but the truth was, he was worried. This wasn't just a cold, and he knew it.

As they drove home, Larry made a promise to himself—he would get it checked out. No more excuses, no more pretending it was nothing. He owed it to himself, to Tiffany, and to his kids.

He didn't know it yet, but that promise would change everything.

Christmas was just around the corner, and Tiffany was in her element. The house was transformed into a holiday wonderland, every inch decorated with love and care. The large Christmas tree still stood proudly in front of the massive window, its lights twinkling for the whole neighborhood to see. But this year, Tiffany had added even more magic—a second tree by the fireplace, its warm glow creating the perfect backdrop for cozy holiday evenings.

Manger scenes were carefully displayed, garlands draped along the staircase, and stockings were hung with perfect precision. Christmas music played softly in the background, and the smell of freshly baked cookies occupied the air. Tiffany was in her happy place. Christmas and the Fourth of July were her two favorite holidays, times of year she looked forward to with childlike excitement.

For Tiffany, it wasn't just about the decorations or the presents. It was about creating memories, about filling the house with laughter, love, and joy. She relished every moment, every tradition, every smile on her children's faces. It was her way of giving them magic, of giving them love.

Amid all the holiday cheer, Larry couldn't shake the nagging cough that had been bothering him for months. True to his promise, he finally made an appointment to see the doctor.

Ten days before Christmas, Larry sat in the office of Dr. Daniela Sikoski in Valparaiso, Indiana. He described his symptoms—the persistent cough, the endless phlegm, the tightness in his chest. Dr. Sikoski listened carefully, her eyes full of concern.

She prescribed a Z-pack, an antibiotic to clear what Larry was convinced was just a lingering flu or respiratory infection. But before he could leave, she asked him to go for a chest X-ray. She didn't like the sound of his cough, and she wanted to be sure he didn't have fluid in his lungs.

Larry agreed, but as he walked to the lab, he saw the waiting room overflowing with patients. The line was long, and the thought of sitting there for hours didn't appeal to him.

He hesitated, glancing back at the lab before deciding he'd come back another day. There was too much to do before Christmas, too much to prepare. He didn't have time to sit around waiting for an X-ray.

Besides, he felt fine. The Z-pack would do the trick.

He walked out of the hospital, the cold winter air biting at his face. His chest felt tight, his cough still nagging, but he brushed it off. There were trees to decorate, presents to wrap, and cookies to eat.

And Tiffany was waiting for him at home, her smile brighter than any Christmas light.

Christmas was magical, just as it always was in their house. Tiffany outdid herself once again, making the season festive and fun, filling their home with love and warmth. The lights twinkled, the fireplace crackled, and the laughter of Patrick, Rylee, and little Brennan echoed through every room.

Larry cherished this time of year. He made it a tradition to stay away from the office during the holidays, dedicating these precious weeks to his family. He traveled a lot for work, and this downtime was his way of making up for the missed dinners, the bedtime stories, and the little moments that made life beautiful.

They laughed, they played, and they celebrated. It was a Christmas filled with joy, love, and unforgettable memories. But in the back of Larry's mind, the nagging cough was still there.

The day after Christmas, Larry decided to keep his promise to himself and get the chest X-ray Dr. Sikoski had ordered. He figured the lab would be empty the day after the holiday, and he could get in and out quickly.

He walked into the clinic, handed over the paperwork, and went through the motions, his mind already drifting to plans for New Year's Eve. It was routine, nothing to worry about. Just checking off a box.

As soon as he returned home, the phone rang. Tiffany picked it up, her cheerful voice echoing from the kitchen. Her expression changed as she turned to Larry, her eyes wide with concern. "They need to speak with you," she said, handing him the phone. Her voice wavered, the smile fading from her face.

Larry took the phone, his heart starting to race. He could feel the anxiety building, a tight knot forming in his chest. He could see the worry in Tiffany's eyes, and for the first time, he felt a ripple of fear.

The voice on the other end was clinical, detached. They needed him to come back for another X-ray. "We saw something," they said. "We need more images to confirm."

Larry tried to play it off, telling Tiffany it was probably just his necklace. Maybe he forgot to take it off. It was nothing.

He drove back to the lab, his mind racing but his heart full of hope. It was just a precaution, just a second look. He stood still as they took more images, his chest pressed against the cold metal plate, his breath held tight.

As he walked back into the house, Tiffany was waiting for him, the phone pressed to her ear. She looked at him, her face pale, her hands trembling. "They need to speak with you," she whispered, her voice breaking.

Larry took the phone, his hands shaking as he put it to his ear. The voice on the other end was somber, careful with their words. "We found a large mass in your chest," they said. "You need to see a surgeon as soon as possible."

The words hit him like a punch to the gut. A mass? A surgeon? The room started to spin, his knees went weak, and he sank to the floor, his back against the wall, the phone slipping from his hand.

Tiffany was there in an instant, her face etched with fear, her arms wrapping around him. But Larry couldn't move, couldn't speak. His mind was swirling, his thoughts a jumbled mess of panic and disbelief.

A mass. A surgeon. It felt like the end of the world.

He thought about Tiffany, about Patrick, Rylee, and Brennan. He thought about all the Christmases they were supposed to share, all the memories they were supposed to make. Was this it? Was it time to say goodbye?

He looked up at Tiffany, tears in his eyes, his heart breaking. "I'm not ready," he whispered, his voice cracking. "I can't leave you. I can't leave them."

Tiffany held him close, her own tears falling, her body shaking with fear. But even through the pain, she stayed strong, her love wrapping around him like a shield.

"We're going to get through this," she said, her voice steady, her heart unbreakable. "Together."

In that moment, Larry realized that no matter what lay ahead, no matter how dark the days might become, Tiffany would be by his side. She was his light, his strength, his hope.

And together, they would face whatever came next.

In a state of panic and disbelief, Larry made the only call that made sense. He reached out to Dr. Patrick McCarthy, the world-renowned surgeon who had cared for Tiffany's dad just a few years earlier. Dr. McCarthy remembered Pat and Vicki well, his voice warm and familiar as he spoke to Larry.

He didn't hesitate. "You need to see Dr. Matthew Blum," Dr. McCarthy said, his voice firm and certain. "He's the head of thoracic surgery at Northwestern University. He's the best there is."

Larry listened intently, his heart pounding in his chest. Dr. McCarthy explained that Dr. Blum was in high demand, and his waiting list was long and daunting. But he would make a call, a personal plea on Larry's behalf, and ensure that he was seen immediately.

A wave of relief came over Larry. If Dr. McCarthy trusted this man, then so could he.

FOREVER TIFFANY

In early January, Larry made the drive to Northwestern University, his mind hopeful. He told Tiffany to stay at home with the kids, assuring her that everything would be fine. It was just a precaution, just a checkup to clear up the scare.

He walked into the towering hospital, his steps confident, his heart steady. But the moment the elevator doors opened, and he stepped into the hallway, his world shifted.

There, staring back at him in bold letters, were the words: Robert H. Lurie Cancer Center.

His heart stopped. His breath caught in his chest. The word "cancer" echoed in his mind, taunting him, terrifying him.

Cancer? Why was he in a cancer center? He was told it was a mass, nothing about cancer. Was this some sort of mistake? A mix-up? Surely, he was in the wrong place.

Larry sank into one of the waiting room chairs, his eyes glued to the words on the wall. He could feel his hands shaking, his vision blurring as tears welled up. But he forced himself to breathe, to stay calm. It had to be a mistake. He was going to see Dr. Blum; they'd clear it all up, and he would go home to Tiffany and the kids.

After what felt like an eternity, his name was called. He stood up on shaky legs and followed the nurse down the long hallway, each step heavier than the last.

When he entered the office, he was greeted by Dr. Matthew Blum, a man who exuded confidence and compassion. He was tall, calm, and had a gentle demeanor that immediately put Larry at ease.

As they began to talk, Larry felt a strange sense of familiarity, as if he was meant to be there, at that moment, with this doctor. It was as if something beyond himself had guided him to this place, to this man.

Dr. Blum spoke with authority, explaining the findings with clarity and care. He didn't sugarcoat it, but his voice was steady, his words precise. Larry could feel the fear tightening in his chest, but he also felt safe.

He trusted Dr. Blum, the man who had been handpicked by Dr. McCarthy, and trusted the doctor who was now looking him in the eyes and telling him that they would face this together.

Larry didn't fully understand what was happening, but he knew he was in the right place. He knew that somehow, someway, he was being watched over, guided through the darkness.

As he left the hospital, he took one last look at the words on the wall. Robert H. Lurie Cancer Center.

They still terrified him. But with Dr. Blum on his side, he felt a glimmer of hope, a light in the darkness.

He would fight. He would go home to Tiffany and the kids.

And he would not give up.

Dr. Blum's words were clear and unyielding, each syllable hitting Larry like a punch to the gut. There was a mass in his chest—a large one, about the size of a pineapple. It was nestled dangerously close to his heart and lungs, its tendrils seemingly hooked onto the very organs keeping him alive.

The news was devastating, his world spinning as he tried to process it. But Dr. Blum was calm, his presence steady and reassuring. He explained the plan with precision: chemotherapy needed to start immediately.

The goal was to shrink the tumor, to see if they could peel it away from his heart, to determine whether it was truly attached or just resting against it. Either way, it was too close, too dangerous, and it needed to be dealt with quickly.

The treatment would be brutal—five days of chemotherapy, each session lasting several hours. It would be an aggressive attack on the tumor, and Dr. Blum made no promises. He spoke with honesty and care, giving Larry the facts while allowing him the space to process the fear, the worry, and the fight that lay ahead.

The first day of chemotherapy was like nothing Larry had ever experienced. The cold, sterile room, the hum of machines, the quiet murmur of nurses moving about. He felt the IV prick his arm, the cold fluid rushing through his veins. It felt like ice, burning and freezing at the same time.

By the time he got home, he was exhausted, his body weak, his spirit heavy. Tiffany was waiting for him, her eyes full of love and worry. She held him close, her presence the only thing that kept him from falling apart.

The days dragged on, each one more grueling than the last. He could barely move, his limbs heavy, his muscles aching. He felt sick, nauseous, and drained of every ounce of strength. But he kept going, one day at a time, one breath at a time.

He was fighting—not just for himself, but for his children, for his angel, for the life he had built with Tiffany. He thought about Patrick, Rylee, and Brennan. He thought about all the moments he still wanted to share with them—all the birthdays, the graduations, the weddings.

He thought about Tiffany, about her laughter, her smile, her love. He thought about all the Christmases he still wanted to spend with her, all the mornings he wanted to wake up by her side.

But no matter how hard he fought, Larry knew that he couldn't do this alone. The weight was too heavy, the fear too great. He needed help. He needed strength.

And he knew there was only one place he could find it.

Each night, as the world grew dark and the pain became unbearable, Larry prayed. He fell to his knees, his body weak but his heart strong. He prayed to God, to the only one who could truly save him.

He prayed for strength, for healing, for the chance to keep living, to keep loving. He prayed for his children, for his wife, for his family.

He put his trust in God, surrendering his fear, his worry, his pain. He let go of the anger, the disbelief, the confusion. He gave it all to God, knowing that no matter what happened, he was in His hands.

The fight had started. The fight to stay alive, to be there for his children, to walk through life with Tiffany.

But he wasn't fighting alone. He was fighting with faith, with love, and with the power of God on his side.

And he was ready to face whatever came next.

In moments like this, when your world is shattered and the very foundation of your life is shaken, you need an anchor. You need someone who can keep you from drifting too far into the darkness, someone who can pull you back when the fear threatens to consume you.

You need someone who knows when to let you have your quiet moments of pain and reflection but who also knows when to kick you in the ass and push you to keep fighting.

In the gym, they call them a trainer. On the field, they call them a coach. In the office, they call them a boss.

But when you're fighting for your life, when the battle isn't just physical but emotional and spiritual—what do you call them?

Larry called her his wife.

Tiffany was his angel, his guide, his hope, and his strength. She was his anchor.

Through every tear, every moment of doubt, every sleepless night, she stood by his side. She held him when he needed comfort, encouraged him when he wanted to give up, and fought for him when he couldn't fight for himself.

FOREVER TIFFANY

She never showed fear, never wavered. Even when her heart was breaking, she put on a brave face, her smile unwavering, her love unyielding.

She kept him tethered to the shore, kept him grounded in faith and hope, and kept him fighting even when the pain was too much to bear.

She was his strength when he was weak, his light when the darkness closed in, and his hope when fear tried to take over.

She was his everything. His wife. His angel. His anchor.

And with her by his side, Larry knew he could keep fighting. He could keep living.

Because no matter how hard the battle, no matter how dark the night, Tiffany was his reason to keep going.

At just twenty eight years old, Tiffany was carrying a weight most people twice her age could never bear. She was maintaining a large home, raising three young children, and caring for a husband who was fighting for his life, all while keeping a smile on her face and hope in her heart.

It didn't make sense. How could someone so young be so strong, so wise, so untiring? How could she carry the weight of the world on her small shoulders and never falter, never complain?

Larry watched her in awe, day after day, holding everything together, keeping their family intact. She was the glue, the heartbeat, the light that kept the darkness at bay.

She was wise beyond her years, wise in a way that defied logic. At her age, most people were out at clubs, dancing the nights away, carefree and wild. Larry knew—because that's exactly what he was doing at her age. At twenty, he wouldn't have been ready for this, wouldn't have been strong enough to face this kind of pressure.

But Tiffany was different. She had a strength that couldn't be explained, a power that seemed to come from somewhere beyond herself.

Larry often wondered where that strength came from. How could someone so young be so fearless, so resilient, so full of grace?

It was as if it was built into her very DNA, as if she was created for this moment, for this purpose. It was as if God had sent her straight from heaven, knowing that her life would one day intersect with Larry's, knowing that Larry would face this battle and that he would need her to survive it.

She was his angel. His light. His strength.

In every whispered prayer, in every quiet tear, Larry thanked God for Tiffany. For her love, for her courage, for her unwavering faith.

She was more than just his wife. She was his miracle. She was truly an angel in spirit.

Late in February of 2009, the day of surgery loomed heavy on Larry's heart. After enduring grueling chemotherapy, the tumor was still there, large, ominous, and dangerously close to his heart. Despite all the treatments, Dr. Blum still couldn't determine if the mass was merely pressing against Larry's heart or if it was actually attached to it.

The plan was to go in through the right side of his chest, making three precise incisions. They would see if the tumor could be removed safely and if they could peel it away without causing damage to the heart or lungs.

Larry was terrified. It wasn't just the thought of surgery or the pain he knew was coming. It was the fear of the unknown, of being put under, of closing his eyes and not knowing if he would wake up again.

He tried to stay strong for Tiffany, to keep his fear hidden beneath forced smiles and soft reassurances. But as the day grew closer, he knew he needed to say something, to share the thoughts that were weighing heavily on his heart.

One evening, as they sat quietly together, the kids finally asleep, Larry took Tiffany's hand. He looked at her, his eyes filled with love and worry, his heart heavy with words he didn't want to say.

"Tiff," he began, his voice cracking, "if something happens to me... if I don't make it through this..."

Tiffany's face immediately tightened, her eyes narrowing. "Don't talk like that," she snapped, shaking her head. "You're going to be fine. We don't need to talk about this."

But Larry persisted. He had to. He needed her to hear it, to understand. "I need you to be happy," he whispered, his voice trembling. "I need you to find someone... someone who will love you, who will walk through life with you, who will be there for you and the kids."

Tears welled up in Tiffany's eyes, her body shaking as she tried to hold them back. "Stop it," she pleaded, her voice breaking. "I don't want to hear this."

But Larry continued, his voice growing stronger. "You deserve to be loved, Tiff. You deserve to be happy. If he loves you even half as much as I do, that's more love than most people get in a lifetime."

She threw her arms around him, her body shaking as she cried into his chest. "You're crazy," she whispered through the tears. "You're not going anywhere. You're going to be fine. We're going to get through this."

Larry held her close, his own tears falling as he buried his face in her hair. He prayed silently, begging God to let him stay, to let him keep walking through life with her, to let him be there for his children.

He didn't want to leave. He didn't want to say goodbye.

The day of surgery arrived, the hospital cold and sterile, the air heavy with fear and hope. Tiffany kissed him softly, her blue eyes filled with love and strength. "I'll be right here when you wake up," she whispered. "I love you."

Larry felt the tears sting his eyes as he whispered back, "I love you too. Always."

Then everything went black.

The surgery was long, brutal, and complicated. They made three incisions on the right side of his chest, working carefully around his ribs and muscles. His right lung was deflated, cleaned, and treated, but the mass was still there, clinging stubbornly to his heart.

Dr. Blum and his team did everything they could, but the tumor was hooked on, deeply embedded, entangled with his heart in a way that made removal impossible.

When Larry woke up, the pain was unbearable. Every muscle on the right side of his chest felt like it was on fire, every breath sending searing pain through his body. He could barely move, his chest heavy, his body broken.

Tiffany was there, her face pale and drawn, her eyes swollen from crying. But she smiled when she saw him, relief flooding her features. "You made it," she whispered, her voice trembling. "You're here. You're alive."

Larry tried to smile, his lips cracking with the effort. "I told you I wasn't going anywhere," he whispered, his voice weak and raspy.

But the battle was far from over. The mass was still there, still attached to his heart.

Dr. Blum came in, his face serious, his eyes heavy with concern. "We couldn't remove it," he explained softly. "It's hooked on... too close to your heart. We need to come up with another plan."

Another plan. Another battle. Another fight.

FOREVER TIFFANY

Larry looked at Tiffany, her face pale but strong, her love solid. She took his hand, holding it tight, her fingers laced through his.

"We're going to get through this," she said, her voice steady, her heart strong. "We're not giving up."

Larry looked into her eyes, his own heart swelling with love, with gratitude, with hope. She was his reason to keep fighting.

He wasn't ready to say goodbye. Not yet.

And as long as Tiffany was by his side, he would keep fighting. No matter how hard the battle, no matter how painful the journey.

Because she was his forever – FOREVER TIFFANY!

Dr. Blum and his team devised a new plan—a bold, risky, and complex plan. The next surgery was scheduled for March 26, 2009, and this time, they were going in from the front, just as they would for open-heart surgery.

This wasn't just another surgery. This was the battle of Larry's life.

A full cardiology team would join Dr. Blum in the operating room. They were prepared for anything. They were ready to replace the valves in Larry's heart if needed and to hook him up to a bypass machine if his heart had to be stopped. They were preparing for a fight, and it was a fight they intended to win.

The night before surgery, Larry and Tiffany drove to Chicago, checking into the Warwick Hotel. They tried to make it feel like just another getaway, tried to find some semblance of normalcy amidst the chaos.

But this wasn't just another trip. This wasn't just another night.

As they stood at the front desk, checking in, the clerk looked at the reservation details and then at the couple standing before her. She smiled politely, her voice cheerful. "I see you've booked one of our suites with a king bed. But don't worry, we have space available—I'll move you to a room with two queens."

Larry burst out laughing, shaking his head. "No, no, the king is perfect," he said, his eyes twinkling. "This is my wife."

The clerk's face turned pale, her eyes widening as she realized her mistake. She stammered, apologizing, her cheeks flushing with embarrassment. She had mistaken them for father and daughter, something that had been happening since they first got together.

Larry just laughed, his heart lightening for a moment. He glanced over at Tiffany, her golden hair flowing softly around her face, her eyes sparkling with amusement. She looked as young and beautiful as the day he met her.

This was a scene they had experienced countless times before. People never seemed to believe that Tiffany was his wife, not with the age difference and not with how young she looked. But it never bothered them. It was just another reminder of how special, how rare, how perfect their love was.

They checked into their room, a spacious suite with large windows overlooking the city. It was beautiful, but their hearts were heavy. They were just a few blocks away from the hotel where they spent their honeymoon nine years earlier, the place where they had dreamed about their future, about a life full of love, laughter, and memories.

But this trip was different. The air was heavy, the night cold and unforgiving. This wasn't a honeymoon. This was a farewell—at least, that's how it felt to Larry.

They went out for an early dinner, the last meal Larry could have before surgery. They chose something light, something filling but not heavy. They talked, they laughed, they tried to pretend everything was normal. But beneath the surface, fear gripped Larry's heart, refusing to let go.

They returned to the room, the night growing darker, the city lights twinkling outside the window. Tiffany changed into her pajamas, her delicate frame curling up on the bed, her head resting on the pillow. Larry watched her, his heart aching, his eyes filling with tears.

FOREVER TIFFANY

She looked so peaceful, so beautiful.

He leaned down, kissing her softly, his lips lingering as he whispered, "I love you."

Tiffany smiled, her eyes fluttering closed. "I love you too," she whispered, her voice soft and full of trust.

He watched her fall asleep, her breathing slow and steady, her body relaxed. She needed the rest. She had been holding everything together, keeping the house running, taking care of the kids, holding him up when he felt like falling apart.

She was exhausted, her strength drained by the worry, the fear, the never-ending fight.

Once she was asleep, Larry slipped out of bed and went into the bathroom, closing the door quietly behind him. He flicked on the light and stared at his reflection in the mirror.

His hair was gone, stolen by the chemotherapy that had ravaged his body. His face was pale, his eyes sunken, his body weak. He looked like a stranger, like a man he didn't recognize.

He paced back and forth, his bare feet cold against the tiled floor. He thought about his parents, Larry and Diana, who had given him love and strength his whole life. He thought about his sister, Holly, and her family, about Amanda and her family, about all the people he loved.

But mostly, he thought about Tiffany.

He thought about her laugh, about her smile, about the way her eyes sparkled when she looked at him. He thought about every moment they had shared, every memory they had made, every dream they still hadn't realized.

He thought about Patrick, about Rylee, about little Brennan. He thought about all the birthdays, the graduations, the weddings, the Christmases they were supposed to share. He thought about Tiffany raising their children alone, about her crying herself to sleep, about her feeling lost without him. He couldn't stand the thought.

Larry fell to his knees, his hands clasped, his head bowed. He prayed.

He prayed for strength, for courage, for the chance to keep living, to keep loving. He prayed for his children, for his parents, for his family. But mostly, he prayed for Tiffany. He prayed that God would let him stay so that he could be there to hold her hand, to kiss her goodnight, to grow old with her.

He prayed for a *miracle*.

He wiped his tears, took a deep breath, and walked back to the bed. He curled up next to Tiffany, his arms wrapping around her, his face buried in her hair.

He closed his eyes, listening to her breathe, feeling her warmth, her love, her life.

And he knew he had to keep fighting. Not for himself but for her. For his angel. For his forever: FOREVER TIFFANY.

****

The morning of surgery arrived with a sense of dread and anticipation. Larry and Tiffany checked in at Northwestern University at 4:45 a.m., the air was cold and still, the world not yet awake. The hospital was quiet, the halls dimly lit, the sterile smell sharp and unwelcoming.

Larry was prepped for surgery, changed into a hospital gown, and an IV was placed in his arm. As he sat in the pre-op room, he began to shake uncontrollably. His hands trembled, his body shivering despite the warm blankets piled on top of him.

His fear was palpable. It wasn't just nerves; it was raw, unfiltered terror. This wasn't just another surgery. This was his heart—his life—on the line.

FOREVER TIFFANY

Tiffany watched him closely, her heart breaking as she saw the man she loved unraveling before her. She reached out, taking his hand, her fingers lacing through his, her grip firm.

But her touch wasn't enough. His shaking grew worse, his eyes wide with panic, his breaths coming fast and shallow. Tiffany looked around frantically before spotting a nurse nearby. She waved her over, her voice firm and urgent.

"He's scared," she said, her eyes pleading. "He's really scared. Can you do something?"

The nurse offered a sympathetic smile, her voice calm. "It's normal to be nervous before surgery," she said gently. "He'll be okay once we get him into the operating room."

But Tiffany wasn't satisfied. She knew Larry, knew his fear, knew this was more than just nerves. She wouldn't allow him to suffer like this.

She stood her ground, her voice stronger this time. "No. He needs something to calm him down. Please."

The nurse's expression softened, understanding the depth of Tiffany's love and concern. She nodded and walked over to Larry's IV, administering a relaxant to help ease his anxiety.

Within seconds, Larry's body began to relax. His muscles softened, his breathing slowed, and his eyes grew heavy. The edges of the room blurred, the lights dimming, the noise fading.

He felt a strange sense of peace, his fear melting away as the medication did its work. His eyes drifted to Tiffany, her face hazy but beautiful, her love the last thing he saw before everything went dark.

The surgical team arrived, their faces masked, their eyes serious. They wheeled Larry out of the pre-op room and down the long hallway toward the operating room.

Tiffany stood there, her heart in her throat, her hands shaking. She watched him disappear through the double doors, her world crumbling around her.

She took a deep breath, steeling herself. She had to be strong—for Larry, for her children, for herself.

She made her way to the waiting room, where friends and family were already gathered, their faces tight with worry, their eyes red with unshed tears. They hugged her, held her, and prayed with her. But Tiffany stayed strong, her face calm, her heart steady.

They settled in for the long wait. The surgery was expected to last eight to nine hours, a taxing, complicated procedure that required a team of the best surgeons in the world.

They knew Dr. Blum was their best hope. They trusted him. They prayed for him.

Hours dragged by, each minute feeling like an eternity. Tiffany watched the clock, her eyes never leaving the hands as they moved so painfully slowly. She whispered silent prayers, her hands clutched together, her heart begging God to bring Larry back to her.

After what felt like a lifetime, Dr. Blum walked into the waiting room. His surgical cap was off, his face drawn and tired, his eyes weary but bright. Tiffany's heart stopped, her breath catching in her throat. She stood up, her legs weak, her body trembling.

Dr. Blum looked at her, his eyes softening. "We got it," he said, his voice calm and steady. "We were able to remove the mass. It was hooked onto his heart, but we managed to get it off without damaging any valves."

A collective sigh of relief filled the room, tears falling, arms wrapping around each other.

Dr. Blum continued, his voice warm, "We did have to replace the pericardium sac around his heart. We used bovine tissue… from a cow."

There was a moment of stunned silence as everyone processed the information. Then, in classic Tiffany fashion, she looked straight at Dr. Blum, her eyes sparkling with mischief. "Does this mean he's going to be mooing all the time?" she asked, her voice deadpan, her face perfectly serious.

For a moment, Dr. Blum stared at her, his mouth hanging open. Then, he burst into laughter, his shoulders shaking, his eyes crinkling at the corners. "What is it with you two?" he asked, shaking his head. "You're such jokesters."

Tiffany's laughter was like music, her smile lighting up the room. It was classic Tiffany—finding humor in the darkness, light in the shadows, and joy in the pain.

It was how they survived. It was how they loved.

Larry spent the next few days in the ICU, his body weak, his chest in agony. Every muscle on the right side of his chest had been cut, his heart stitched together with tissue from a cow. His breaths were shallow, his movements slow and painful.

But he was alive.

Tiffany stayed by his side, holding his hand, whispering words of love and encouragement. She watched over him, her love fierce and unwavering.

The day finally came for Larry to go home. It was the day he had been dreaming about, the day he had fought so hard for, the day he thought might never come. But as the morning light crept through the hospital window, Larry made a decision that surprised everyone—he didn't want Tiffany to come pick him up.

He loved her more than anything, but he needed this day to be about something else. He needed to feel normal again, to feel like himself, to reconnect with the life he had before the diagnosis, before the fear, before the fight.

He needed to be with George.

George was one of his best friends, his confidant, his work buddy. They had worked together for years, shared laughs, shared stories, shared life. During Larry's fight, he had been away from work, away from his passion, away from the part of his life that made him feel normal.

That's why he asked George to come. He needed that sense of familiarity, of friendship, of laughter. He needed to feel alive again.

George didn't hesitate. When Larry called and asked him to pick him up, he was there without question. He arrived at Northwestern, his large, six-foot-four frame making him easy to spot as he weaved his way through the hospital corridors.

When he found Larry, he wrapped him in a bear hug, his eyes wet with emotion. "You did it, man," George whispered, his voice cracking. "You fought like hell, and you made it."

Larry smiled, his body weak but his spirit strong. He looked at George, his eyes twinkling. "I want to go to Gino's East," he said firmly. "I want some damn pizza."

George laughed, his booming voice echoing down the hallway. "You're crazy," he said, shaking his head. "But hell, let's do it."

Before they left, George found Dr. Blum, who was making his rounds. "Doc, can we take him to Gino's East? He wants pizza."

Dr. Blum's eyes widened, his mouth opening in shock. "Are you serious?" he asked in utter disbelief.

George nodded, his face serious. "It's all he's been talking about. He wants pizza."

Dr. Blum looked at Larry, his eyes narrowing. Then, after a moment, he shook his head and laughed. "You know what? If Larry wants pizza, then Larry gets pizza. Whatever he wants, he deserves it."

FOREVER TIFFANY

Larry's face lit up, his heart soaring. This wasn't just about food. This was about freedom, about life, about stepping out of the shadow of cancer and back into the light of living.

George helped him into the car, his big hands gentle and careful as he buckled Larry in. They drove the short distance to Gino's East, the famous Chicago pizzeria that Larry had been dreaming about for weeks.

As they walked in, George cleared a path through the crowd, his tall frame towering over everyone else. People moved aside, their eyes widening as they saw Larry, pale and thin but standing tall.

They found a booth near the window, the city bustling outside, the smell of pizza filling the air. Larry took a deep breath, his eyes watering as he realized just how much he had missed this.

George took charge of the ordering, waving over the waitress and grinning. "We'll take six personal pizzas," he said confidently. "One of everything."

Larry looked at him, his eyes wide. "Six?" he asked, laughing. "There's no way I can eat all that."

George shrugged, his face serious. "You don't have to eat it all. I just want you to taste it all. I want you to feel alive. I want you to feel like you're back in the game."

Back in the game.

Larry felt a lump rise in his throat, his heart swelling with gratitude and love for his friend. George understood. He knew what Larry needed, what this day meant, and what this pizza symbolized.

It wasn't just about food. It was about life. About second chances. About new beginnings.

When the pizzas arrived, Larry stared at them, his eyes wide with wonder. There were six different flavors, each one more delicious than the last. The deep-dish crust was golden and flaky, and the cheese melted to perfection, the sauce rich and tangy.

He took his first bite, the flavors exploding in his mouth, his senses coming alive. It was the best pizza he had ever tasted.

Tears filled his eyes as he chewed, the emotion overwhelming him. He had eaten Chicago-style pizza his whole life, but this was different. This was victory. This was survival. This was life.

He looked at George, his voice cracking as he whispered, "I didn't think I'd ever taste this again."

George's eyes softened, his smile gentle. "You're back, man. You're back in the game."

They ate together, laughing and joking like old times. For a few hours, they forgot about cancer, about hospitals, about fear. For a few hours, they were just two friends, eating pizza, living life.

It was the start of something new, the beginning of Larry's second chance.

And as he savored each bite, he made a silent promise to himself—to never take another moment for granted, to never let fear control his life, to always find joy in the simple things.

Because life is precious. Life is fragile. Life is beautiful.

And sometimes, life tastes like deep-dish pizza at Gino's East.

Larry was determined to get back to normal life. He knew the road to recovery would be long, filled with months of radiation and the lingering pain from surgery, but he was alive. He was home. And he was ready to live again.

There was nothing quite like the feeling of sleeping in his own bed, the warmth of Tiffany by his side, her breath soft and steady as she slept. He would lay there at night, his body aching but his heart full, listening to the gentle rhythm of her breathing, feeling the steady beat of his own heart—a heart that was still fighting, still beating, still alive.

It took several weeks before Larry felt strong enough to return to work full-time. His body was still weak, his energy low, but his spirit was stronger than ever. He was eager to get back to his routine, to feel useful, to feel normal.

He was incredibly fortunate to work for the company he did—a company led by a man named Dan L., a giant of a man in every sense of the word. At six feet eight inches tall, Dan commanded attention when he walked into a room, his presence undeniable, his authority unquestionable.

But Dan was more than just a powerful leader. He was a man of compassion, integrity, and vision. He had been in the energy business for a long time, weathered every storm, faced every challenge, and led the company to success time and time again.

From the moment Larry met Dan, they hit it off. They were cut from the same cloth—both driven, both passionate, and both loyal. Dan saw Larry's dedication, his relentless work ethic, his passion for the job. And Larry saw Dan's heart, his compassion for his employees, and his foresight to lead the company into the future.

When Dan first heard of Larry's diagnosis, he was shocked. He couldn't believe that Larry was still out on the road, visiting clients, working long hours, all while carrying the weight of cancer on his shoulders.

Dan called Larry immediately. His voice was firm but gentle, his words heavy with concern. "Go home, Larry," he said. "Go home and be with your family. Take all the time you need. We'll be here when you get back."

And Dan meant every word. He made sure Larry never missed a paycheck, never missed a bonus, and never had to use a single day of PTO. He took care of everything, handling the paperwork, the benefits, the insurance. He removed every ounce of financial pressure from Larry's life, allowing him to focus solely on his fight, on his recovery, on his family.

Larry couldn't believe it. In a world where loyalty was rare and compassion even rarer, Dan was a force of nature—a man who led not just with power but with heart.

When Larry returned to work, his body was weaker, but his spirit stronger; the first thing he did was find Dan.

He called Dan's office, his heart pounding, his emotions raw. "Thank you," he said, his voice breaking. "Thank you for everything. If it weren't for you, for what you did for my family… I don't know if I would have made it."

Dan looked at him, his tall frame leaning forward, his eyes softening. "You're part of the team, Larry," he said simply. "We take care of our own."

Larry felt tears sting his eyes, his throat tightening. He realized that Dan wasn't just his boss. He was his silent partner in this fight, the rock he didn't even know he needed.

Dan had taken care of him when he couldn't take care of himself. He had taken care of Tiffany, of Patrick, of Rylee, of Brennan. He had lifted the weight from Larry's shoulders, allowing him to fight without fear, without worry, without distraction.

He was a silent hero, a man who showed his strength not just in boardrooms but in acts of kindness, acts of love.

Larry knew he was lucky. Lucky to be alive, lucky to have Tiffany by his side, lucky to have friends like George who brought him back to life over pizza.

And lucky to have Dan L., a giant of a man with a heart even bigger than his frame.

Life was different now. It was more precious, more fragile, more beautiful.

FOREVER TIFFANY

And Larry knew he would never take another moment for granted.

Because of people like Tiffany. Because of people like George.

And because of people like Dan.

CHAPTER 6.
Grace Despite Hard Race

In the fall of 2009, life took an unexpected and thrilling turn for Larry. One day at work, he was called into a meeting, his heart pounding as he sat down at the long conference table, his mind racing with possibilities. What he didn't expect was the incredible opportunity that awaited him.

The company had decided to offer him, along with a select few others, ownership stock. It was a rare chance to own a piece of the very company he had dedicated so much of his life to—a company that was privately held but was already looking toward the future, toward either selling or going public.

It was a life-changing opportunity. If things went well, this could be the very thing that set Larry and Tiffany up for an early retirement, a chance to live out every dream they had ever dared to dream.

He sat there, stunned, his mind reeling with the possibilities. He thought about Tiffany, about Patrick, Rylee, and Brennan. He thought about the life they could build, the memories they could make, the future they could secure.

It felt like the break they deserved, a reward for all the battles they had fought, all the hardships they had overcome.

Larry accepted the offer with a heart full of gratitude, his smile wide, his spirit soaring.

By early 2010, Larry was on the road to a full recovery. His strength was returning, his energy rebuilding, and his spirit stronger than ever. He still had his battle scars, the physical reminders of the fight he had survived, but they were proof that he was alive, proof that he was a warrior.

It was during this time that he received bittersweet news—Dr. Matthew Blum, the man who had saved his life, the man he trusted more than anyone, was leaving Chicago. He had accepted a prestigious role as the head of thoracic surgery at UC Health in Colorado Springs, Colorado.

Larry was happy for him, proud to see his hero moving on to bigger and better things. But a part of him felt lost, afraid even. Dr. Blum wasn't just his surgeon; he was his safety net, his guardian angel, his friend. It felt like losing a lifeline, a security blanket, a piece of his recovery that he wasn't ready to let go of. But Tiffany, being the rock she always was, reassured him. She reminded him of how strong he was, of how far he had come, of how Dr. Blum had given him the greatest gift of all—a second chance.

And she was right. Larry was alive, and his life was moving forward.

Patrick was excelling in both baseball and basketball, his natural athleticism shining brighter with each passing season. But the real surprise was BMX. Patrick had always been fearless, always been driven, and his hard work was paying off.

He secured a factory sponsorship in BMX, a huge accomplishment, and proof of his determination and talent.

Larry watched with pride as his son soared over jumps, his body flying through the air, his heart fearless. Patrick was living his dreams, and Larry was alive to witness it.

Life was clicking along, the pieces falling into place, the world bright and full of promise.

Meanwhile, Amanda and her husband Bob were thriving on the East Coast, living just outside Washington, D.C. Bob was excelling in his government job, his career taking off, his future full of opportunity.

Their three boys—Jacob, John, and Josh—were growing up fast, each one more brilliant than the last. They were thriving, happy, and full of life.

Larry and Tiffany made the trip to visit, knowing how precious family time truly was. Watching Tiffany with Amanda was like watching a reflection—two sisters so close, so connected, so full of love for one another.

They laughed, they cried, they shared memories and dreams. But as the days passed and the visit came to an end, both women felt the ache of distance. Life had grown busy, time had grown short, and they couldn't see each other as often as they wanted to.

They hugged tightly, their hearts heavy, their eyes wet with tears. But they promised to stay close, to visit more often, to never let distance weaken their bond.

Tiffany held on to Amanda, her heart full of love, her soul full of hope. It was a promise she intended to keep, a bond she would never let go of.

Life was moving forward, full of joy, full of hope, full of dreams waiting to come true.

And for the first time in a long time, Larry felt like he was truly living again.

With Tiffany by his side, with his children thriving, with his family close, with his career blossoming, with a second chance at life, Rylee was soaring in the world of gymnastics. Her talent was undeniable, her passion unmatched. She was fearless on the beam, graceful on the floor, and powerful on the vault. With each meet, she grew stronger, more confident, and more determined.

Tiffany was there for every routine, every practice, every moment. She watched with pride as Rylee flipped and twisted, as she pushed herself harder and chased her dreams with relentless drive.

FOREVER TIFFANY

Tiffany saw the spark in Rylee's eyes, the same spark she remembered in Amanda's eyes all those years ago. Amanda had been a state champion, a gymnastics prodigy, and now it seemed Rylee was following in her footsteps.

Who knew? Maybe one day, Rylee would be a state champion, too.

But for Tiffany, it wasn't just about winning. It was about building character, teaching resilience, and fostering passion. It was about giving Rylee the tools she needed to succeed in life, not just in gymnastics.

Tiffany was dedicated, sacrificing her own time, her own needs, and her own dreams to ensure Rylee could pursue hers. She was at every practice, every meet, cheering the loudest, supporting the hardest.

She wasn't just Rylee's mom—she was her biggest fan, her rock, her guide.

But Tiffany's love and support didn't stop at Rylee. She built beautiful, lasting friendships with the other moms, forming bonds that would carry on long after the last dismount or the last medal ceremony. She was the glue that held the group together, leading by example, choosing friendship over rivalry, kindness over competition.

Tiffany cheered for every girl as loudly as she did for Rylee, her voice full of love, her heart full of pride. She showed Rylee and everyone around her that success wasn't just about winning. It was about lifting each other up, celebrating each other's victories, supporting each other's dreams.

In a world that often pitted parents against each other, Tiffany was a beacon of light, a reminder that there was enough room for everyone to shine.

Larry watched her with awe, his heart swelling with love and admiration. He would stand back, just watching her—watching the way she cared, the way she loved, the way she supported.

He remembered the day he first met her, the day he looked into those blue eyes and knew, without a doubt, that she was the one. He remembered thinking that she would be the most amazing mother, the most loving wife, the most beautiful soul.

He was right.

Watching Tiffany dedicate herself to Rylee, watching her sacrifice without hesitation, watching her pour every ounce of love into their children, Larry knew. He knew she was the greatest of all time. The GOAT of motherhood. She was everything he had ever dreamed of and more. She was his heart, his hero.

And every time she smiled at Rylee, every time she cheered, every time she hugged the other moms, Larry fell in love with her all over again.

Because Tiffany wasn't just a mother. She was a legend.

Around this time, Tiffany began to notice something that tugged at her heart. Brennan, now two years old, wasn't talking much. While other toddlers his age were stringing words together, his vocabulary was limited, his words few and far between.

At first, she tried not to worry. He was sweet, loving, playful—everything a two-year-old should be. But the words just weren't coming.

Tiffany did what any concerned mother would do—she brought it up to their pediatrician. "He's just a late bloomer," the doctor said with a reassuring smile. "Boys sometimes take longer to talk. Don't worry."

But Tiffany couldn't shake the feeling. She watched him carefully, day after day, noticing how he would look at her, his big eyes curious and bright, but his lips silent.

Trusting her instincts, Tiffany decided to get a second opinion. She took Brennan to another pediatrician who, after a brief evaluation, dropped a bombshell—"He's autistic."

The words hung heavy in the air, echoing in her mind. But what made it worse was the doctor's lack of direction, his cold, clinical delivery. No resources, no guidance, no hope—just a diagnosis that hit like a punch to the gut.

Larry was devastated. The room spun, his knees went weak, his heart shattered. He thought back to everything they had been through—his cancer, the surgeries, the fear. He thought about all the battles they had fought, all the pain they had endured.

"Here we go again," he thought, his spirit sinking. "We just can't catch a break."

But Tiffany? She didn't flinch. She didn't cry. She didn't panic.

Instead, she took a deep breath, squared her shoulders, and did what she always did. She fought.

Tiffany picked up the phone and made two calls—one to Rush University in Chicago and the other to Children's Hospital in Chicago. She wasn't about to accept a diagnosis without facts, without evidence, without exhausting every resource.

She was a warrior, and Brennan was her son.

They took Brennan to both hospitals, undergoing a battery of tests, evaluations, and consultations with specialists. They watched him interact, play, respond, and react.

Finally, the truth came out. Brennan wasn't autistic. He wasn't withdrawn or unengaged. He just couldn't hear. It was as simple as that.

The doctors explained that fluid was trapped behind his eardrums, blocking sound and making it difficult for him to process language.

He wasn't quiet because he didn't want to speak—he was quiet because he couldn't hear the words to repeat them.

The solution? A simple surgery to insert tubes in his ears, allowing the fluid to drain, clearing his hearing, and opening his world.

The surgery was scheduled, and Tiffany never left his side. She held his hand as he was wheeled into the operating room, her heart strong, her love fierce.

The surgery was quick and successful. And the change? It was immediate.

As soon as the tubes were placed, Brennan's face lit up, his eyes widening as the world opened up around him. Sounds became clearer, voices more distinct, and laughter more musical.

And then the words started to pour out. It was like a floodgate had been opened. Brennan became a chatterbox, his little voice filling the house, his words spilling out faster than they could keep up.

There were days when Larry and Tiffany would look at each other and laugh, wishing he would slow down just for a moment. But deep down, they were thrilled. Brennan was communicating, connecting, living.

But he was behind in speech. There was no denying that. Nonetheless, Brennan had something most kids didn't have. He had Tiffany.

Tiffany, who would run through a brick wall for her children. Tiffany, who would climb the highest mountain to give them every opportunity, every chance, every ounce of love.

She wasn't about to let Brennan fall behind.

She threw herself into research, diving into articles, books, and studies about speech development. She wasn't a speech therapist, but she would learn. She wasn't a teacher, but she would teach. She wasn't a miracle worker, but she would make miracles happen.

FOREVER TIFFANY

Tiffany found a speech therapy group that would come to their home twice a week, working one-on-one with Brennan, teaching him words, sounds, and sentences. She was at every session, cheering him on, encouraging him, loving him.

She was his mother, his warrior, his champion.

Larry watched in awe, his heart full of love and admiration. He remembered the day he first saw her, that beautiful blonde with sparkling blue eyes. He remembered knowing, in that moment, that she was special, that she was meant to change his life.

He was right.

Tiffany was more than just his wife. She wasn't just his hero. She was their children's hero.

She was a fighter, a warrior, a queen.

She was the GOAT of motherhood.

She was a woman who never backed down, never gave up, never stopped fighting for her children.

She was the angel God sent to save them all.

And as Brennan's voice filled the house, his words poured out, and his laughter echoed through the rooms, Larry knew.

He knew that every miracle, every moment, every memory—they were all because of her.

It was something people said, a metaphor, a phrase people used to describe someone who was extraordinary, someone who changed lives, someone who made the world a better place.

Larry had heard it his whole life. People called teachers angels, nurses angels, and mothers angels. He knew it was just a way to describe someone kind, someone selfless, someone good.

But Tiffany was different.

From the day he met her, he felt it—something otherworldly, something divine, something he couldn't explain. When he looked into her blue eyes, he saw light, a light so pure, so beautiful, it felt like it was shining straight from heaven.

He didn't think much of it then. He was young, in love, captivated by her smile, her laugh, her beauty. He thought he was just lucky that he had found his soulmate, his forever.

But as the years went by, as they built a life together, as they faced every battle, every challenge, every storm, Larry began to wonder.

It was more than luck. It was more than fate. It was more than just a love story.

It was destiny.

Because Tiffany was more than just his wife. She was his light, his hope, his heart. She was the strength that carried him, the courage that held him up, the love that saved him.

He started to believe it when she stood by his side during his battle with cancer, never once showing fear, never once letting him feel alone. She was his rock, his fighter, his reason to keep living when she noticed Brennan's silence, her heart so attuned to her children that she could see what no one else could. She was his voice, his advocate, his star.

He started to believe it when he watched her sacrifice everything—her time, her dreams, her life—for her children. A mother, a teacher, and their protector.

As the years went by, life found a rhythm. The family settled into a good routine, days flowing into nights, nights into mornings, each one a gift they never took for granted.

Patrick was growing up fast, his interests evolving, his passions shifting. He made the difficult decision to hang up his BMX bike and put away his baseball glove, choosing instead to dedicate himself fully to the sport his grandfather had coached with so much pride and passion—basketball.

In Indiana, basketball is more than just a game. It's a religion, a way of life, a legacy passed down through generations. It's where legends are born, where rivalries are fierce, where dreams are made.

Patrick understood this. He felt the weight of that legacy, felt it coursing through his veins, felt it in his bones. He was his grandfather's grandson, and he was determined to honor that name, that history, that tradition.

He pushed himself hard, practicing day and night, perfecting his shot, his dribble, his speed, and his agility. He played with heart, grit, and determination that reminded Larry of Tiffany. That drive, that passion, that refusal to quit—it was his mother's spirit shining through.

Patrick's hard work paid off. He earned a starting spot on the 7th-grade A team—a huge accomplishment in any state but monumental in Indiana, where basketball reigns supreme.

And not just any A team. This was the A team at one of the largest junior high schools in the state, a school where competition was fierce, where only the best made the cut, and where only the greatest earned a starting spot.

This was everything.

The team was stacked with talent, filled with players who were destined for greatness. Maurion, Jalen, Nick, Anthony, Aaron, Sharod—each one a powerhouse, each one a game-changer, each one a star.

Together, they were unstoppable.

They dominated the court with speed, power, and precision. They played with an intensity that was unmatched, a chemistry that was undeniable, a hunger that was unrelenting.

They went on a tear, winning game after game, leaving their opponents in the dust. They moved as one, playing with heart, with courage, with passion.

They were special. They were electric. They were a team destined for greatness.

They finished the season with an extraordinary record, somewhere around 20-1, a nearly perfect season, a testament to their talent, their hard work, their unity. They won the conference, a title that had eluded their school for over a decade. They brought pride back to their community, hope back to their school, and joy back to their fans.

Larry watched from the stands, his heart swelling with pride, his eyes welling with tears. He saw himself in Patrick, saw his own dreams, his own memories, his own legacy. But more than that, he saw Tiffany. He saw her love, her dedication, and her forever support. He saw her cheering the loudest, her smile the widest, her pride the greatest.

He saw the way she hugged Patrick after every game, the way she wiped his tears after every loss, the way she encouraged him, believed in him, and loved him.

He saw the way she led the other moms, cheering not just for Patrick but for every boy on that team, supporting them, lifting them up, making sure they knew they were all champions.

He saw the way she celebrated not just the wins but the effort, the teamwork, and the journey.

Because that's who Tiffany was.

She was love. She was light. She was everything.

Patrick shone on that court. He played his heart out, honoring his grandfather, honoring his team, honoring himself.

But Larry knew that the reason Patrick was great, the reason he was brave, the reason he was strong, was because of her.

FOREVER TIFFANY

Because Tiffany was the champion. She was the reason they all kept fighting, the reason they all kept winning, the reason they all kept living. She was the heart of their family, the glue that held them together, the love that kept them strong.

And as Patrick held up that conference trophy, his face beaming with pride, his heart bursting with joy, Larry looked at Tiffany, her blue eyes sparkling with tears, her smile brighter than the sun.

He looked at her and whispered, "You did this."

Because Tiffany wasn't just raising children. She was raising champions.

Rylee continued to excel in gymnastics, her routines more powerful and graceful with each passing season. She followed in Aunt Amanda's footsteps, proving herself a fierce competitor and a dedicated athlete. Tiffany was there for every practice, every meet, cheering the loudest and loving the hardest.

Brennan found his passion on the soccer field and basketball court. He was fast, fearless, and full of joy. Whether dribbling down the court or scoring goals on the field, his energy was infectious, his spirit unbreakable.

Larry and Tiffany watched their children compete, learning to be part of something bigger than themselves. It was everything they wanted for them—discipline, teamwork, character. They made memories the way families are meant to—together, laughing, living, loving.

Disney was a magical tradition, a promise kept, a place where dreams came to life. They walked down Main Street hand in hand, the castle towering before them, the air alive with excitement. Patrick's face lit up as he met Buzz Lightyear, his hero. Rylee spun in circles, her princess dress flowing, her eyes sparkling with wonder. Brennan's laughter echoed as he raced through Adventureland, his energy boundless, his spirit free.

Tiffany planned every detail with the precision of a magician, ensuring each child's dream came true. Character breakfasts where Mickey himself would visit the table rides perfectly timed to avoid long lines, and fireworks viewed from the best spot in the park.

Larry watched in awe, his heart full, his gratitude endless. It wasn't just the magic of Disney—it was the magic of Tiffany.

They returned to Wisconsin Dells year after year, a place of endless fun, of water slides and lazy rivers, of laughter that echoed through hotel hallways late into the night. They raced down giant slides, their screams of joy mingling with the rush of water. They floated together on rafts, the sun warming their faces, their hearts light and happy.

Nights were spent in cozy cabins, playing board games, eating popcorn, and sharing stories. Tiffany always made it special, finding ways to turn the simplest moments into cherished memories.

Then there were the trips to Florida, the sun-drenched days spent with Uncle Dan and Aunt Susan. They would head out on the boat, the ocean stretching endlessly before them, the waves dancing beneath the sun. Patrick would cast his line, his face full of concentration, his heart full of hope. Brennan would jump off the side of the boat, his laughter echoing across the water, his joy uncontainable. Rylee would curl up next to Tiffany, her head resting on her shoulder, the two of them whispering secrets, sharing dreams.

Evenings were filled with laughter, dinners around large tables, the family close, the love closer. They watched sunsets paint the sky in hues of pink and gold, the ocean reflecting the beauty above. They held hands, wrapped in blankets, watching the stars appear, feeling the world slow down, feeling time stand still.

They were moments that would live forever.

Tiffany captured it all, her camera clicking, her heart full, her smile wide. She made scrapbooks for each child, pages filled with photographs, memories, and love. She wanted them to remember it all—the adventures, the laughter, the togetherness.

For Tiffany, memories were more than just moments frozen in time. They were gifts. They were proof that they had lived, that they had laughed, that they had loved deeply and completely.

Larry watched her, his heart swelling as she hugged the children, held them close, and made every moment magical.

****

May 26, 2012, was supposed to be the day their lives changed forever.

Larry had poured his heart and soul into his company, dedicating countless hours, endless energy, and unwavering passion. He believed in the mission, believed in the vision, believed in the future. He worked harder than anyone, traveling coast to coast, building relationships, closing deals, pushing the company forward.

The company's Initial Public Offering (IPO) was the dream. It was the reward for all the late nights, all the missed birthdays, all the sacrifices. It was the key to financial freedom, the ticket to early retirement, and the promise of everything he had ever wanted for his family.

But dreams don't always come true.

The stock price didn't soar. It sank. Fast.

Larry watched in disbelief as the numbers plummeted, his heart dropping with each tick, each fall, each loss. It was brutal, devastating, soul-crushing. He watched everything he had worked so hard for slip through his fingers, powerless to stop it, helpless to change it.

Over the coming days, the reality sank in. The company was struggling, and Larry knew what that meant. He knew changes were coming.

In July of 2012, the call came. He was asked to leave the company he had given everything to.

He was being let go. Just like that.

A career he had built from the ground up, a future he had envisioned, a dream he had nurtured—it was all gone.

As he packed his office, his hands trembling, his heart breaking, Larry felt a burden of emotions crash over him—anger, confusion, fear, shame.

How could this be happening? How could everything he had worked for just disappear? How could he go home and look Tiffany in the eyes and tell her he failed?

That's how he felt, like a failure.

He sat in his car for what felt like hours, his head resting on the steering wheel, his heart shattered.

He thought about Tiffany, about Patrick, Rylee, and Brennan. He thought about the life they had built together, the dreams they had dreamed, the future he had promised her.

He had promised to take care of her, to give her everything, to protect her from the hardships of life. And now, he was coming home empty-handed.

When he walked through the door, his shoulders slumped, his face pale, his heart heavy, Tiffany knew. She could see it in his eyes, in his posture, in his silence.

She walked over to him, her eyes soft, her heart strong. She reached for his hand, her fingers wrapping around his, her touch warm and steady.

"I lost my job," Larry whispered, his voice breaking, his tears falling. "I failed you. I failed us. I don't know how we're going to get through this."

FOREVER TIFFANY

But Tiffany didn't cringe. She didn't cry. She didn't panic.

She was a rock. Solid, strong, unbreakable.

She looked at him the way a young fan looks at Michael Jordan hitting the game-winning shot, the way a kid looks at Tom Brady throwing the perfect pass. She looked at him like he was her hero, her champion, her everything. Because he was.

She believed in him, even when he didn't believe in himself. She had faith in him, even when he had lost all hope. She trusted him, even when he felt like the ground was crumbling beneath his feet.

She wrapped her arms around him, holding him tight, her love fierce, her heart full. She kissed his cheek, her lips soft, her voice strong.

"We've got this," she whispered, her words a promise, a vow, a truth. "We're going to be okay. I believe in you. I always have. I always will."

Larry sobbed, his body shaking, his fear melting away in her embrace. He felt the weight lift, the darkness fade, the hope return.

Tiffany offered to go back to work and reenter the workforce without hesitation. She was willing to do whatever it took to keep their family safe, happy, and whole.

She wasn't afraid to get her hands dirty, wasn't afraid of hard work, and wasn't afraid of sacrifice.

She was even willing to sell the house, to downsize, to give up the life they had built, if that's what it took to keep their family strong.

Because Tiffany's love was never about things. It was never about money, success, or status. It was about family. It was about faith. It was about fighting through the hard times together.

Larry looked at her, his tears falling, his heart overflowing with love. He knew she meant every word. She would stand by his side no matter what. She would love him no matter what. She would fight for him no matter what.

She was his rock.

And in that moment, Larry realized something he had known all along. Tiffany was the reason he fought, the reason he survived, the reason he kept going. He didn't fail. He didn't lose. Because he had her.

And with her by his side, he had already won.

Together, they could face anything.

Together, they were unstoppable.

Tiffany was right again. She had a way of always being right, of seeing the light even in the darkest moments, of believing in miracles even when all seemed lost.

Just two short weeks after losing his job, Larry received a phone call that changed everything. A company based in Denver, Colorado, reached out with an incredible offer. They wanted him to open an office in the Chicagoland area, to grow their footprint in the Midwest, to lead their expansion, to take his experience and passion, and to build something extraordinary.

It was everything he had hoped for. Everything he had prayed for.

He could stay in the energy business, the industry he loved, the career he had built, the passion that fueled him. He could continue living in the home he adored, the place where memories were made, where laughter echoed, where love grew.

And most importantly, Tiffany could continue to do what she did best—pour her heart and soul into their children, love them fiercely, guide them gently, and keep their family strong.

Larry was overjoyed. The relief was overwhelming, the gratitude uncontainable. He looked at Tiffany, her blue eyes sparkling, her smile wide, her heart full.

FOREVER TIFFANY

She never doubted him. Not once. Not even for a moment.

Larry chose to put the office in downtown Valparaiso, Indiana—a picturesque little town that felt like something out of a movie.

It was charming, beautiful, and perfect. A quaint downtown filled with shops and boutiques, cozy coffee houses, top-rated restaurants, and a vibrant community. The university added youthful energy, the parks offered peaceful escapes, and the streets were lined with character and charm.

It was the perfect place to grow a business, to build a dream, to start again.

Larry threw himself into the work, his passion reignited, and his confidence restored. He grew the company quickly, making connections, closing deals, building a team.

The family settled back into their routine, laughter filling the house, joy filling their hearts, and love filling their lives.

They had overcome another hurdle, faced another challenge, and survived another storm.

They were stronger, braver, closer.

But as the sun shone brightly on their lives, change was brewing on the horizon. Change so big, so monumental, so life-altering that it would affect everyone. It would affect Holly and Steve, whose lives were knotted with Larry and Tiffany's, whose children grew up side by side, a family that cooperated like friends. It would affect Larry's parents, Larry and Diana, who were the foundation, the roots, the legacy. It would affect Tiffany's mom, Vicki, who has always sacrificed so much for her children and grandchildren.

It would affect everyone.

In May 2014, Larry received another call, this time from his boss in Denver. "I'd like to talk," he said, his voice serious, his tone heavy.

Larry's heart sank, his mind racing. Was it happening again? Was he about to lose another job? Was the company struggling? Was he failing again?

His hands shook, his heart pounded, his fear returned.

But it wasn't bad news. It was the opportunity of a lifetime.

His boss wanted him to take on a larger role—a leadership position that would put him at the forefront of the company, a promotion that would elevate his career, a challenge that would test his skills and showcase his talent.

But it came with a cost.

He had to move to Denver.

The corporate office needed him there. They wanted him in the room, at the table, leading the charge, driving the vision. This wasn't just a job—it was a calling. But it meant leaving everything behind. Their beautiful home. Their picturesque neighborhood. The life they had built. The roots they had planted. The friendships they cherished. The memories they treasured.

It meant leaving Holly and Steve, whose children were like siblings to Patrick, Rylee, and Brennan. It meant leaving his parents, whose support was unwavering and whose love was unconditional.

It meant leaving Vicki, who had dedicated her life to helping Tiffany, who was the rock, the constant, the heart of their family.

It meant starting over again.

Larry looked at Tiffany, his eyes filled with uncertainty, his heart heavy with fear. "What do we do?" he asked, his voice trembling. "How do we leave all of this behind?"

Tiffany looked at him, her blue eyes steady, her heart strong. She took his hand, her fingers warm and firm, her love unshakable.

"We go," she said softly, her voice calm, her faith firm. "We follow our hearts. We follow our dreams. We do what we always do—we do it together."

Larry felt the fear melt away, and the doubt disappeared; the hope returned.

Tiffany was his guide, his lifeline. She always knew. She always believed. She always led.

They would follow this new dream, this new adventure, this new life. Together. Because as long as they were together, they were home. Home wasn't a place. It wasn't a house, or a neighborhood, or a town. Home was Tiffany.

It was always FOREVER TIFFANY.

Larry and Tiffany had planned everything out perfectly. The kids would finish one last school year with their friends, creating memories that would last a lifetime, and they would make the big move to Colorado in June of 2015.

They hadn't even put the house up for sale when they received an unexpected phone call early one morning. The kids were rushing off to school, breakfast dishes still on the table, toys scattered across the living room, the typical chaos of a busy household.

It was a local realtor. She had heard they were thinking about moving and asked if she could bring a potential buyer by to see the house.

Larry was caught off guard but didn't hesitate. "That would be fantastic," he said, glancing around the cluttered kitchen. "When were you thinking?"

"How about fifteen minutes?" she asked.

Fifteen minutes? Larry's eyes widened. He hung up the phone, his heart racing, his mind spinning.

"Tiffany!" he shouted, his voice urgent. "We have fifteen minutes!"

They sprang into action, moving with the speed and precision of a well-trained team. Dirty dishes were tossed into the dishwasher, toys shoved under beds, and dirty laundry baskets hidden in closets. They wiped down countertops, fluffed pillows, made beds.

In fifteen minutes, they performed a miracle. The house looked clean, beautiful, and picture-perfect.

The doorbell rang. The realtor stood there with a gentleman who looked serious, thoughtful, and quiet.

Larry and Tiffany stayed in the house, trying to appear calm and casual, their hearts pounding, their nerves frayed.

The man walked in, his eyes sweeping over the rooms, his expression unreadable. He moved slowly, glancing here and there, taking it all in.

After five minutes, he walked out without saying a word.

Larry and Tiffany looked at each other, their shoulders sinking, their hope fading.

"Well, that was fast," Larry said, his voice heavy with disappointment. "He didn't like it."

They shrugged it off, sending the kids to school, heading off to work, trying not to think about it.

Larry was driving to the office when his phone rang. It was the realtor.

She was almost breathless with excitement. "He wants to make an offer," she said quickly. "He wants to offer more than the asking price as long as you can close in thirty days."

Larry almost swerved off the road, his mouth dropping open, his heart leaping. "Wait, what? He was there for five minutes! What happened?"

The realtor's voice softened. "He walked in and was overcome with emotion. He said he just knew. He felt it. He said he knew this was home. He could see himself raising his three daughters here. He felt like it was meant to be."

Larry's heart swelled, his eyes misting. He thought about all the memories they had made in that house—all the laughter, all the love, all the moments.

It was a special place.

Just like that, the house was sold.

They suddenly had to move, and they had no idea where to go.

They decided to move in with Vicki, who opened her doors without hesitation, welcoming them with open arms and embracing them with love.

Mayflower arrived to pack up the house. Every single item, from the smallest pencil to the largest piece of furniture, was carefully wrapped, boxed, and loaded into the truck. It was surreal, watching their life being packed away, watching the house grow emptier and emptier.

Everything was going to be stored in Colorado, waiting for them to find a new home.

Larry and Tiffany now had to make a trip to Colorado to find that new home and choose the place where their new memories would be made, where their new life would begin.

But before they left, they spent one last Saturday morning in the house they were selling.

LARRY BLAKE

They lay in bed, the morning sun pouring through the giant window in their master bedroom—a window six or seven feet wide, seven feet tall, with a beautiful half-moon arch at the top.

The sunlight bathed the room in golden light, warm and soft, peaceful and perfect.

Tiffany lay on her stomach, her long blonde hair over her shoulders, her skin glowing in the sunlight. She wore nothing but her underwear, her back smooth and flawless, her beauty breathtaking.

Larry lay beside her, his hand softly rubbing her back, his fingers tracing circles, his heart full of love.

This was his favorite place in the world. Right here, in this bed, in this room, in this house, with her.

He knew every inch of her beautiful skin, every curve, every mark. He had memorized the three tiny beauty marks on her back, knew their exact location, and knew the way they looked in the morning light.

He watched her breathe, watched her smile, watched her eyes sparkle as they talked about their plans for the day, about love, about life, about dreams.

She was his dream. She was his life. She was his ultimate love.

He knew, without a doubt, that no words could ever describe the way he felt about her.

They were deeply, beautifully, magically in love.

It was more than love. It was destiny. It was forever.

As he softly rubbed her back, as she rested peacefully, her eyes looking out the window, Larry felt his heart ache.

He was going to miss this house.

This was the house where they made their life, raised their children, loved fiercely, and laughed loudly. This was the house where they created memories, found joy, and where they lived fully.

FOREVER TIFFANY

But most of all, this was the house where he loved her, where he watched her, where he held her.

He watched the sunlight dance on her skin, his fingers memorizing the feel of her back, his heart capturing this moment, this memory, this love.

He didn't know where life would take them, what the future would hold, or where they would end up.

But he knew one thing. As long as he had her, as long as she was by his side, as long as he could lie next to her and love her, he was home.

Because the home wasn't this house. Home was Tiffany. It was always Tiffany.

Larry and Tiffany knew exactly where they wanted to begin their next chapter—Castle Rock, Colorado.

They had made a few trips in October and November of 2014, exploring neighborhoods, feeling the pulse of the town, and picturing their family growing and thriving in this beautiful place.

Castle Rock was perfect.

A charming town with a population of 42,000, nestled just twenty-five miles south of Denver, it was a community on the rise. It had a picturesque downtown with boutique shops and cozy cafés, the kind of place where you'd know your neighbors, where children could grow up safely, where memories could be made.

The outlet mall was a dream come true for Tiffany. She loved to shop, and she did it with the precision of a seasoned pro. Her eyes lit up as she walked through the stores, already imagining holiday shopping sprees, back-to-school outings, and lazy Sunday afternoons spent hunting for the perfect pair of shoes.

Castle Rock felt like home.

In December of 2014, they flew out one last time, ready to make it official, ready to find the house where their new life would begin.

They worked with a realtor named Steve, who had been handpicked for them by Tiffany's Aunt Susan in Florida.

Susan was a powerhouse, one of the most successful real estate agents in the state, a woman who built her empire with grace, grit, and brilliance. Tiffany had been her flower girl years ago when Susan and Dan married, a little blonde angel scattering petals down the aisle.

Susan loved Tiffany fiercely, and she wanted nothing but the best for her niece. So, she made sure Larry and Tiffany were represented by the best of the best.

Steve was exactly that. He was kind, patient, knowledgeable, and dedicated. He understood their vision, respected their budget, and treated them like family.

There was only one problem—Tiffany had come down with the flu.

She was exhausted, weak, and feverish. Her body ached, her head throbbed, and her energy was drained. But that wasn't about to stop her.

She was a warrior, a fighter, a woman who never backed down, never gave up, and never let anything get in the way of her family's happiness.

They had traveled all this way, they were ready to buy a house, and Tiffany was going to find their home—flu or no flu.

On Friday, Steve showed them fourteen or fifteen houses. Tiffany pushed through, her smile never fading, her heart never uncommitted. She walked through every room, mentally decorating, imagining her children playing, picturing holidays and birthdays and memories yet to come.

FOREVER TIFFANY

On Saturday, they saw another dozen houses. They were tired, exhausted, and emotionally drained.

But then, they found it. Their dream home.

It was everything they wanted, everything they needed, everything they had dreamed of.

The home had high ceilings that soared above them, making the space feel open, airy, and grand. The main foyer was elegant and inviting, leading to a formal sitting room that was both beautiful and cozy. A formal dining room with large windows overlooked the street, filling the room with sunlight, warmth, and charm.

The kitchen was breathtaking—tall cabinets with crown molding, granite countertops that sparkled in the light, and a large island perfect for family breakfasts, holiday baking, and late-night snacks.

There was a formal office for Larry, a place where he could work, dream, and build his career.

A large loft overlooked the main living space, a perfect spot for the kids to play, to laugh, to grow.

The basement was fully finished, complete with a gorgeous bar, a workout room, and plenty of space for game nights, movie marathons, and sleepovers.

The backyard was beautifully landscaped with a large patio, perfect for summer BBQs, birthday parties, and lazy evenings under the stars.

Tiffany fell in love.

She could already see where each child would sleep, hear their laughter echoing through the halls, and feel their joy as they made this house a home.

She imagined Christmas morning, the grand staircase wrapped in garland, the fireplace glowing, the tree twinkling, the house filled with magic and love.

She pictured summer nights on the patio, the kids playing tag, Larry grilling burgers, and the sunset painting the sky in shades of pink and gold.

She imagined every holiday, every birthday, every memory they would make.

She saw it all. This wasn't just a house. This was home.

Larry watched her eyes light up, watched her smile grow, watched her heart fill with love and hope.

This was it. This was the place where their new life would begin, where they would build their future, where they would raise their children.

He could see it, too.

They put in an offer that night, their hearts excited, their fingers crossed.

They went back to the hotel, exhausted and hungry. The long day of house hunting had taken its toll, and Tiffany was visibly worn out, her body aching, her fever relentless.

She was too weak to even consider going out for dinner. Her face was pale, her eyes heavy, her energy drained.

"I need a hot bath," she whispered, her voice fragile, her spirit still strong. She shuffled off to the bathroom, the door clicking softly behind her. Larry watched her go, his heart aching, his love overwhelming. He hated seeing her like this—weak, sick, vulnerable. She was always so strong, so full of life, so full of love.

But tonight, she needed him. And Larry knew what to do.

He picked up the phone and called a nearby Chinese restaurant, ordering enough food to feed a small army. He knew her favorites—sweet and sour chicken, fried rice, wonton soup, and egg rolls. He ordered it all, wanting to make sure she had options, wanting to give her anything that would bring a smile to her face.

When the food arrived, he set it up like a buffet, spreading it across the table in the hotel room, arranging it with care, making sure it looked perfect.

He knew how much she loved Chinese food, how the smell alone could lift her spirits, and how her eyes would light up when she saw the spread.

Larry had always taken care of her from the first day they met. It was just who he was. It was who he would always be.

After what felt like an eternity, Tiffany finally emerged from the bathroom, her hair wrapped in a towel, her face flushed from the hot bath, and her body still weary. She stopped in her tracks, her eyes wide, her mouth dropping open.

The smell hit her first—the sweet, savory aroma of her favorite dishes. Then she saw the table overflowing with takeout boxes, sauces, chopsticks, and fortune cookies.

Her smile grew. "Are you crazy?" she laughed, her voice soft, her love loud. "You ordered enough food for twenty people!"

Larry just shrugged, his smile mischievous, his heart proud. "You need to eat," he said simply. "You love Chinese food. And I love you."

Tiffany walked over to him, her arms wrapping around his waist, her head resting on his chest. "I don't deserve you," she whispered, her voice cracking. "You're my prince. You always take care of me. You always make everything better."

Larry held her close, his fingers brushing her hair, his heart full of love. "I'll always take care of you," he whispered back. "Always."

They sat down and ate together, laughing, talking, and relishing each bite. For a moment, she forgot she was sick. And exhausted. In that moment, everything was perfect.

The next morning, they boarded the flight back to Chicago. The sun was rising, the sky pink and gold, the mountains a silhouette against the dawn.

Tiffany was feeling better, her fever fading, her strength returning. She leaned her head on Larry's shoulder, her heart content, her mind peaceful.

But as the plane took off, she suddenly turned to him, her eyes wide, her face confused.

"Did we buy a house?" she asked, her words hesitant.

Larry's head snapped toward her, his jaw dropping. "What?" he asked, his voice loud, eyes wide. "Are you serious?"

Tiffany's cheeks flushed, her eyes blinking in confusion. "I don't remember. Did we put in an offer?"

Larry's heart sprinted, his mind spinning. How could she not remember? Was she really that sick? Was she just that exhausted?

He stared at her, trying to process her question. "Yes, we did," he said slowly, his voice cautious. "They accepted our offer. We bought the house."

Tiffany's eyes grew even wider, her face even more confused. "Which house?" she asked, her voice trembling. "Was it the one with the big kitchen? Or was it the one with the marble foyer?"

Larry felt his heart skip a beat, his palms growing sweaty. Had they really forgotten which house they bought? Were they really that overwhelmed, that exhausted, that delirious?

His hands shook as he reached for his bag, pulling out the paperwork, flipping through the pages, finding the photos of the house.

He held up the pictures, his fear rising. "This one," he said. "This is the one we bought."

Tiffany stared at the photos, her eyes scanning the rooms, her mind confused, her heart drubbing.

And then she exhaled, her shoulders sinking, her face relaxing. "Oh, thank God," she sighed, her voice full of relief, her heart full of joy. "That's the one I wanted the most. I was just afraid you put an offer on the other one."

Larry's heart finally slowed down, his fear disappearing, his relief overwhelming. He burst out laughing, his head falling back, his laughter echoing through the plane.

Tiffany joined him, her famous laugh.

They were fatigued, excited, overwhelmed. But they were together. They were happy. They were in love.

And they had just bought their dream home.

Together, they were ready to start this new chapter. And live this new adventure. Together, they were unstoppable. Because together, they were home.

CHAPTER 7.
Angels and Fathers

Just before the end of 2014, Larry and Tiffany faced another tragedy, one that hit them harder than they could have imagined.

Max, the little black pug who had been part of their family for over a decade, wasn't doing well. His eyesight was nearly gone, his movements slow and strained. Just walking outside to go to the bathroom was a struggle. His tail, once curly and full of life, hung limp. His eyes, once bright and mischievous, looked tired and defeated.

Max had been there through it all. He was there when Patrick was just a boy, when Rylee was learning to walk, and when Brennan was learning to talk. He was there for every birthday, every Christmas morning, every bedtime story. He was there for every laugh, every tear, every moment.

He was family.

One morning, after the kids went off to school, Larry and Tiffany made the difficult decision to take Max to the veterinarian. They knew something was wrong, something more than just old age. They knew he was suffering, even if he tried to hide it.

They drove in silence, their hearts heavy, their fears mounting. Max lay quietly in Tiffany's lap, his little body curled up, his breathing soft and shallow.

At the vet, they were led into a small room, sterile and cold. The veterinarian examined Max carefully, gently, and lovingly. He looked at Larry and Tiffany, his eyes sad, his voice heavy.

Max had cancer. Tumors were spread throughout his little body, silent and deadly. His spine was damaged beyond repair, leaving his rear legs numb and his movements labored. He was in pain—deep, unrelenting pain.

They were faced with an impossible choice. They could take him home, give him a few more days, try to make him comfortable, and try to pretend that everything was okay. Or they could say goodbye. Today. Right here. Right now.

The room was suffocating and silent. They found it hard to breathe, hard to think, hard to move. They were lost, shattered, broken.

How could they say goodbye to him? How could they let him go? How could they live without him?

They looked at Max, his eyes tired but trusting, his body weak but loving. They knew. They knew they couldn't let him suffer. They knew they had to do the right thing.

They knew they had to say goodbye.

Tears poured down their faces, their hands trembling, their hearts breaking. They held Max close, their faces buried in his fur, their voices soft and loving. They told him how much they loved him, how much he meant to them, and how he would always be a part of their family. They whispered memories, shared stories, and kissed him over and over again.

They were there for him, just as he had always been there for them.

The veterinarian was gentle, his voice kind, his heart empathetic. He explained every step, every movement, every moment. He gave them time, gave them space, gave them love.

Max's breathing slowed, his body relaxed, his eyes closed. He looked peaceful, calm, loved.

And then, he was gone.

Larry and Tiffany sat there, holding him, crying, whispering, mourning. They stayed for over an hour, unable to let go, unwilling to say goodbye.

It was another blow, another loss, another heartbreak.

They didn't just lose a dog. They lost a family member.

As they drove home, the silence was deafening, the pain choking. They were heartbroken for themselves and for each other, but mostly, they were heartbroken for their children.

How would they tell them? How would they break the news that their best friend, their buddy, their constant companion was gone? How would they find the words to explain the unexplainable?

Later that afternoon, they attended a parent/player meeting with Patrick and his eighth-grade basketball team. Patrick knew they had taken Max to the vet but didn't know what had happened.

As he sat with his teammates, he looked across the room and caught his parents' eyes. He stared at them, his face full of hope, his heart full of fear.

He mouthed the words, "How's Max?"

Larry and Tiffany froze. They felt the tears rush back, felt the pain hit again, felt their hearts break all over.

They didn't have to say a word. Their faces said it all.

Patrick's eyes filled with tears, his heart breaking, his world shattering. But he didn't want his teammates to see him cry. He tried to hold it together, tried to stay strong, tried to be brave.

But as soon as they got in the car, he broke.

Patrick lost it; his body was shaking, his sobs loud, and his tears unstoppable. He was devastated, heartbroken, shattered.

He was sad, but he was also angry. Angry that Max was gone. Angry that he didn't get to say goodbye. Angry that his parents made the decision without him. He shouted, his voice cracking, his tears falling. "Why didn't you wait? Why didn't you let me see him one last time? Why didn't you give me one more day?"

Larry and Tiffany were gutted, their guilt overwhelming, their sorrow uncontainable. They tried to explain. They tried to make him understand. They tried to comfort him. But they were sad, too. They were heartbroken, too. They were disappointed in themselves, too.

They thought they were doing the right thing by sparing Max the pain and understood they were making the best choice.

But now, they were doubly sad.

Sad that Max was gone. Sad that they lost a member of their family. Sad that Patrick was hurting. Sad that their hearts were broken.

Max was more than just a pet. He was family. He was love. He was home. He was there through it all, through the good times and the bad, through the laughter and the tears, through the wins and the losses.

He was loyal, loving, and perfect. But now, he was gone.

And nothing would ever be the same.

But then again, Max would live on. In their hearts, in their memories, in their love.

In January of 2015, Larry and Tiffany closed on their new home in Castle Rock, Colorado. It was the beginning of a new adventure, a new chapter, a new life.

The house was perfect—a place where dreams could be lived, where memories could be made, where love could grow. It was everything they had envisioned, everything they had hoped for, everything they had prayed for.

Mayflower arrived with all their belongings, every box carefully labeled, every piece of furniture carefully wrapped. The moving team followed Tiffany's instructions with precision, placing each item exactly where she wanted it and arranging each room just the way she imagined.

The house was coming together, transforming from empty walls and vacant rooms into a warm, welcoming home.

But it wasn't finished. Not yet.

Tiffany had a vision, and she was determined to make it a reality. She was on a mission to turn this house into a masterpiece, to make it not just beautiful but magical, to make it feel like home.

She discovered a local furniture store that quickly became her favorite place. It was a decorator's paradise, filled with gorgeous pieces, stunning decor, and everything she needed to complete her vision.

Tiffany shopped like only Tiffany could.

She had an eye for beauty, a talent for style, and an instinct for design. She knew exactly what she wanted, where each piece would go, and how it would all come together.

She picked out elegant couches, plush rugs, cozy chairs. She found gorgeous lamps, stunning artwork, beautiful mirrors. She chose table settings, throw pillows, and curtains.

She spared no detail and left nothing to chance. She worked tirelessly, arranging and rearranging, decorating and designing, perfecting every corner, every wall, every room.

She did it all with love, with care, with passion.

Larry watched in awe, his heart full of admiration.

This was Tiffany's gift. She had a way of turning the ordinary into the extraordinary, a way of transforming a house into a home, a way of making everything more beautiful.

She had done it before. She was doing it again.

And she made it perfect. She made it warm, inviting, and elegant. She made it magical, charming, breathtaking. She made it home.

They stood in the living room one evening, the sun setting over the mountains. Tiffany wrapped her arms around Larry, her head resting on his chest and her heart full of love.

"Welcome home," she whispered, her words full of promise.

Larry kissed her forehead, his eyes wet, his heart overflowing with love.

They had done it.

Together, they had built another dream, created another chapter, started another adventure. Together, they were ready for whatever life had in store. Together, they were home.

In February of 2015, Larry and Tiffany returned to their new home in Castle Rock, Colorado. They wanted to spend their anniversary and Valentine's Day in their new house, explore the area even more, and start making memories in the place they would now call home.

It was the beginning of a new chapter, and they wanted to celebrate it right.

Holly and Steve decided to join them on the trip. Holly and Tiffany weren't just sisters-in-law—they were best friends. They had been inseparable since they were twelve years old, sharing dreams, secrets, laughter, and life.

Holly and Steve had never visited Colorado before and were eager to see where Larry and Tiffany would be living, to explore the town, to picture their best friends' new life.

When they arrived, they were blown away.

The beauty of Colorado was breathtaking. The majestic mountains stood tall against the clear blue sky, the rolling hills were covered in snow, and the fresh, crisp air smelled of pine and adventure.

And then there was Castle Rock.

Driving south from Denver, the iconic butte seemed to rise out of nowhere, standing proudly above the town, a symbol of strength, of history, of home.

It was charming, picturesque, perfect. The downtown was quaint and inviting, and the neighborhoods were beautiful; the community was warm and welcoming.

It felt like something out of a storybook. Holly and Steve were mesmerized. Valentine's Day was magical.

They spent the evening at a cozy restaurant, the lights dim, the candles flickering, the atmosphere romantic. The food was delicious, the wine flowing, and the company was perfect.

They laughed, reminisced, and shared stories of the past, memories of childhood, and dreams of the future. But as the night went on, the reality of the situation began to sink in. This wasn't just a vacation. This wasn't just a visit. This was goodbye.

Larry and Tiffany were moving. Really moving. They were leaving Indiana. They were leaving their family, their friends, their life. They were leaving Holly and Steve.

Holly tried to hold it together, tried to be strong, tried to be brave. But she couldn't help it. Tears welled up in her eyes. She looked at Tiffany, her best friend, her sister, her person.

She thought about all the birthdays she would miss, all the holidays they wouldn't share, all the proms, all the graduations, all the moments, all the memories. All the times they wouldn't have together, all the laughs they wouldn't share, all the tears they wouldn't cry.

She thought about losing her best friend.

Larry watched his sister, his heart aching. He knew how close Holly and Tiffany were, knew how much they loved each other, knew how much this hurt. It hurt him, too. He was emotional, just like his sister. They wore their hearts on their sleeves, loved deeply, and felt strongly.

He didn't want to leave, didn't want to say goodbye, didn't want to break his sister's heart. But he also knew he had to follow his dream, his heart, and his destiny.

The next morning, Larry and Tiffany were still reeling from the emotions of the night before, still heavy-hearted, still sad.

But then, everything changed.

Holly and Steve dropped a bombshell, a surprise so shocking, so unexpected, so wonderful that Larry and Tiffany could hardly believe it.

Holly and Steve had fallen in love with Colorado in just twenty-four short hours.

They loved the mountains, the beauty, and the lifestyle. They loved Castle Rock, the charm, the community, and the promise of adventure. They loved it all. And they decided, right then and there, to move their family to Colorado, too.

Holly couldn't imagine life without Tiffany, couldn't imagine her kids growing up without their cousins, couldn't imagine her heart living half a country away. They were best friends, they were sisters, they were family. And they were going on this adventure together.

Tiffany was over the moon, her eyes sparkling, her tears falling, her heart bursting.

Her best friend, who had been coming with her since she was twelve years old, was coming with her. Her partner in crime, her sister in spirit, her person. They would be together.

Their children would grow up together, go to school together, and celebrate birthdays together. They would share holidays, vacations, and weekends. They would make memories together. They would build their lives together.

Tiffany hugged Holly, her heart full, her soul happy. "I can't believe this is happening," she whispered, her voice trembling. "I thought I was losing you."

Holly hugged her back, her tears falling, her love strong. "You'll never lose me," she whispered back. "Not now. Not ever."

They laughed, they cried, they hugged. And then they got to work.

Holly and Steve started house hunting that very day. They called Steve, the same realtor who helped Larry and Tiffany, the man who made dreams come true.

They toured houses, walked through neighborhoods, and planned their future.

They were doing it. They were really doing it. Together.

Larry and Tiffany stood on the back deck of their new home that evening, looking out at the mountains, the sun setting behind the peaks, the sky glowing.

Tiffany rested her head on Larry's shoulder. "You see?" she whispered, her voice soft, her words accurate. "Everything works out the way it's supposed to."

Larry kissed her head. She was right. She was always right. They weren't just starting a new adventure. They were bringing their family with them. They weren't just building a new life. They were building it together. And that made all the difference.

After returning to their temporary home in Indiana, Larry and Tiffany continued to prepare for the final move to Colorado. The countdown had begun, and with each passing day, the reality of leaving became more real, heavier, and more emotional.

The kids were rolling along in school, trying to soak up every last moment, trying to absorb memories that would last a lifetime. They played at recess, laughed in the hallways, and whispered secrets in the cafeteria.

FOREVER TIFFANY

But even at their young age, they understood that goodbyes were coming. They knew that these goodbyes would be different. These weren't the "see you tomorrow" goodbyes or the "catch you this weekend" goodbyes. These were the kind of goodbyes that would most likely be the last time they saw their friends, the kids they grew up with, the kids they loved. They were leaving behind more than just a school—they were leaving behind a piece of their childhood.

Larry and Tiffany watched them closely, knowing how hard this was. They knew how painful it was to say goodbye; they were feeling it, too.

Tiffany especially felt the weight of it all. She had built a community, a tribe, a family. Her home was always full of kids, friends, laughter, and love.

But not every child who walked through her door came from a loving home. Not every child who played in her backyard went home to a warm meal, a kind word, a loving hug.

Tiffany knew this, and she made it her mission to fill in the gaps, to be the love those kids were missing, to be the light in their darkness.

She was fairylike that way.

She had a way of seeing people—their pain, their struggles, their needs. She didn't just look at them; she saw them.

She saw the little boy who wore the same clothes every week, who looked at the lunch menu with hungry eyes but never enough money. She saw the little girl who came over every day after school, who laughed loudly but cried quietly, who never wanted to go home.

Tiffany loved them all unconditionally, wholeheartedly, and beautifully. She took them under her wing, made them feel special, and made them feel loved. She was the mom they needed, the friend they were missing, the hope they were searching for.

If a kid needed a meal, Tiffany made sure they were fed. But she didn't just hand them a sandwich or throw them a snack. She took them out to a restaurant, treated them to dinner, made them feel special. She watched as they looked at the menu, their eyes wide, their faces cautious, their fear of costing too much or asking for too much evident in every movement. They would always order the cheapest item on the menu, just the bare minimum. They would speak quietly, hesitantly, embarrassed.

But Tiffany wouldn't stand for that.

She would lean in, her voice soft, her heart big. "What do you really want?" she would ask, her eyes kind, her smile warm.

The kids would look up, their eyes wide, their faces shocked. "Really?" they would ask, their voices shuddering, their hearts hopeful.

"Really," Tiffany would say, her voice firm, her love fierce. "Get whatever you want. Get as much as you need."

She would then order more food than necessary—enough for them to take home, enough for their siblings to eat, enough to help their family, even if just for one night.

She did it with grace, with love, with humility. She never made them feel ashamed or small. She never made them feel like charity. She made them feel special. She made them feel loved. She made them feel seen. She didn't just feed their bodies—she fed their souls. She didn't just change their day—she changed their lives.

Maybe she wasn't changing the world in some huge, extraordinary way. Maybe she wasn't ending hunger, solving poverty, or saving the planet.

But she was changing the world in a way that mattered. She was changing it for one person, for one child, for one moment. And to that child, she was a hero. To that child, she was everything.

Tiffany loved to love.

She loved fiercely, beautifully, completely. She gave without expecting anything in return. She poured out her heart, her soul, her kindness.

She did it because she believed in love, kindness, and helping others. She did it because she knew there might come a day when she needed a helping hand. She did it because that was who she was.

She was light. She was love.

And her love would live on in the hearts of those children, in the lives she touched, in the world she changed.

Larry's father, Larry Sr., had always been a coach. It wasn't just his job—it was his calling, his passion, his life.

He had spent years as the men's head basketball coach at Purdue Northwest, leading teams, mentoring players, and building a legacy. But a few years back, he decided to retire from basketball, stepping away from the sidelines, stepping away from the game he loved.

But Larry Sr. wasn't ready to give up coaching. Not yet.

The school knew this. They also knew they had just hired a young, inexperienced head coach to lead the baseball team—a team with potential, a team that needed guidance, a team that needed leadership.

They saw the opportunity, the perfect fit, the ideal mentor. They asked Larry Sr. to stay on as the head assistant baseball coach, to be the steady hand, the wise voice, the guiding light. Larry Sr. agreed, his heart soaring, his excitement returning. Baseball was where he started his coaching career, his first love, his first passion. He was back on the field, back in the dugout, back in the game.

He was coaching again, teaching again, and leading again. And he loved every minute of it. He loved the sound of the bat cracking against the ball, the smell of freshly cut grass, the dirt under his shoes. He loved working with the players, molding young men, teaching them not just about baseball but about life.

LARRY BLAKE

He was exactly where he was meant to be.

But then, things turned in the opposite direction.

He heard the news that his son, Larry, was moving to Colorado.

It was tough, painful, heartbreaking. But he understood. He was proud of his son, of the man he became, and of the father and husband he was.

But then, just as he was coming to terms with it, just as he was preparing to say goodbye, he heard the second piece of news.

His daughter, Holly, was moving to Colorado, too.

That was the breaking point. It hit him hard, shook him to his core, and shattered his heart. It was one thing to lose his son, but to lose his daughter too? To lose both of his children? To watch them take his grandchildren across the country, miles and miles away?

He sat at the kitchen table, his head in his hands, his heart aching.

Diana sat across from him, her face sad, her eyes moist. She watched him, knowing how deeply he was hurting, knowing how much this was tearing him apart.

"They're leaving," he whispered, his voice breaking, his tears falling. "They're really leaving."

Diana's heart broke for him, for herself, for the family they had built, the life they had shared, the memories they had made. She reached across the table, her fingers wrapping around his, her love persistent.

"What do you want to do?" she asked, her voice steady, her heart strong. "Where do you want to be?"

He looked up, his eyes red, his face wet. He didn't hesitate. "With them," he said simply, his voice firm, his love fierce. "I want to be with them."

FOREVER TIFFANY

They made the decision together, sitting at that kitchen table, their hands clasped, their hearts aligned.

They were putting their house up for sale. They were leaving Indiana. They were moving, sight unseen, to Colorado. They were going to be with their children, with their grandchildren, with their family. Because nothing mattered more than family.

The news spread quickly, like wildfire, like a shockwave, like a farewell.

All the local media outlets featured stories on Larry Sr.'s career, his impact, and his legacy. They celebrated his years as the men's head basketball coach, his dedication, his success, and his love for the game. They told stories of his leadership, his mentorship, and his influence on young athletes. They spoke of his kindness, patience, and wisdom.

They talked about his return to the baseball field, his second career, his new chapter. Purdue Northwest was going to miss him.

He was inducted into the Athletic Hall of Fame at the university, his name forever carved into the history of the school, his legacy secured, his career celebrated.

Larry Sr. stood on the stage, his voice cracking as he thanked everyone who had supported him, believed in him, and loved him.

He looked out at the audience, his former players, his fellow coaches, his colleagues, his friends. He thought about all the years he spent on that campus, all the games he coached, all the lives he touched, all the memories he made. He loved that school. He loved that campus. He loved being there every day, loved the feeling of walking through those hallways, loved the sound of the basketball bouncing, the crack of the bat, the roar of the crowd.

He loved coaching. He loved teaching. He loved leading. But he loved his family more. And he wanted to be with them more than he wanted to stay.

LARRY BLAKE

Larry Sr. and Diana made the announcement quietly, privately, without fanfare, without spectacle. They weren't leaving because they were unhappy. They weren't leaving because they were tired. They were leaving because they were in love. In love with their children. In love with their grandchildren. In love with their family.

They wanted to be there for every birthday, every holiday, every milestone. They wanted to be there for every basketball game, every track meet, every dance routine. They wanted to watch their grandchildren grow up. They wanted to share in the laughter, in the memories, in the love.

So, they were moving to Colorado without hesitation, without regret, without fear.

Larry Sr. was walking away from the school he loved, the career he cherished, the life he built.

But he was walking toward his family, his heart, his home.

And that made all the difference. Because to Larry Sr., the home wasn't a place. Home was where his family was.

And his family was in Colorado. So that's where he would be.

CHAPTER 8.
Light in the Storm

June of 2015 was fast approaching, and for Vicki, the reality of it all was finally sinking in.

Tiffany was leaving.

Her baby girl, her best friend, her everything—was leaving Indiana, moving across the country, starting a new life in Colorado.

Tiffany had been her rock, her joy, her light. From the moment she was born, from the first cry, from the first smile, Tiffany had filled Vicki's heart with love, her soul with hope, and her life with purpose.

She was the one who made her laugh, the one who shared her life.

But now, she was leaving.

Vicki tried to be strong, brave, and supportive. She didn't want to make Tiffany feel guilty, didn't want to hold her back, didn't want to keep her from chasing her dreams. She was happy for her, proud of her, and excited for her.

But she was also heartbroken. Because this wasn't just Tiffany leaving. This was Vicki losing her daughter, her friend, her reason for living.

Years ago, Amanda moved away, following her heart and her dreams and building her life in Ohio.

And now Tiffany was leaving, too. Vicki was going to be alone.

She sat in her living room one evening. The house was quiet, and the air was heavy. She looked around at the pictures on the wall, the memories frozen in time, the laughter, the love, the moments. She thought about all the birthdays she celebrated, all the Christmas mornings she shared, and all the bedtime stories she read. She thought about all the times she kissed their boo-boos, wiped their tears, and held them close.

She thought about her life, her love, her heart. She thought about Tiffany. She thought about losing her. Her heart sank, her tears fell, her fears rose. She needed Tiffany. She needed her laughter, her smile, her love. She wanted to be close to her daughter and grandchildren.

And then, in that quiet room, in that heavy air, Vicki made a decision. A decision that would change everything. This decision would be the most wonderful surprise that Tiffany could ever receive.

She was going to Colorado, too.

She was leaving Indiana, leaving the life she had built, leaving the school she taught at for so many years. She was submitting her retirement papers, closing that chapter, ending that story. She was moving to Colorado to be with her daughter, to be with her grandchildren, to be with her family.

She was going to start over, to begin again, to live this new adventure. She was choosing Tiffany.

Vicki didn't hesitate, didn't waver, didn't doubt. She quickly sold her house.

She didn't even visit Colorado first and didn't even consider the risks. If it was good enough for Tiffany, it was good enough for her.

Vicki dialed the phone, and Tiffany picked up. Her voice was bright, and her laughter was warm and beautiful. "Hi, Mom," she said. "What's up?"

Vicki took a deep breath, her heart beating faster, her love strong. She smiled, her soul full of hope, her voice full of love.

"I'm coming with you," she whispered, her words soft, her promise true. "I'm moving to Colorado, too."

There was silence on the other end, a pause, a breath, a beat.

FOREVER TIFFANY

And then, Tiffany's scream, her laughter, her joy.

"Are you serious? Are you really coming?" she cried, her voice bursting with excitement, her heart exploding with love. "Oh my God, Mom! I can't believe it! I can't believe you're coming!"

Tiffany and Larry had always been planners. They thought ahead, they dreamed big, and they built their life with purpose and intention.

When they bought their new home in Castle Rock, they chose it carefully, thoughtfully, and lovingly. They wanted it to be beautiful, to be welcoming, to be perfect. But they also wanted it to be big enough for one more.

They chose a house with a guest suite, complete with a private bathroom, a cozy sitting area, and plenty of space. They chose it with Vicki in mind.

Early June of 2015 finally arrived, and the day they had been planning, dreaming, and dreading was here.

The car was packed, every suitcase neatly arranged, every belonging carefully stowed. The kids piled into the back seat, Larry in the driver's seat, Tiffany by his side. They were ready to go.

But first, they took one last pass through their old neighborhood, one last drive down the familiar streets, one last look at the place they had called home. They waved to neighbors, smiled at friends, and said goodbyes that were more than just goodbyes. They were goodbyes to a chapter, to a life, to a dream. They were goodbyes to a past they loved, to a place they cherished, to a community that had been their foundation. They were goodbyes that were most likely final, goodbyes that hurt, goodbyes that were hard.

But they were ready.

They were ready for a new adventure, a new chapter, a new life. They planned to break the one-thousand-mile journey into two days, taking their time, making memories, and appreciating the moment.

Their first stop would be in Lincoln, Nebraska, a quiet town, a place to rest, a night to reflect.

The kids were genuinely happy, their faces bright, their eyes wide. They were slightly nervous, unsure of what was to come, unsure of what to expect. But they were excited, hopeful, and organized for the next escapade.

They had traveled across the United States and Mexico, seen beaches and deserts, mountains and valleys. But they had never been to Colorado. They had never seen the snow-capped mountains, never smelled the crisp, clean air, never felt the magic of the Rockies. They had never seen the place that would become their new home.

They were excited, curious, eager. But first, they had to get through Nebraska. No offense to Nebraska or Iowa, but that stretch of highway was long, flat, and boring. The kids were restless, fidgety, complaining. They fought over the iPad, whined about the radio station, and kicked the back of Larry's seat. They were bored. Really bored.

After what felt like forever, they finally arrived in Lincoln, exhausted, hungry, and ready for a break.

They checked into the Embassy Suites, their bodies weary, their minds tired. But the excitement of the adventure was still there, the thrill of the unknown, the magic of the journey.

Later that night, Rylee and Larry decided to head downstairs for a late-night snack. The restaurant was quiet, the lights dim, the air warm.

They sat at the table, eating chips and salsa, talking about the move, laughing about the trip. And then Rylee's eyes grew wide, her face shocked, her mouth dropping open. "Dad," she whispered, her voice excited, her words quick. "That's the 'Despacito' guy! That's Luis Fonsi!"

FOREVER TIFFANY

Larry looked over, his eyes squinting, his face confused. He knew the song—everyone knew the song—but he had no idea who the singer was.

Rylee pulled out her phone, her fingers flying, her eyes wide. She looked at the pictures, then looked at the man. He was a dead ringer.

Rylee was only eleven years old, but she was brave, confident, and fearless. She walked up to the man, her voice soft, her face smiling. "Excuse me, are you...?"

The man cut her off, his eyes twinkling, his smile playful. "The 'Despacito' singer?" he asked, his voice teasing, his words light.

Rylee's eyes grew even wider, her smile even bigger. "Yes!" she shouted, her excitement overflowing, her heart drumming.

The man leaned in, his voice low, his face serious. "Maybe," he said, his words mysterious, his eyes twinkling.

Rylee knew it was him. She was sure of it. She shook his hand, her heart racing, her smile bright. She went back to the table, her face glowing.

Larry looked at her, his face curious, his heart full. "Was it him?" he asked, his voice low, his words careful. Rylee shrugged, her smile wide, her heart full. "I don't know," she said, her voice playful. "But it was still pretty cool."

Larry laughed, his head falling back. They would never know for sure if it was him. But that didn't matter. They were making memories, building moments, living life.

They were on an adventure. They were on their way home.

Getting ready in the morning—this was Larry's favorite time to watch Tiffany. There was something magical about the way she moved, the way she brushed her hair, the way she put on her makeup, the way she got ready for the day. It was graceful, effortless, and fascinating.

LARRY BLAKE

He loved the way she looked in the mirror, her eyes focused, her smile soft, her beauty undeniable.

She was small in stature but mighty in strength, fierce in love, powerful in presence.

To the world, she was a mother, a wife, a friend. But to Larry, she was everything.

He loved watching her get ready, loved the way she moved about, loved the way she made the ordinary look extraordinary. And on that morning, as they prepared for the second leg of their journey to Colorado, she looked especially beautiful. She wore tiny jean shorts that showed off her beautiful tan legs, a white t-shirt that fit her perfectly, and a white baseball cap that sat just right on her head. Her Ray-Ban sunglasses were perched on her nose, and her flip-flops dangled off her feet.

She was effortlessly beautiful, effortlessly sexy, not in a flashy way, but in an elegant, timeless way. She carried herself with confidence, with grace, with humility. She walked into a room and lit it up, brightened it, and made it better.

But she never acted like she knew that. She never demanded attention, never craved the spotlight, and never needed validation.

She was just herself. And that was enough.

Larry watched her as she moved about, his love overflowing.

She was his wife, his partner, his soulmate. She was his angel.

They packed up the car, loaded up the kids, and got back on the road, ready for another eight hours of driving, ready to be in their new home.

The highway seemed long and slow, the minutes dragging, the miles endless. But they were excited, eager, and optimistic.

They approached the split from Highway 80 onto Highway 76 with anticipation, knowing that this was the road that would take them to Colorado. They were almost there. When they finally crossed the state line into Colorado, the car erupted in cheers, in laughter, in celebration.

They had made it. They were in Colorado.

But then, the cheering stopped, the smiles faded, the excitement dimmed.

The kids looked out the windows, their faces confused, their eyes disappointed.

Where were the mountains? Where was the beauty, the majesty, the magic?

They had heard so much about Colorado—the grand mountains, the breathtaking scenery, the snow-capped peaks. They expected to see it all, expected to be in awe, expected to be amazed. But all they saw were endless plains, flat land, and empty fields.

They were disappointed. Really disappointed.

They turned to Tiffany, their faces sad, their hearts heavy. "Where are the mountains?" they asked, their voices confused, their words sad.

Tiffany laughed, her eyes twinkling, her smile bright. She turned to face them, her voice soft, her love strong. "They're coming," she said, her words filled with promise, her heart full of hope. "Just be patient. We've got three more hours to go. But once we get closer, once we get to the front range, you'll see them. And they're more beautiful than you can even imagine."

The kids sat back in their seats, their faces still unsure, their hearts still doubtful. But they believed her. They always believed her. Because Tiffany never let them down.

They looked out the windows again, this time with hope, with anticipation, with excitement.

The Colorado plains were nice, quiet, and calm. But they weren't the front range. They weren't the mountains. Not yet. But they were coming. And Tiffany couldn't wait to see the looks on their faces when they finally saw them.

As late afternoon fell and the sun began to dip below the horizon, the light softened, the sky painted in shades of pink and gold.

And then, there they were. The mountains.

They rose up before them, majestic, breathtaking, powerful.

Snow-capped peaks touched the sky, their white tops glowing in the evening light. The rugged slopes stood tall, unyielding, magnificent. The front range stretched out endlessly, the Rockies forming a wall of beauty, a gateway to a new life, a new home.

The kids' eyes grew wide, their mouths falling open, their hearts pounding. It was more beautiful than they could have ever imagined. They pressed their faces to the glass, their fingers pointing, their voices excited.

"There they are!" Rylee shouted, her eyes sparkling, her face glowing. "There are the mountains!"

Brennan's mouth dropped open, his voice filled with awe. "They're huge!" he whispered, his words quiet, his heart running.

Patrick stared without blinking. "They're amazing," he said, his voice and soul full.

Larry looked over at Tiffany. She was smiling, her eyes bright, her face peaceful. She looked at the mountains, then back at her children, her heart overflowing with love. She knew this was a moment they would never forget, a memory they would carry with them forever.

This was the start of their new life. This was the beginning of their new journey.

This was the place they would call home.

They drove closer, the mountains growing bigger, stronger, more beautiful. The sun dipped lower, the light fading, the peaks glowing in the golden dusk. It was breathtaking. It was magical. It was everything they dreamed of and more.

Their smiles widened, their hearts buzzed with excitement. They were almost there. They were almost home.

Tiffany turned to face the kids, her voice soft, her words gentle. "This is just the beginning," she whispered.

Larry reached over, his hand finding hers, his fingers wrapping around hers. He gave her hand a gentle squeeze, his love silent, his promise unspoken. She squeezed back, her eyes meeting his, her heart happy.

They looked out at the mountains, the journey before them, the life ahead of them. They were ready. Ready for the change. Ready for the journey that would change them all in ways they could never imagine.

The journey was just beginning. And it was beautiful.

When they finally arrived at their new house in Castle Rock, the sun had set, and the air was cool, crisp, and refreshing.

The house was situated up a shared driveway off a quiet neighborhood road, nestled among three other beautiful homes. It was private, peaceful, and perfect.

The headlights illuminated the driveway, shadows dancing across the yard, and excitement palpable. Before the car even came to a complete stop, the kids were unbuckling their seatbelts, bursting out of the car, running up the steps, and racing to the front door.

They were finally here. They were finally home.

The door swung open, and the kids scattered, their laughter echoing through the halls, their footsteps thundering up the stairs. They explored every corner, every room, every space. They found their bedrooms, their beds neatly made, their toys waiting, their clothes folded. They hadn't slept in those beds in months. It felt good. It felt right. It felt like home.

The house was set up to perfection—of course, it was. Tiffany had taken care of every little detail, planned every piece, and arranged every item. Pictures were hung, dishes were put away, and towels were neatly folded in the bathrooms. It was perfect. She always made it perfect.

Larry watched his children run from room to room, their laughter filling the house, their joy bursting. He looked over at Tiffany, his love, his home.

She smiled at him. They had made it. They were here. They were home.

It was late, and they were exhausted from the long drive, the emotional goodbyes, and the anticipation of the new adventure.

They finally settled in, their heads hitting the pillows, their eyes closing, their hearts happy. They fell asleep with dreams full of possibilities, excitement, and hope.

But the next morning came early. Too early.

Larry's phone rang, waking him from a deep sleep, his head foggy, his body heavy.

It was Earl, a former NBA player who spent years in the league.

Before they moved to Colorado, Larry had spoken with Earl, who was coaching a local high school team and an AAU team in the summer. Earl had invited Patrick to be a part of his program, to join his team, to learn from one of the best.

And Earl wasn't wasting any time.

He called to check on their trip, to see how they were settling in, and to welcome them to Colorado. But he also called to invite Patrick to play in a tournament just north of Denver—game time at 9:00 am.

Patrick, groggy from the late-night arrival, his body still tired, his eyes still heavy, didn't hesitate. He jumped at the invitation. His love for basketball was stronger than his fatigue. His excitement for his new team was greater than his exhaustion. He was ready. They quickly dressed, grabbed a quick breakfast, and headed out the door.

Patrick was nervous, his mind buzzing. He wanted to make a good impression, wanted to show Earl that he belonged, and wanted to prove himself to his new teammates.

When Earl put Patrick into the game, he sprinted up and down the court, his legs pumping, his heart pounding.

He played with great hustle, with energy, with passion.

He was determined to impress his new coach and show Earl that he was worth the opportunity and the chance.

But then, something happened.

Just three or four minutes into the game, Patrick felt like he was going to die.

His chest was tight; his breathing was labored, and his legs were heavy. His vision blurred, his head spun, and his heart raced. He looked up into the stands, his eyes wide, his face pale, his body weak. He looked at his parents, his eyes desperate, his heart panicking.

Something was wrong. Something was seriously wrong.

Earl called a timeout, waving Patrick over, his face calm, his voice steady.

Patrick stumbled to the bench, gasping for air, his hands on his knees, his head hanging low.

Earl put his hand on Patrick's shoulder, his voice gentle, his smile kind. "Welcome to Colorado," he said, his laughter light. "That's the thin air. It takes some getting used to."

Patrick looked up with questioning eyes, his face confused.

Earl explained the elevation, the thin air, and the lack of oxygen. He told Patrick that it happens to everyone, that it's normal, that it's just a part of playing at a mile high.

Patrick nodded, his breath finally steadying, his heart slowing.

Earl clapped him on the back, his words encouraging, his confidence reassuring. "Give it a couple of weeks," Earl said. "You'll adjust. You'll be fine."

Patrick looked over at his parents in the stands, his face red, his smile shy. Larry gave him a thumbs up, his eyes proud, his love obvious. Tiffany blew him a kiss, her eyes smiling.

They were so proud of him.

He sat on the bench, his body recovering, his heart and mind still racing.

He looked around at his new team, his new coach, his new life.

He was in Colorado. He was on a new team. He was on a new adventure.

The team went on to easily win the tournament that weekend, their energy high, their confidence soaring.

Patrick felt the excitement, the anticipation, and the promise of new opportunities, new dreams, and new memories.

He felt he belonged. He was home.

CHAPTER 9.
Legacy of Love

Two weeks. They had only been in Colorado for two weeks, and Tiffany was already planning an addition to their family.

It wasn't the house, it wasn't the furniture, it wasn't the routine. It was Max. They all missed him—their old friend, their loyal companion, the little black pug who had been with them for so many years.

They missed his snorts, his wiggles, his lazy afternoons lying in the sun. They missed his presence, his love, his warmth.

The house was beautiful, perfect, everything they dreamed of. But it didn't quite feel like home. Not yet. Without Max.

Tiffany thought another little black pug might help. She thought it might help the kids adjust and feel more settled, more comfortable, and more at ease. She thought it might help them feel more at home, so she didn't hesitate.

She did some research, made some phone calls, and found a breeder in Denver who had pug puppies ready to be sold. She hopped in the car with Rylee, the excitement tangible, the anticipation budding.

It was a warm summer day; the sun was shining, the air was warm, and the drive was easy. They arrived at the breeder's house, the puppies waddling around, their tiny faces wrinkled, their eyes big and round. Tiffany's heart melted. Rylee's eyes sparkled, her smile wide, her laughter loud.

They crouched down, letting the puppies crawl all over them, their tails wagging, their tongues licking, their little paws prancing.

And then they saw her.

A tiny black pug with a small white stripe on her chest, her face mischievous, her eyes bright. She was full of life, full of energy, full of love.

Rylee scooped her up, her arms cradling the little pup with her heart bursting.

Tiffany looked at her daughter, looked at the puppy, looked at the smile on Rylee's face. She knew this was the one. They named her Mya, but Mya was no Max.

She was wild, energetic, and full of life. She wiggled, jumped, and ran in circles. She nipped at fingers, barked at shadows, and bounced off walls. She was a handful, but Tiffany loved every ounce of that little dog's energy.

She snuggled her, kissed her, cradled her. She fed her treats, rubbed her belly, and spoiled her rotten. Mya was pampered. She slept in bed with Tiffany and Larry, curling up at their feet, snoring softly, dreaming sweetly.

She loved being close, loved being warm, loved being loved.

Larry wasn't exactly thrilled. He had been hopeful that their dog ownership days were over, that Max was their one and only, that they could live a life free of pet hair and dog slobber. But Larry loved Tiffany more than he loved his clean sheets or quiet mornings. He could never tell her no. Especially not when she looked at him with those big, beautiful blue eyes, her smile playful, and her voice sweet.

Especially not when she was snuggling that little black pug, her heart full, her love strong. Larry watched her; his heart melted, and his resolve broke. He could never say no to her.

He never could.

Mya was home, and with her, the house felt complete.

The laughter was louder, the joy was stronger, the love was fuller.

The house felt more alive, more like home.

Mya wiggled her way into their lives, into their hearts, into their family. She wasn't Max. But she was perfect. And Tiffany loved her.

Larry watched Tiffany as she played with Mya. He didn't love dogs, but he loved Tiffany, and that was enough.

Tiffany was not exactly what you'd call "outdoorsy."

Her idea of roughing it was staying at a hotel that didn't offer spa services or have a five-star restaurant.

She loved the finer things in life—elegant dinners, luxurious bedding, designer clothes. She was classy, sophisticated, and beautiful. But she was also adaptable, adventurous, and fearless.

So, when they moved to Colorado, it didn't take long for Tiffany to embrace the Colorado lifestyle. In fact, she dove in headfirst.

She and Larry made a trip to Cabela's, the giant outdoor retailer that seemed to have everything you could ever need for the great outdoors. They bought sleeping bags, cots, and tents. They picked up camping chairs, lanterns, coolers, and all the cooking gear they'd need for a weekend in the wilderness.

They were going camping. Yes, camping.

And not just camping—they were doing it with their brand new puppy, Mya, who had been with them for just two weeks. They were diving into the Colorado way of life with no reservations and no looking back. Holly and Steve were joining them, bringing their kids along for the adventure.

It was going to be a weekend full of laughter, love, and memories.

They found the perfect campsite on the southern end of Lake Granby at the Arapaho Bay Campground. It was breathtaking.

They pitched their tents just feet from the water, the crystal-clear lake stretching out before them, the towering mountains standing tall behind them. The air was crisp, clean, fresh. The pine trees swayed in the breeze, and the water lapped at the shore; the sun sparkled off the waves.

It was flawless.

The kids ran down to the water, their laughter echoing off the mountains, their joy contagious. They played, they splashed, they swam. They were free and absolutely happy.

Tiffany watched them, her heart full, her love packed. She saw their smiles, heard their laughter, and felt their joy. This was what she wanted. This was what she dreamed of.

They cooked out, grilling hot dogs and hamburgers over an open flame. They sat around the campfire, toasting marshmallows, making s'mores, and telling ghost stories.

The stars came out, bright, beautiful, endless. The air grew cool, and as the night grew quiet, the world grew peaceful.

Tiffany looked up at the sky. This was Colorado. This was beautiful. This was life.

On Saturday, they rented a large pontoon boat and spent the day on the water. The kids were excited. They swam, they jumped off the boat, they laughed. They fished, waiting patiently, hoping for a bite. Rylee was determined, her eyes focused, her heart set. And then, she felt a tug. Her rod bent, her line tightened, her heart raced. She pulled, she reeled, she fought.

She caught a large trout, its body thrashing, its scales shimmering in the sunlight. Her face lit up. She showed it off to the boys, her head held high, her pride undeniable. She had out-fished them all. Larry watched her, pride smiling in his eyes.

He looked over at Tiffany, the woman who made all of this possible, the woman who gave him everything. She was standing at the edge of the boat, her hair blowing in the wind, her eyes glittering, her face glowing. She was smiling, laughing, loving.

FOREVER TIFFANY

She looked out at the water, at the mountains, at her children. She was happy. She was peaceful. She was beautiful. Larry just watched her endlessly.

He knew she felt loved, safe, and happy. He knew she was happy they had moved to Colorado and that they had made the right decision.

This was where they were meant to be.

And they were just getting started.

A few weeks later, Larry's company had planned an employee night out at Coors Field to see the Rockies play.

That night at Coors Field was one of those memories that would live forever in the hearts of Larry, Tiffany, and their children. It was more than just a baseball game—it was an experience, a reminder of why family time mattered so much.

Larry's company had pulled out all the stops, inviting employees and their families to enjoy the game from one of the most exclusive spots in the entire ballpark—the private suite inside the right-field wall. It wasn't just any suite. It was massive, decked out with everything a baseball-loving family could dream of.

The kids immediately ran to the pool table, challenging each other to games between innings. There were arcade games, oversized leather chairs, and enough food and drinks to last well beyond nine innings. The energy inside was electric, the chatter of coworkers mixing with the laughter of children. Outside, the smell of freshly cut grass and the hum of the crowd gave that unmistakable feeling of summer baseball in Colorado.

For the family, baseball had always been something special. With their cousin Elliot having played Major League Baseball, they had grown up around the sport in a way most families never got to experience. They had been on big league fields before, standing in dugouts, watching batting practice from behind the cage. But tonight was different. This wasn't just about the game—it was about a memory in the making, one that would become a "remember when" story for years to come.

As the final out was recorded and the Rockies secured the win, the real magic was just beginning. The announcer invited those with special field passes to make their way down to the warning track. Larry and Tiffany exchanged excited glances. This was going to be special.

Hand in hand, Tiffany led the children down the tunnel and out onto the perfectly manicured grass of Coors Field. The field lights beamed overhead, illuminating the vast stadium, now mostly empty of fans. It was a surreal feeling, standing in the outfield of a Major League park, looking up at the massive scoreboards and towering seats, feeling the history beneath their feet.

Tiffany, as effortlessly beautiful as ever, spread out a large blanket in centerfield. The family laid back, staring up at the endless Colorado sky, waiting for the show to begin.

And then—BOOM!

The first explosion of color filled the night sky, a burst of gold and red raining down over the stadium. The crowd on the field gasped in unison, and then it began—one of the most breathtaking fireworks displays they had ever seen.

Larry stole a glance at Tiffany, who was mesmerized by the light show, her face glowing in the reflection of the bursts above. She had always been beautiful, but there was something about this moment—her with the kids, their laughter mixing with the echoes of fireworks, the joy in her eyes—that made him fall in love with her all over again.

The kids lay beside them, eyes wide with wonder, pointing at the sky as the show reached its grand finale. It was one of those moments where time seemed to stand still, where nothing else in the world mattered except being together, right there, in that exact moment.

As the fireworks faded and the field lights flickered back on, Brennan sat up and turned to his parents.

"That was the coolest thing ever," he said, still in awe.

Rylee and Patrick nodded in agreement, all three of them knowing that this night was something they'd remember forever.

Walking off the field, Larry slipped his arm around Tiffany's waist and pulled her close.

"Welcome to Colorado," he whispered.

She smiled, resting her head against his shoulder. Yeah, this was home now. And this was a memory they'd cherish for the rest of their lives.

August finally arrived, bringing with it the excitement and nerves that come with the first day of school.

This year was different. This year, they were starting at new schools, in a new state, in a new life. They were starting over.

Patrick was excited, optimistic, and ready for the adventure.

He was starting high school, a freshman at a school where everything was unfamiliar, where the hallways were different, the faces were new, and the journey was just beginning.

But he was lucky.

He had been playing basketball all summer with his AAU team, and some of his teammates were attending the same high school.

He already had friends, already had connections, already had a place to belong.

He walked into the building with confidence, his head high, his heart steady. He knew what to do.

Rylee was starting sixth grade, the last year of elementary school, the bridge between being a kid and becoming a teenager.

She was confident, bubbly, outgoing. She had always had a way of making friends easily, of lighting up a room, of walking in and making everyone feel comfortable. She was excited. She was ready for the challenge, the fun, and the friendships.

Brennan was starting first grade. He was young, innocent, sweet. He was sensitive, thoughtful, and tender-hearted.

He had never been to any school other than the one in Indiana, and he had never known anything other than the life they left behind.

He was quiet that morning, his eyes wide, his heart heavy. He had yet to make any new friends in Colorado, hadn't found his place, hadn't found his people. He was nervous, scared, unsure. Larry and Tiffany could see it, could feel it, could sense it. They knew this was different for him, knew this was hard, and knew he needed them.

They drove him to school, the air tense, the car quiet.

They parked the car and walked him to the playground area where all the parents were gathering, the noise loud, the crowd big.

Brennan's eyes grew even wider, his fingers digging into Tiffany's hand, his body leaning into hers. Tiffany squatted down, her eyes meeting his, her hands on his shoulders, her voice gentle.

She needed him to feel her love, needed him to feel her strength, needed him to feel her confidence.

She needed him to know he could do this. "Brennan," she whispered, her voice soft, her words warm. "You're going to do awesome. I know it. You're brave, you're smart, you're strong."

He looked at her, his eyes big, his face worried.

"You know I love you, right?" she said, her voice steady.

Brennan nodded, his chin trembling, his eyes glistening.

"And you know I'll be right out here waiting for you at the end of the day, don't you?" she continued, her words soothing, her love solid.

He nodded again, his shoulders straightening, his heart calming.

He always fed off Tiffany's calmness, always leaned on her strength, and always trusted her love.

She made him feel safe. She made him feel strong. She made him feel brave.

With glossy eyes and a face that looked like he might cry, Brennan took a deep breath, squared his shoulders, and walked toward the door.

He didn't look back. He didn't hesitate. He didn't cry. He just walked in, his back straight, his head high, his courage leading the way. Tiffany watched him go, her love overflowing.

She smiled. "Never a doubt," she said with a chuckle, her eyes drizzly, her pride overwhelming.

Larry watched her, so strong, so brave, so beautiful. She was everything to him.

They stood there together, watching Brennan disappear into the building, watching him begin his journey and face his fear. They stood there, hand in hand, heart to heart, soul to soul.

They were proud. They were hopeful.

It didn't take long for the kids to settle in and make new friends. They were thriving in Colorado, their laughter echoing through the house, their joy contagious, their lives full of adventure. They were happy. Rylee, especially, was fitting right in. A few weeks into the school year, she made a new friend—Mackenzie. They were instant besties, inseparable from the moment they met. They laughed together, played together, talked about everything and nothing.

They were just kids, being kids, living life.

Rylee was excited to have her first Colorado sleepover, to spend more time with her new friend, and to share her home with Mackenzie.

Tiffany and Larry agreed, happy to see Rylee making connections, adjusting, and smiling.

Friday night came quickly, the anticipation building, the excitement growing. Around 5:00 pm, the doorbell rang. Rylee's face lit up. She ran to the door, flinging it open, her smile widespread.

Mackenzie stood there with her overnight bag in hand, her face glowing, her joy overflowing. Beside her was her mom, doing what any good mother would do—checking the place out, meeting the parents, and ensuring her daughter would be safe.

Rylee's face beamed with pride, her love loud, her excitement deep.

Tiffany walked into the foyer, her face warm, her smile genuine.

"Hello, I'm Tiffany, Rylee's mom," she said in a sweet voice, her words kind. "Nice to meet you."

"Hello," Mackenzie's mom replied, her face friendly, her demeanor calm. "My name is Stacy. Thanks for having her over."

They exchanged pleasantries, small talk flowed easily, and laughter was light.

Larry was in a distant room, but he could hear the conversation, could hear Tiffany's voice, could hear the welcome in her words.

He figured it was the right thing to do, the polite thing to do, the good-dad thing to do, so he walked in to say hello.

"Hello, I'm Rylee's dad—Larry," he said, his voice cheerful, his smile wide.

Stacy's eyes wandered to a piece of art on the wall—a large wooden piece showing the Chicago skyline from the beach where Larry and Tiffany once lived.

Stacy's face brightened, her curiosity piqued. "Oh, are you from Chicago?"

FOREVER TIFFANY

Tiffany nodded, her eyes fond, her heart nostalgic. "Just outside the city, not too far away," she said. "That's where we moved from."

Stacy smiled, her face understanding, her heart relating. "It seems like no one in Colorado is actually from Colorado," she laughed. "I grew up in Bangor, Maine."

Without hesitation, Larry jumped in. "Well, if you can't screw her in Brewer, you take her over the bridge and Bangor," he said with his face deadpan and voice casual.

Time stopped.

Tiffany's eyes went wide, her face pale, her jaw dropping open.

Did he just say that?

Did he just say that in front of Rylee's new friend's mom?

Did he just ruin Rylee's friendship before it even began?

Her face turned red, her mouth opened, her words sharp.

"Excuse him," she said, her voice clipped, her eyes narrowing. "He's a moron."

Larry froze, his heart dropping, his mind racing.

What did he just do?

Stacy stood there, her face blank, her eyes still, her body rigid.

Tiffany braced herself, her heart heavy, her apology ready.

And then, Stacy started to laugh. A loud, hearty, genuine laugh.

She laughed so hard she held her stomach, her body shaking, her face glowing.

Through her laughter, she managed to say, "How do you know that saying?"

Larry's face broke into a grin, his tension easing, his relief profound.

"I was just in Bangor with my friend George," he explained, his smile wide, his love loud. "We spent a week fishing and hanging out. I heard everyone saying that at the bars."

Stacy laughed even harder, her joy contagious, her spirit light.

She knew exactly what he was talking about and what he meant.

And she loved it.

Tiffany's shoulders dropped, her tension melted, and her heart calmed. She let out a breath.

Larry didn't ruin Rylee's friendship. He just created a new one.

Tiffany and Stacy clicked immediately, their bond instant, their friendship strong. They were tied at the hip, spending time together, laughing, talking, and sharing life.

They became best friends. All thanks to Larry's trip to Bangor.

CHAPTER 10.
To Infinity and Beyond

Tiffany and Stacy were inseparable.

They were two peas in a pod, two souls who found each other in a world of chaos, two hearts that connected in an instant. It was as if they had been waiting their whole lives to meet each other.

They spent more and more time together, their bond growing stronger, their friendship growing deeper. They laughed together, cried together, supported each other, and trusted each other.

They were more than just best friends. They were sisters.

Stacy was married to Brian, a man she had met at her sister Amy's wedding.

Much like Tiffany and Larry, she knew from the first moment she saw him.

"I knew I was going to marry him the day I first met him," she once told Tiffany, her eyes sparkling, her love glowing.

Tiffany smiled. She knew that feeling all too well. She knew exactly how Stacy felt. Tiffany and Stacy's friendship was more than just a blessing. It was a lifeline. It was a saving grace. It was meant to be.

It wasn't by chance. It wasn't luck. It wasn't random. It was fate. Larry knew that, too.

He watched their friendship grow, watched the way they laughed together, watched the way they leaned on each other.

And it brought him immense comfort.

He knew that when he was away for work, Tiffany had Stacy.

Yes, Tiffany had Holly, her childhood best friend, her soulmate, and her sister-in-law. Yes, she had Diana and Vicki, her mother-in-law, her mom, her foundation, and her family. Yes, she had love all around her. But she needed something more. She needed someone to confide in, someone to share secrets with, someone to cry with when the world felt heavy. She needed someone who wasn't family, someone who could listen without judgment, someone who could stand by her side without obligation.

She needed a friend. She needed Stacy. Stacy was more than just a friend. She was the missing piece, the perfect fit, the answer to an unspoken prayer. She was the sister Tiffany didn't know she needed, the confidant she didn't know she was missing, the partner she didn't know she was waiting for.

Their friendship was special, rare, and beautiful. It was magical. It was forever.

It didn't take long for Stacy to introduce Brian to Larry. They hit it off quickly, the way only two men with similar souls can. They were easy together, comfortable, and relaxed. They shared a love of craft beer, spending hours talking about hops and malts, and brewing techniques. They shared the same political views, finding comfort in their aligned perspectives and finding humor in the chaos of the world.

They just got along.

They were both family men, dedicated to their wives, loving their children, and wanting the best for their families. They were both hard workers, passionate about their jobs, and driven to succeed. They were both good men, strong men, loyal men.

It didn't take long for the two couples to start spending more time together, their lives linking, their memories building.

They dined out together, trying new restaurants, exploring new flavors, and laughing over shared meals. They spent quiet nights on each other's patios, sitting around a fire, sipping cocktails, talking about life, about love, about dreams. They found comfort, joy, and a friend in each other.

They were two couples who came together by fate, by destiny, by magic.

They were more than friends. They were family. Tiffany and Stacy. Larry and Brian. They were together. And they were happy.

It didn't take long for the couples to discover something strange, something uncanny, something that made them all stop and wonder. It was the kind of thing that made you believe in fate. That may be, just maybe, the universe had a hand in bringing them together.

Larry and Tiffany were married on February 15th.

February 15th was Brian's birthday.

And Brian and Stacy were married on June 27th.

June 27th was Larry's birthday.

It was bizarre, surreal, and impossible to ignore.

Two couples, two weddings, two birthdays, perfectly connected.

It was the kind of coincidence that confronted logic, the kind of coincidence that made you question everything.

It was the kind of coincidence that made you believe.

Larry and Tiffany stared at each other, their faces stunned. Brian and Stacy looked at each other, their mouths open, their hearts beating at the same pace – fast.

It was eerie, magical, beautiful. It was meant to be.

They laughed about it, joked about it, and marveled at it.

They tried to make sense of it, tried to find some explanation, tried to wrap their minds around it.

But there was no explanation. There was no reason. There was only fate. I'm not one to read too much into horoscopes or numerology or signs from the universe. I'm not one to look for meaning in dates, numbers, or coincidences.

But this was different. This was special.

This was real. Surely, there was something more to this.

Surely, there was a reason they found each other, a reason they became friends, a reason they became family.

Surely, they were meant to be together.

Surely, they were meant to share this journey, meant to share this life, meant to share this love.

Surely, it was destiny.

In the not-too-distant future, the couples would come to realize the reasons they were brought together.

There were several reasons—small moments, shared laughter, common dreams, deep connections.

There were reasons that seemed insignificant at the time but would prove to be monumental.

There were reasons that made them stronger, reasons that made them better, reasons that made them whole.

But one reason stood out far bigger than they could have ever imagined.

One reason would overshadow all the rest.

One reason would shake them to their core, test them in ways they never thought possible, and push them to the very edge.

It was a reason so big, so powerful, so unimaginable that it would change everything.

It was a reason that would bring them to their knees, a reason that would break them, a reason that would save them. A reason so significant that had they not been in each other's lives, well... I'm not sure what would have happened. I'm not sure Larry would have survived. I'm not sure he would have made it through. I'm not sure they would have found the strength, the courage, the hope. I'm not sure they would have found the light.

But they were brought together for this reason, this purpose, this destiny. They were brought together to face the storm, to weather the darkness, to stand strong in the face of the impossible. They were brought together to love, fight, and save each other.

They were brought together because they needed each other, because they belonged together, and because they were meant to be together.

And when the time came, when the reason revealed itself, when the unthinkable happened...

They were together.

Dr. Blum had long since settled into his new role in Colorado Springs, and with Larry now living in Castle Rock, it made perfect sense for him to schedule his bi-annual appointments with the man who had once saved his life. It had been over six years since they had last seen each other, and though time had passed, Larry still held Dr. Blum in the highest regard. To him, Dr. Blum was more than just a doctor—he was the person who had given him a second chance at life.

Larry had made a habit of keeping up with his routine scans, always cautious but optimistic. He knew the importance of staying ahead of anything that could resurface, but with each passing appointment, the news remained the same—he was still cancer-free. It was a phrase he never grew tired of hearing. Six years without a recurrence, six years of waking up every morning knowing he had defied the odds.

LARRY BLAKE

On the day of his check-up, Larry arrived at the hospital for his routine CT scan with contrast, a process that had become familiar to him. He went through the motions, checked in at radiology, drank the barium solution, and waited for the imaging to be complete. Once finished, he made his way through the hospital toward Dr. Blum's office to hear the results.

As he walked down the long, sterile hallway, memories of his past treatments, surgeries, and hospital stays flooded his mind. So much had changed since those days at Northwestern. He had survived what once felt insurmountable, built an incredible life in Colorado, and watched his children grow. He had so much to be grateful for.

Then, in the distance, he spotted a familiar figure walking briskly in the opposite direction. Without hesitation, Larry called out, "Hi, Matt."

Dr. Blum, caught in the middle of his routine, instinctively responded with a polite but distracted greeting, offering a quick hello as he continued walking past.

Larry smiled to himself as he continued toward the office, understanding that doctors had busy schedules. He checked in at the front desk, took a seat in the waiting room, and settled in, expecting to wait as usual. But just a few minutes later, Dr. Blum came hustling back into the room, scanning the faces of the waiting patients until his eyes locked onto Larry's. His expression immediately changed from professional to one of pure surprise and recognition.

"Larry? No way!" he said, a look of disbelief spreading across his face. "I saw your name on the patient list this week and thought there's no way that could be my Larry from Northwestern!"

Larry grinned as they shook hands. "We moved to Castle Rock a few years ago. I'm back under the care of my hero."

Dr. Blum smiled warmly, clearly pleased to see his former patient thriving after all these years. They caught up quickly, reminiscing about the long journey that had brought them to this moment. Dr.

Blum reviewed the scan results, confirming what Larry had hoped to hear—everything looked good. He was still cancer-free.

The words settled in Larry's mind with a familiar sense of relief. He had been blessed with six years of clear scans, six years of making memories with his family, and six years of living without the shadow of fear that had once loomed over him.

Neither he nor Dr. Blum had any idea at the time, but this was not the last major moment they would share. In just a few short years, Dr. Blum would go on to play a role in Larry's life—a role that neither of them could have possibly foreseen.

CHAPTER 11.
More Than a Mom

The summer of 2016 was one to remember.

Patrick was playing on one of the best AAU basketball teams in the country.

They traveled coast to coast, playing in the most competitive tournaments, going up against the best of the best. And they were winning. Nearly every tournament they entered, they left as champions.

Earl had assembled an elite squad—some of the top players in Colorado, along with standout athletes from across the country.

They were special. They were dominant. And Patrick was right in the middle of it all.

For Larry and Tiffany, it was a dream.

Every weekend was an adventure: another city, another tournament, another opportunity to watch their son grow, compete, and thrive.

They sat courtside, their hearts full, their voices cheering.

They watched as Patrick poured everything he had into the game, as he fought for every rebound and battled for every point.

It was surreal. It was everything they had hoped for him.

In July, the team flew to Las Vegas to compete in the AAU West Coast National Championship tournament.

It was a big moment, a high-stakes competition, a chance for Patrick and his team to prove they were among the best.

But for the family, the weekend was about more than just basketball.

FOREVER TIFFANY

Patrick was turning sixteen. Sixteen.

A milestone birthday, a moment that felt like time was moving too fast, a reminder that their little boy wasn't so little anymore.

Larry wanted to make it special.

He wanted Patrick to feel celebrated, to feel appreciated, to feel like a king—even if just for a moment. So, he planned a surprise.

As soon as they landed in Vegas, a long-stretch limo was waiting at the airport, gleaming under the bright desert sun. The driver stood outside, holding a sign with Patrick's name. Patrick froze, his face turning red, his eyes darting to his parents.

He shook his head, muttering under his breath, "No way."

Larry grinned, Tiffany laughed, and the driver opened the door. Patrick climbed in, shaking his head, rolling his eyes, pretending to be embarrassed.

But underneath it all, he loved it.

He loved that his parents had thought of this. He loved that they went out of their way to make him feel special. He loved that they were always there, always supporting him, always making moments like this unforgettable.

As the limo cruised down the Vegas Strip, neon lights flashed, music played, and the city buzzed with life. Patrick sat back, his face softening, and a small smile maintained on his lips.

He appreciated it. He appreciated everything.

He appreciated the sacrifices, the endless hours in the gym, the flights, the hotels, and the long weekends spent watching him chase his dream.

He appreciated his parents more than they would ever know.

And deep down, he knew this wasn't just a special weekend. This was a memory that would last forever.

Larry and Tiffany wanted to make Patrick's sixteenth birthday unforgettable, and what better way to celebrate than with his teammates in the heart of Las Vegas?

They rented out a large private room at Circus Circus, filling it with everything a group of teenage basketball players could ever want—pizza, wings, snacks, and unlimited access to the indoor amusement park.

It was loud, chaotic, and full of laughter.

Patrick and his teammates ran wild, jumping from ride to ride, challenging each other at arcade games, and living in the moment.

It was the kind of night every sixteen-year-old dreams of—no parents, no rules (within reason), just pure fun.

Larry had been shocked when Tiffany agreed to let it be a players-only event. That wasn't usually her style—she loved to be involved, to be hands-on, to be there for every moment. But she also understood that this was Patrick's night.

So, while Patrick and his teammates were off being teenagers, Larry had something else planned—something just for him and Tiffany.

A special night. A Vegas night.

Larry had made reservations for just the two of them: a romantic dinner at an elegant restaurant, a moment away from the madness, a chance to celebrate their love.

After all, it wasn't just a special night for Patrick—it was a special night for them, too.

After dinner, they walked hand in hand along the Las Vegas Strip, the neon lights flashing, the warm desert air wrapping around them, the energy of the city buzzing.

For Tiffany, this was her first time seeing Vegas in person. And Larry was more than happy to show her everything.

FOREVER TIFFANY

She looked around, her eyes wide, taking in the massive hotels, the fountains, the street performers, the glitz, the chaos, the magic.

Larry watched her, watched the way her face lit up, watched the way her blonde hair shimmered under the glow of the lights, watched the way her smile widened with every new sight.

She was incredible. Vegas was dazzling, but nothing was more beautiful than her.

Larry had always believed that every moment with Tiffany was a moment worth remembering, but that night—walking the Strip, soaking in the energy, feeling the pulse of the city—felt different.

It was seamless.

They stopped in front of the Bellagio Fountains just as the water erupted into the night sky, dancing to the music, shimmering under the moonlight.

Larry pulled Tiffany close, wrapping his arms around her, feeling the warmth of her body against his. She leaned into him, resting her head on his shoulder, sighing softly.

He kissed the top of her head, breathing her in, holding her tight.

At that moment, nothing else in the world mattered.

Not the lights, not the noise, not the chaos of Vegas. Just them. Just this moment. Just this love.

Larry knew that no matter where they were, no matter what city they stood in, no matter how bright the lights were around them, Tiffany was always the brightest entity in his life.

After pool play was over, the team remained undefeated. Saturday night was a time for the players to relax, have an early dinner, and prepare for the semifinals on Sunday.

Tiffany had made a friend in Denise, whose son was a standout point guard on the team. He would later go on to lead his high school to a state championship and then have a successful college career in Oregon. Tiffany, Denise, and Larry decided to go out for dinner that night, enjoying good food and conversation.

At some point during the meal, Tiffany started talking about something she had always wanted—a figure-eight tattoo on her foot. Within the figure eight, she wanted each of her children's names in cursive: Patrick, Rylee, and Brennan.

Larry chuckled, shaking his head. "You'll never do it," he said, knowing her fear of needles all too well.

Denise leaned in, eyes twinkling with excitement. "Tiffany, do it tonight! What a great Vegas memory that would be."

Larry grinned and decided to up the stakes. As they walked through the hotel, he spotted a tattoo shop. He pointed to it and said, "Now's your time. I'll bet you $300 you won't go through with it."

It was a bold move, but Larry was betting from their shared account, and Tiffany was the CFO of the family. She didn't need his permission for the money—or the tattoo.

To Larry's shock, Tiffany didn't hesitate.

She rolled right into that tattoo shop, sat down, and got the tattoo. Denise sat beside her, taking videos and snapping photos, capturing every moment of Tiffany's unexpected act of spontaneity.

When it was done, Tiffany looked down at the fresh ink on her foot, her children's names beautifully matted within the figure eight.

It was her only tattoo.

She was never one for ink, never someone who needed permanent markings to express herself. But this one was different. This one was for her children—the three souls who made her world go round, the three names that held her heart, the three people she would stop at nothing to protect.

She wore that tattoo with pride.

It wasn't just a Vegas memory. It was a symbol of her love, her devotion, and the unbreakable bond she had with her children.

****

Sunday arrived, and the team was ready. They won their first two games, securing their spot in the championship.

The tournament took place at the Las Vegas Convention Center, where the courts were old NBA floors. The championship game would be played on an old Miami Heat floor, adding to the intensity and excitement of the moment.

Patrick's team was preparing to take on a talented squad from New Orleans, a team loaded with athleticism and size. Two of their players had already committed to NCAA Division I programs, making them a formidable opponent.

From the start, the game was tight. Patrick's team trailed by five to seven points most of the way, unable to quite catch up. But Earl had a strategy, one he had implemented from the opening tip with the hope it would pay off in the final minutes.

With most of the team living and training in Colorado, they had a conditioning advantage. Las Vegas sits at 2,000 feet above sea level, a 4,500-foot drop from where they trained every day. For the New Orleans team, used to playing at just 20 feet above sea level, the elevation was going to take a toll.

Earl kept the pressure relentless, rotating his first and second teams every five minutes and running a full-court press the entire game.

With five minutes to go, the game shifted. The New Orleans team, exhausted from the constant pressure, started to break down. Their legs were heavy, their lungs burning. But Patrick's team looked as if the game had just started, still moving with energy and intensity.

The lead shrank.

They were down by one.

Tiffany sat in the front row, chair-back seats with the other moms, right at center court.

The final seconds ticked away.

They had the ball.

Ten seconds left.

TJ found himself wide open in the left corner. He caught the pass.

Tiffany, unable to stay seated, was halfway out of her chair, her heart racing, every fiber of her being wanting this moment for her son.

Patrick was on the bench now, watching, waiting, hoping.

The ball left TJ's fingertips.

A deep three from the NBA line.

Time seemed to freeze.

Swish.

All net.

The crowd erupted.

Tiffany jumped what seemed like fifteen feet in the air, pure joy bursting from her.

Patrick ran onto the court, the team mobbing TJ, celebrating a massive win.

They had done it.

They were the first team from Colorado to ever win the tournament.

It was a moment for the history books, a moment Patrick would never forget.

Tiffany sat back, her eyes shining with pride.

FOREVER TIFFANY

She loved the fact that Patrick had this moment.

But as the celebration roared around her, she did what she always did.

She slipped into the background, not wanting to take one second of glory away from her son. This was his time. And she wouldn't change a thing.

CHAPTER 12.
The Silent Strength

Late July 2016, at Tiffany's request, the family set off for a long-awaited vacation in Mexico. It was the perfect way to close out the summer, a chance to step away from the routines of life and just enjoy time together.

Tiffany had taken charge of all the planning, as she always did, ensuring that everything was just right. She had booked breathtaking ocean-view rooms, each with a private pool, the kind of place where you could sit for hours, listening to the waves and feeling the soft ocean breeze. She wanted this trip to be unforgettable, and she succeeded. Mexico would soon become a destination forever etched in their hearts; a place filled with memories they would cherish for years to come.

After a couple of days at the resort, they set out on a snorkeling excursion, something the entire family had been looking forward to. The idea of drifting through crystal-clear waters, surrounded by tropical fish and the beauty of the ocean, was exactly the kind of adventure Tiffany had envisioned.

But as they arrived at the dock and took in the sight of the boat, Tiffany immediately had a feeling that this wasn't quite what she had expected. The boat was large, sleek, and inviting, but there was something about the atmosphere that caught her attention. This didn't look like a quiet, family-friendly excursion—it looked more like a party.

It didn't take long for her suspicions to be confirmed.

The other passengers were mostly young couples, full of energy and ready to let loose. The music was already blasting from the speakers, and the staff had wasted no time passing out rounds of tequila shots. The vibe was electric, the kind of energy that even the most reserved person would struggle not to get caught up in.

Tiffany, however, was still processing the scene. This wasn't exactly the relaxing family getaway she had pictured.

The women on board were wearing bikinis that could barely be called swimsuits, and the men were already tossing back drinks like it was spring break in Cancun.

Larry, on the other hand, was grinning ear to ear, already amused by the entire situation. He knew Tiffany well enough to read her thoughts without her even saying a word.

But before she could say anything, the boat captain, a charismatic man with infectious energy, grabbed a microphone and started hyping up the crowd. His crew, all just as lively, moved through the boat, engaging with guests, making jokes, and ensuring that no one—absolutely no one—would leave that trip without having an amazing time.

Even Tiffany had to admit it was impossible not to smile.

The guests, though clearly here for a different kind of adventure, were incredibly kind and welcoming to the family. They recognized that maybe Larry and Tiffany had mistakenly booked the wrong excursion, but instead of making them feel out of place, they embraced them.

Some of the women, dressed in their tiny bikinis, approached Tiffany and complimented her on her own swimsuit, laughing and chatting as if they had known each other for years. A group of men, mid-drink, raised their glasses and said to Larry, "Best mistake ever, right?" Larry just laughed and nodded.

As the boat started moving, the warm Caribbean breeze swept across the deck, lifting Tiffany's golden hair and carrying the scent of the ocean.

She sat back, closing her eyes for just a moment, feeling the wind against her skin, listening to the waves crashing against the boat and the laughter of her children nearby.

Maybe this wasn't the trip she had expected, but maybe that was okay.

At the first snorkeling stop, Patrick and Larry jumped in immediately, eager to explore the water. It was clear and blue, the kind of water that didn't seem real, like something out of a travel magazine.

Tiffany stayed back on the boat with Brennan, who, at just eight years old, was a little hesitant. Just as they were about to jump in, Rylee—ever the mischief-maker—casually mentioned that she had seen a giant shark.

Brennan froze mid-step, eyes wide, processing what his sister had just said.

Tiffany turned and looked at Rylee, narrowing her eyes.

Whether Rylee had actually seen a shark or just wanted to mess with her little brother was up for debate, but the damage was done.

Brennan was not getting in that water.

Tiffany sighed and laughed to herself.

The next stop was Isla Mujeres, a charming little island just a 45-minute boat ride from Cancun. It was exactly what they all needed—a slower pace, delicious food, and beautiful scenery.

They enjoyed an incredible lunch, soaking in the island's laid-back vibe, before heading to the backside of the island for another snorkeling session.

This time, they all got in.

The water surrounded them, warm and gentle, with colorful fish darting in and out of the coral. Schools of fish swam so close that it felt like you could reach out and touch them.

Larry took a step back, treading water for a moment, just watching his family.

He saw the kids laughing, splashing, and fully immersed in the moment.

Then, his eyes found Tiffany.

She was there in the water, her blonde hair wet from the sea, her sun-kissed skin glowing, her blue eyes filled with joy.

Larry smiled to himself.

He would never get tired of looking at her.

Never.

Tiffany used to laugh at him when he told her that.

"You're crazy," she would say, shaking her head. "How is it that you only see me?"

He never had an answer for her.

Because the truth was simple. There was only her. There had only ever been her.

Their second adventure of the week was one that had been on their bucket list for years—swimming with dolphins.

The excitement started the moment they arrived at the marine center. The air smelled of saltwater, the sun was high, and the distant sound of splashing dolphins echoed through the air. This was going to be a day to remember.

After a short introduction from the trainers, the family suited up in life jackets and waded into the cool, clear water. A group of dolphins swam in circles, their sleek gray bodies cutting through the surface, clicking and whistling as if they were just as excited for the interaction.

Their instructor explained that each of them would get to play trainer for the day, commanding the dolphins through different tricks and activities.

Brennan went first, his little hands clapping with excitement. He held his arms out just like the trainer showed him, and within seconds, a dolphin leapt out of the water, spinning in the air before splashing back down. Brennan's face lit up as he let out a loud, "Did you see that!?"

Next was Rylee, who was eager to take control. She signaled with her hands, and her dolphin swam up, stopping inches from her. She held out a fish, and the dolphin gobbled it up before flipping onto its back and letting out a high-pitched squeak. Rylee laughed, rubbing its belly like she had just made a new best friend.

Patrick, always the competitor, wanted to try something more exciting. He was up for the foot push, where two dolphins would press their noses against the bottom of his feet and rocket him across the pool like a human torpedo. The trainer gave him the signal, and suddenly, two dolphins shot toward him. Patrick stiffened his body as they pushed him forward, water spraying all around. He flew across the water, arms out like Superman, before coming to a stop and sliding back into the pool.

The whole family erupted in cheers.

Larry was up next, and of course, he had to go big. He asked to do the dorsal tow, where he'd grab onto the fins of two dolphins and let them pull him through the water. He took a deep breath, positioned himself, and before he knew it, he was flying. The dolphins dragged him effortlessly, the wind whipping past his face as he skimmed across the surface. It felt like something straight out of a movie.

Then, it was Tiffany's turn.

Larry watched as she stepped forward, her confidence showing in the effortless way she always carried herself. The trainer instructed her to hold her hands out, palms down. A dolphin swam right up to her, pausing inches from her fingertips.

She smiled and gently placed her hands on its smooth, wet skin, running her fingers along its head. The dolphin closed its eyes, clearly enjoying the attention.

It was an incredible sight.

Tiffany, holding a dolphin and rubbing its head, was completely lost in the moment.

Then came her turn to be pulled through the water. She grabbed onto the dolphin's dorsal fin, and with a quick flick of its tail, it pulled her forward, gliding smoothly across the pool.

The kids applauded.

Larry watched, shaking his head. She made everything look so effortless.

The experience was beyond what they had imagined. The dolphins were playful, intelligent, and full of personality, making it feel like they were interacting with old friends rather than marine animals.

By the time they left, the kids were completely exhausted, still buzzing with excitement as they replayed their favorite moments over and over.

It was another perfect day. Another memory safe in their hearts.

And the trip was still far from over.

The week in Mexico ended with an unforgettable Friday night white party, a tradition at the resort that brought guests together under the stars for a night of music, dancing, and celebration.

As the sun set, the resort transformed. White lights draped over palm trees, illuminating the night with a soft glow. A massive stage stood at the center of it all, surrounded by an open-air dance floor filled with people dressed in crisp, elegant white attire. The energy in the air was electric.

The entertainment was nonstop. Singers filled the air with beautiful melodies, dancers in elaborate costumes moved with effortless grace, and traditional Mexican performers kept the crowd captivated. At one point, fire dancers lit up the stage, their flames flickering against the dark sky, mesmerizing the audience with their daring routines.

The ocean breeze was perfect—just enough to cool the warm night air without taking away from the heat of the celebration. It carried the scent of the sea, mixing with the faint aroma of tropical cocktails and fresh flowers lining the venue.

Tiffany was absolutely stunning.

She wore a flowing white dress that moved smoothly as she danced, catching the light just right, making her glow even more than usual. Her blonde hair fell over her shoulders, and every time she smiled, it was as if she made the whole night shine a little brighter.

Larry couldn't have enough of her.

They danced together, spinning under the lights, laughing as they moved to the music. The kids joined in, too, twirling around and feeling the energy of the night. Everyone was caught up in the magic, the kind of joy that makes time feel like it's standing still.

They didn't know it yet, but this was only the beginning.

This white party, this resort, this experience—it would become a place that meant so much more.

It would become a tradition.

It would become a place of memories, of love, of moments they would cherish forever.

But on this night, they were simply living in it, dancing the night away, unaware that they had just found a new home away from home.

CHAPTER 13.
Faith Without Limits

2016 ended on a high note with another wonderful Christmas and an even better New Year's Eve celebration. Tiffany and Larry always made sure to welcome the new year in style, throwing parties that were filled with friends, laughter, and an endless spread of food and drinks. Their home had become the go-to place for gatherings, and they took great pride in creating a warm, inviting space where people could come together and celebrate. The decorations were always perfect, thanks to Tiffany's eye for detail, and the atmosphere was filled with joy. Whether it was watching the countdown on television, clinking glasses at midnight, or dancing in the living room, these were the moments that made life feel full.

As the new year began, life was shifting in new and exciting ways. Brennan had moved up to second grade, full of energy and curiosity, still discovering the world around him. Rylee had made the big transition into middle school, growing more independent, making new friends, and getting involved in school activities. Patrick was now a sophomore in high school, fully occupied in basketball and, perhaps most notably, driving. Larry and Tiffany had purchased a car for him, something he had been anticipating for what felt like forever. It was an exciting milestone, one that gave him a new sense of freedom but also left his parents feeling a little uneasy. Letting go, even just a little, was never easy, but they were proud of the young man he was becoming.

As time moved forward, they found themselves thinking less and less about Indiana. While their roots would always be there, Colorado had fully become home. They had built a life here, one filled with new traditions, new friendships, and a deep love for their community.

Larry's career continued to grow, requiring him to travel frequently, which meant Tiffany was home, holding everything together. While she loved being a stay-at-home mom, she had started considering the idea of reentering the workforce, feeling the pull to contribute in a new way. Still, she never let it interfere with her role as the heart of the household. No matter how busy life became, she made sure their family remained the top priority.

Patrick was thriving in basketball, playing on a strong team and working hard to improve his game. Brennan had also fallen in love with the sport and had made the roster of a local AAU team, eager to follow in his older brother's footsteps. Rylee had shifted her focus from gymnastics to cheerleading and was enjoying every minute of middle school, forming friendships, and fully embracing this new phase of her life.

Beyond their own children's activities, Larry and Tiffany themselves on a larger role in the high school community. They had volunteered to run the school's booster club, which quickly became a major responsibility. It wasn't just about fundraising; it was about supporting student-athletes, ensuring the concession stands were fully stocked, making sure uniforms were ordered, and organizing team events. They spent countless hours planning, managing, and overseeing every detail, but they loved every minute of it.

One of Tiffany's favorite contributions was bringing an Indiana basketball tradition to Patrick's team—team dinners.

Back in Indiana, it had been common for basketball teams to gather for a meal the night before a big game, a way to bond and build team chemistry. Tiffany had always loved the idea of these gatherings, and she wanted to bring that same sense of camaraderie to Patrick's team in Colorado. She took it upon herself to organize the meals, ensuring that the boys had a home-cooked dinner before stepping onto the court. Some nights, she would cook huge pots of spaghetti with garlic bread, filling the house with the comforting smell of Italian food. On other nights, she would make chicken Alfredo, a favorite among the players. When things were hectic, she would order pizzas and wings, knowing that the boys didn't care as much about what was being served—what mattered was that they were together.

Their home quickly became the meeting place for the team. The players would gather around the bar downstairs, joking around as they ate, trading stories from practice, and hyping each other up for the next game. After dinner, they would play games—ping pong, foosball, and video games—all of which became a regular part of these pre-game gatherings.

Tiffany and Larry loved having a home that was always full of energy. Their house wasn't just a place to sleep; it was a place where friendships were built, where young athletes bonded, and where laughter echoed through the hallways. It was a home filled with warmth, food, and loving memories being made every single day.

They had created something special, something that wasn't just about their own family but about the community they had embraced. Colorado was no longer just where they lived—it was where their lives had truly begun to flourish.

Larry and Tiffany quickly grew close to their neighbors, forming bonds that made their new home feel even more like *the* place to be. The shared driveway they lived on connected them to three other families, each unique but all welcoming in a way that made them feel like they had known each other for years.

First lived Tim and Julie, a kind and down-to-earth couple with two daughters who went to school with Patrick and Rylee. Their families meshed effortlessly, with the kids becoming fast friends and the parents often stopping to chat outside or catch up during school events.

Just beyond them were Jayce and Mary, another wonderful couple whose youngest son was just a year older than Patrick. Their home was always full of life, and their easygoing nature made them a joy to be around. Whether it was casual conversations at the mailbox or long summer evenings spent outside, it didn't take long for a solid friendship to form.

And then there was Carl and Karen, a couple in their late sixties who had only recently married. Their love story was something special, proof that sometimes it takes a little longer to find the right person, but when you do, it's worth every moment of the wait.

When Carl and Karen invited Larry and Tiffany to their wedding, it felt like more than just an invitation to a celebration—it was an invitation into their lives, into their circle of friends.

The wedding was magnificent, held at an elegant country club nestled in the foothills, surrounded by towering pine trees and rolling hills. As the ceremony began, deer grazed peacefully in the distance, and an elk stood majestically on the ridge as if nature itself had paused to witness their vows.

The ceremony took place on a scenic tee box overlooking the mountains, the sun setting in the background, forming golden light across the landscape. It was one of the most beautiful weddings they had ever attended, not just because of the setting but because of the undeniable love Carl and Karen shared.

Watching them, it was clear how much they truly cherished one another. The way they looked at each other, the way they laughed together—it was a reminder that love has no timeline, that it can find you when you least expect it, and when it does, it's something worth rejoicing.

As the evening carried on, laughter and music filled the air, and Tiffany and Larry were surrounded by new friends, people who had already made them feel so welcome in their new community. The wedding for them was also the start of something more—a sense of belonging.

They had found their place and, with it, a new extended family that made Colorado feel even more like home.

Stacy and Tiffany's friendship continued to deepen, becoming something truly special. Stacy, always looking to bring people together, introduced Tiffany to Jessica and a few other women who shared a passion for helping animals. These women were running a dog rescue, dedicating their time and energy to ensuring that dogs from high-kill shelters or difficult circumstances could find their way to safe, loving homes.

Tiffany, with her naturally giving heart, was immediately drawn to the cause. She had always been someone who wanted to help in any way she could, and the idea of fostering dogs in need resonated with her deeply. She quickly grew into the role, opening their home to pups that needed temporary care while waiting for adoption.

At this point, the couple already had Mya, their energetic little black pug, and had recently added a tiny Chihuahua mix to the family—a feisty but lovable dog they named Luigi. Luigi had a big personality packed into his small frame, and despite Larry's general resistance to the idea of having more dogs in the house, he was also warming up to the little guy.

Still, Larry wasn't exactly thrilled about the revolving door of foster dogs coming and going. Each time Tiffany brought in a new pup, Larry would tense up, knowing full well that what was supposed to be "just a few days" could easily turn into longer.

The foster dogs were usually only in their home for a short while before being placed with their forever families, but that didn't make it any easier for Larry. It wasn't that he disliked dogs—he just wasn't the type to want a house full of them. But at the end of the day, he could never say no to Tiffany.

She had a way of making him see things differently, of reminding him that these little lives were worth saving, that even if they could only help for a short time, it mattered. And deep down, even though he wouldn't always admit it, he admired how much she cared.

So, while he might have sighed dramatically every time she brought in a new dog, he also knew that this was just another part of who Tiffany was—someone who always knew a way to give love to those who needed it most.

Larry and Tiffany, like any couple, had their disagreements.

Their fights were never over anything dramatic—there was no betrayal, no deep-rooted issues like infidelity or substance abuse. Instead, their disagreements were over everyday things, the small frustrations that can feel big in the moment. Maybe it was Tiffany spending a little too much money on one of her shopping sprees. Maybe it was Larry staying out too late with friends. Sometimes, it was about the kids, the pressures of parenting, and making decisions that felt heavier than they actually were.

In the grand scheme of things, their arguments were normal, even trivial. But in the heat of the moment, they could feel like mountains instead of molehills.

Larry had his own way of handling conflict—he was a firm believer in what he jokingly called the "Dr. Phil approach." He would say his piece, make sure his perspective was heard, and if the disagreement started escalating or if he felt like he might say something he'd later regret, he would walk away. Not in a dismissive way, but in a way that allowed space for both of them to cool off. He would retreat to his office or head down to the basement, flipping on the television and giving himself time to breathe.

Despite the intensity of some of their arguments, one thing was certain—Larry never said a hateful word to Tiffany. He never insulted her, never called her names, and certainly never laid a hand on her in anger. And she was the same. Even when they were upset, there was always a deep respect that kept them from crossing any lines they could never take back.

But what truly made their relationship special was the way Tiffany always knew how to fix things.

FOREVER TIFFANY

And she used the same method every single time.

No matter how upset Larry was, no matter how stubborn he tried to be, Tiffany always found a way to break through. She would follow him into whatever room he had escaped to, standing in the doorway with that look on her face, the one that said she wasn't about to let a silly fight get in the way of their love.

Without a word, she would walk over and climb onto his lap, straddling him face to face, wrapping her arms around his neck. She would lean in, trying to kiss him, and Larry, still pretending to be upset, would turn his head away just enough to keep up the act.

That was when she would take his hand, place it gently under her shirt, and in a teasing, playful voice, she'd say, **"Here, feel my boob. It'll make you feel better."**

And it did.

Every. Single. Time.

No matter how frustrated he had been, no matter what had caused the argument, Larry would feel that familiar warmth spread through him, and like magic, the fight would instantly start to fade. A slow smile would illuminate his face, and Tiffany, knowing she had won, would flash that dazzling grin of hers.

"It's me and you, right?" she would whisper. "We love each other."

So simple. So powerful.

With just those words and her touch, everything went back to normal.

That was Tiffany's charm. She had a graceful way of reminding Larry that nothing was more important than their love. She knew him better than anyone and knew exactly how to bring him back from his stubbornness and into her arms.

In the end, their disagreements never mattered because, at the core of everything, it was always them against the world. And no argument, no frustration, no moment of tension could ever change that.

Larry and Tiffany had fully settled into life in Castle Rock, and they embraced everything their new hometown had to offer. It didn't take long for them to realize that Castle Rock was more than just a place to live—it was a community, a town that felt like something out of a storybook.

One of their favorite things about living there was the abundance of local festivals. Every season seemed to bring a new reason to gather in town, and they were more than happy to take part in all of it. Oktoberfest was a particular favorite, a weekend filled with traditional Bavarian music, steins of beer, and the irresistible smell of bratwurst and pretzels in the crisp autumn air. They would walk through the streets, hand in hand, watching families laugh, kids playing games, and local vendors selling handmade goods. Tiffany loved exploring the artisan booths and picking out little decorations for the house, while Larry focused on trying as many different German beers as possible.

But nothing compared to the Star Lighting Celebration in November.

For Tiffany, it was the official beginning of the holiday season and one of the most cherished traditions in Castle Rock.

The iconic star, perched atop the town's namesake rock, had been a symbol of the community for nearly a century. The event itself felt straight out of a Hallmark movie. It was always just cold enough to wear a stylish vest, a cozy hat, and light gloves. More often than not, snow would fall gently, dusting the streets, adding to the already scenic setting.

Every year, they would meet Brian and Stacy at the fire station downtown, where the fire department hosted a chili dinner before the festivities began. It had become their own little tradition—warm bowls of hearty chili, surrounded by friends and neighbors, laughter filling the room as they caught up on life. The fire station was packed, filled with the comforting aroma of spices and fresh cornbread; people huddled around tables, their faces glowing from the warmth of the food and the anticipation of the night ahead.

As the time approached for the star lighting, the streets would become crowded with excited families. The air buzzed with holiday cheer, the sound of carolers singing classic Christmas tunes mixing with the hum of conversation and the occasional ringing of jingle bells from a passing child. Tiffany's eyes would sparkle as she took it all in—this was what she had always dreamed of, a town that truly embraced the spirit of the season.

Meanwhile, Larry and Brian had their own little tradition.

"Let's go find something to keep us warm," Brian would say with a smirk, and that was their signal. The two of them would slip away, cutting through the crowd to find a cozy bar where they could share a glass of whiskey and a little extra warmth to fight off the evening chill—or at least that's what they would say.

With drinks in hand, they would step outside just in time to see the moment everyone had been waiting for.

The crowd would hush, the countdown would begin, and as the final numbers were shouted in unison, the star atop Castle Rock would suddenly illuminate, casting a brilliant glow over the town. At the same moment, fireworks would burst into the sky, reflecting off the snow-dusted rooftops, filling the air with color and the sound of celebration.

Tiffany would squeeze Larry's hand; her face lit up with joy as she watched the display.

And on nights like this, it felt like heaven.

CHAPTER 14.
When Time Stood Still

Holly had climbed the corporate ladder and was now the vice president of a publicly traded IT company. As she was looking to fill a highly skilled and talented business analyst role, only one person came to mind—Tiffany.

Without hesitation, Holly picked up the phone and made Tiffany an offer.

Tiffany had considered going back to work for some time, but now that a real opportunity was in front of her—one she hadn't even applied for—she felt a mixture of excitement and nerves. She had spent years dedicated to raising the kids and running the household, and while she had always been capable of balancing anything life threw at her, stepping back into the professional world was a big decision.

That night, she and Larry went out to dinner to talk it through. They discussed how the additional income would benefit the family, the ways it could provide more flexibility for the kids' futures, and whether this was something she truly wanted. Larry, as always, supported her completely, knowing that whatever she set her mind to, she would excel at.

Tiffany didn't need much time to make up her mind—she was ready to take on this new challenge. But before she accepted, there was one thing she needed to negotiate.

The salary was more than fair, but commuting into Denver every day? That was out of the question. She made it clear that she would only take the job if she could work remotely, and if there ever came a point where she was required to be in the office full-time, she would quit.

Holly didn't hesitate—deal.

FOREVER TIFFANY

And just like that, Tiffany was back in the workforce.

She jumped into the role with the same dedication and intelligence she had applied to everything else in her life. It didn't take long for her to make an impact, proving once again that whether at home or in a high-powered corporate setting, she was a force to be reckoned with.

2018 was cruising by, and life seemed to be moving at an unstoppable pace. The family had settled into a rhythm, balancing school, sports, work, and family time with the ease that came from years of being deeply connected. Patrick was in his junior year of high school, a time filled with excitement, uncertainty, and big decisions about the future. He was actively exploring colleges and universities across the country, visiting campuses, meeting with coaches, and imagining where he would spend the next four years of his life. Larry and Tiffany were by his side every step of the way, offering advice but mostly just taking in the moment, realizing how fast the years had gone by. Their oldest was standing at the edge of adulthood, and while they were immensely proud, there was a bittersweet feeling that came with it.

Rylee, now in eighth grade, was eagerly anticipating her transition to high school. More than anything, she was excited about the fact that she would get to share one year at the same school as Patrick before he left for college. The idea of being in the same building, even for a short time, meant everything to her. She had always looked up to her big brother, and the thought of seeing him in the halls, maybe even catching a ride home together on occasion, made the transition to high school seem a little less scary.

Brennan, still in grade school, was full of boundless energy, bouncing between sports and school, growing more independent by the day. He idolized his older siblings, wanting to be just like Patrick on the basketball court and just like Rylee when it came to making friends effortlessly. He was at that beautiful age where the world still felt big and full of wonder, and Tiffany and Larry cherished every moment with him, knowing how quickly these years would pass.

LARRY BLAKE

One of the greatest joys of living in Colorado was how easy it was to escape into the mountains, and the family took full advantage. They spent as many weekends as possible in Breckenridge and Estes Park, places that had quickly become second homes. There was something about being up in the crisp mountain air, surrounded by towering pines and snow-capped peaks, that made life slow down just enough for them to fully appreciate the moment.

Patrick had started learning to ski, pushing himself to tackle new and more challenging runs each time they visited. While he was carving down the slopes, the rest of the family found just as much joy on the tubing hills, racing each other down the packed snow, laughing so hard that they often forgot about the cold. Tiffany, always one for experiences over extreme sports, preferred watching the kids have fun, bundled up with a warm drink in her hands, completely in her element.

Back home, they had found their favorite local spot, a place that would quickly become their sanctuary: The Office.

The Office wasn't just another bar and grill—it was a place with character, a neighborhood gem that felt like home from the very first visit. Tucked away in town, it had an intimate but lively atmosphere, the kind of place where the hum of conversation mixed perfectly with the sounds of clinking glasses and the occasional burst of laughter. The walls behind the bar were lined with an impressive collection of whiskey, giving it an old-school, refined feel, yet it was never pretentious.

The food was elevated bar fare—nothing fancy, but consistently delicious. Whether it was their signature burgers, crispy wings, or the perfectly seasoned fries that always seemed to disappear too quickly, every meal hit the spot. But it wasn't just about the food or the drinks—it was about the people.

Larry and Tiffany didn't just love The Office—they made it their place.

It became their escape from the routine, the spot where they could unwind after a long day, where they could sit together in a booth and talk about everything and nothing at all. It was where they found moments of peace, where they stole time just for themselves in the middle of busy weeks.

Before long, it wasn't just their go-to date spot—it became a family tradition. Three times a week, when Larry was in town, they met up with Holly and Steve, as well as Larry's parents, Diana and Larry Sr., for lunch. It was something they all looked forward to: a break from the chaos of life, a few hours where they could sit around a table, share stories, and just be together.

The owner, Pablo, was a huge part of what made The Office special. He had a way of making everyone feel like family, greeting them by name, remembering their favorite drinks, and always making sure they felt at home. Over time, he and his staff became more than just familiar faces—they became friends.

Larry and Tiffany didn't realize it at the time, but The Office would become part of their lives in a way they never expected. It wasn't just a restaurant or a bar—it was where they celebrated milestones, toasted to good news, and went when they needed to laugh or even when they needed a quiet moment to reflect. It was their haven, a place that became an extension of home.

The beauty of life is often found in the little things—the places that make you feel at ease, the traditions that happen without planning, the people who turn from strangers into friends.

For Larry and Tiffany, The Office was all of that and more. It was their place, their tradition, their little piece of magic right in the heart of Castle Rock.

2018 was shaping up to be an exciting year, filled with growth, change, and new adventures. Tiffany had stepped back into the workforce and was thriving in her career, proving once again that she could do anything she set her mind to. With her career taking off, she decided it was time to treat herself to something special, something she had dreamed of for years—a luxury SUV.

For as long as she could remember, her dream car had been a white Range Rover. There was something about the sleek lines, the elegant yet powerful presence on the road, that had always fascinated her. It was the perfect mix of sophistication and strength, much like Tiffany herself. So, one afternoon, she made her way to the Land Rover dealership in Littleton, ready to finally make that dream a reality.

As she walked through the showroom, admiring the beautifully crafted vehicles, something unexpected caught her eye. It wasn't the Range Rover she had always envisioned; instead, it was a brand-new, full-size Land Rover Discovery, gleaming under the dealership lights. It had everything she wanted—luxury, space, a third row for the kids, and a commanding presence on the road. She took a seat behind the wheel, running her hands over the premium leather, adjusting the controls, and imagining all the places this car would take her family.

She smiled to herself, knowing in that moment that this was the one. It wasn't just a car—it was a symbol of her hard work, her independence, and her success. It was something she had earned through years of dedication, balancing motherhood, marriage, and now a thriving career. Driving off the lot, she felt an immense sense of pride and accomplishment.

Of course, Tiffany never let herself be the only one in the family to enjoy something new. She always had a way of making sure those she loved had everything they needed—and everything they wanted. So, it wasn't long before she had set her sights on something for Rylee.

From a young age, Rylee had always loved horses, and her passion for them had only grown stronger over the years. She had taken lessons and dreamed of owning a horse of her own, but that was a big commitment, one that Tiffany and Larry had to seriously consider. As always, Tiffany had a way of persuading Larry, a mix of charm and pure logic, and he found himself unable to say no to something that would bring their daughter so much joy.

FOREVER TIFFANY

The search for the perfect horse began, and after looking at several options, they found *him*.

He was a magnificent show-jumping horse with an athletic build, powerful strides, and a temperament that was both gentle and intelligent. His registered name was *Too Kool Kat*, but they quickly decided he needed something simpler, something that felt more personal. They started calling him *Andy*, and from the moment Rylee met him, it was clear they belonged together.

Andy wasn't just a horse—he was a new member of the family.

Rylee took to him immediately, spending every free moment she had at the barn, brushing his coat, learning his movements, and bonding with him in a way indisputable. She started taking lessons with a well-respected local trainer, and it quickly became apparent that she had a natural talent for show jumping. She was fearless, guiding Andy over jumps with grace and confidence that made Tiffany's heart swell with pride.

But something even more special happened between Tiffany and Andy.

Tiffany had never been around horses growing up, yet she had a way of forming connections with animals that was almost magical. She wasn't afraid of Andy's size, his strength, or his power. Instead, she approached him the same way she did with everyone in her life— with kindness, patience, and love.

Whenever she pulled up the long driveway to the barn, her entire demeanor would change. Her face would light up, her excitement palpable. She would step out of her car, call out in her signature, melodic voice—

"ANNNNNDYYY!"

And no matter where he was, no matter how far away, Andy would stop in his tracks. Whether he was grazing in the open field, drinking from the trough, or playing with the other horses, he would lift his head, ears alert, and lock eyes with her. And then, without hesitation, he would break into a full gallop, kicking up dust as he ran straight to her.

It was a sight to behold—the way he responded to her as if he had been waiting for her all day.

The moment he reached her, Tiffany would wrap her arms around his strong neck, pressing her face against his soft coat. He would nuzzle into her, completely at ease in her presence. She would gently stroke his face, whispering to him, her touch making him feel safe and loved.

Larry watched these moments unfold time and time again, in awe of how naturally Tiffany connected with every living thing she encountered. It was as if she radiated a kind of warmth that animals and people alike couldn't help but be drawn to.

Andy had become more than just Rylee's horse; he had become Tiffany's escape, her sanctuary. In the midst of busy schedules, work responsibilities, and the everyday chaos of life, spending time with Andy gave her a sense of peace.

She didn't need to have grown up around horses to understand them. She just *knew*.

And Andy *knew* her too.

Their bond was special, built on trust, respect, and the kind of love that didn't need words.

For Tiffany, Andy wasn't just a horse—he was a cue that she belonged in every space she entered. That her presence mattered. That love, in its purest form, was something she gave without hesitation, without expectation.

And for Larry, watching her with Andy was just another confirmation of something he had always known—Tiffany was gifted.

FOREVER TIFFANY

She had a way of making every single soul, whether human or animal, feel *seen*. Feel *important*. Feel *loved*.

With her new car, a thriving career, and this newfound connection with Andy, Tiffany was stepping into a beautiful new chapter of her life. And as always, she did it with grace, love, and a heart wide open to the magic of it all.

Late July 2018, Larry and Tiffany were once again headed back to Mexico, a place that had become a haven for them over the years. The warm ocean breeze, the soft sand beneath their feet, the endless sound of waves crashing—it all felt like home. This time, they weren't traveling alone. They were joined by Larry's great friend George and his wife, Jamie, making the trip even more memorable. The four of them had planned the kind of getaway that was equal parts adventure and relaxation.

They had booked stunning private villas in the adults-only section of the resort, a secluded area designed for complete tranquility. Their villas were arranged around a large, luxurious private pool, and with only half of the twelve available villas occupied, it felt almost like they had the place to themselves. It was the perfect balance of intimacy and socialization—mornings spent lounging by the pool, afternoons sipping tropical drinks, and evenings filled with laughter, conversation, and treasured moments.

As much as Larry wanted Tiffany to completely unplug and lose herself on the vacation, she had brought her laptop along, as she often did. Work had become a major part of her life again, and she was excelling at it in a way that both amazed and inspired Larry. He would watch her as she sat on the villa's private patio, bathed in the morning sunlight, typing away with that determined look on her face. He both loved and hated it—loved seeing her shine, but hated that she wasn't fully relaxing. But that was Tiffany. She always gave everything her all, and that was one of the many reasons he adored her.

The days slipped by in a beautiful blur. They would wake up each morning to the sound of the waves in the distance, the warmth of the sun streaming through the villa's oversized windows. Mornings were lazy and slow, with fresh fruit, coffee, and long dips in the pool before the heat of the day set in.

Larry and Tiffany found themselves falling into an easy rhythm, one they knew well from all their previous trips together. They would spend hours in the pool, drifting side by side, the cool water keeping them refreshed as they soaked in the tropical sun. Tiffany, with her blonde hair pulled up under a sun hat and oversized sunglasses covering her eyes, looked stunning, as she always did. Larry would watch her, completely mesmerized by the way she moved, the way she laughed, the way she seemed to fit so perfectly into every moment.

They had been together for eighteen years, and yet, when she would float over to him, wrap her arms around his shoulders, and lean in to whisper something just for him, it still gave him that same rush of excitement as it did in the very beginning.

The pool became their all-time favorite place to be. While George and Jamie socialized with other guests, Larry and Tiffany often found themselves wrapped up in their own little world, talking about everything and nothing, reminiscing about past vacations, planning future ones, and simply enjoying being together.

By afternoon, the group would make their way down to the beach, the warm sand beneath their feet as they strolled toward the cabanas. They would sip on margaritas and listen to the waves, sometimes in conversation, other times just sitting in comfortable silence, enjoying the moment.

As evening approached, the energy of the resort shifted. The quiet hum of the day transformed into the vibrant pulse of the night. They would dress for dinner, and Tiffany always looked naturally gorgeous in whatever she chose to wear. Larry loved these moments—watching her get ready, the way she would apply just a touch of makeup, the way she would slide on a dress that hugged her perfectly, the way she would look at him just before they walked out the door, a small, knowing smile on her lips.

Dinners were an experience in themselves. They would sit at candlelit tables overlooking the ocean, the warm breeze rolling in, the sound of live music floating through the air. They enjoyed every bite of fresh seafood, every sip of expertly crafted cocktails, and every second of being in this beautiful place together.

One evening, Larry and George decided to head into downtown Playa del Carmen, eager to experience the energy of the city. The streets were alive with music, laughter, and the scent of delicious food. They were in a lively bar, a local band playing in the corner, the energy infectious. It was the kind of night that reminded them why they loved traveling—submerging themselves in the culture, feeling the heartbeat of a place, letting loose, and simply enjoying life.

While they were out, Tiffany and Jamie were indulging in their own favorite pastime—shopping. The resort had brought in a group of local vendors, setting up a vibrant market filled with handmade goods, colorful dresses, intricate jewelry, and stunning home décor. Tiffany was completely in her element, moving from stall to stall, chatting with the artisans, picking out treasures to bring home.

Larry wasn't sure what he loved more—the joy she found in shopping or the way she would light up when she found the perfect piece. She had an eye for beauty, and everything she chose seemed to tell a story.

Their villa was a paradise in itself. It had white marble floors that felt cool underfoot, a luxurious king-sized bed positioned in the center of the room, a fully stocked bar, and an outdoor shower surrounded by lush palm trees. That shower became one of their favorite places—there was something exhilarating about being under the warm water, surrounded by nature, the night air cool against their skin.

Larry would hold Tiffany close, feeling the weight of the moment, of how deeply he loved her, of how lucky he was to have her.

Nights were spent in each other's arms, talking about life, about their dreams, about their children, and how proud they were of them.

They laughed, they reminisced, and they held onto every second, knowing that these were the moments that mattered.

As the trip neared its end, there was a sense of fulfillment, of gratitude. They had spent five incredible days in paradise, but they were ready to return home. The kids were waiting for them, and as much as they loved their time away, there was no greater joy than coming home to their family.

On their final night, they walked along the beach, hand in hand, the waves gently lapping at their feet. The sky was a canvas of colors—deep purples, fiery oranges, soft pinks fading into the night.

Larry looked at Tiffany, her blonde hair blowing in the breeze, her face glowing under the moonlight, and he knew—he would never stop feeling this way about her.

Eighteen years together, and somehow, she was even more beautiful than the day they met.

The flight home was quiet, both of them lost in their thoughts. The vacation had been perfect, but more than that, it had been a reminder. A reminder of why they worked so well together, of why their love had only grown stronger over the years.

As they landed and stepped off the plane, Larry glanced over at Tiffany, squeezing her hand.

"Ready to go home?" he asked.

She smiled, nodding. "Always."

And with that, they walked forward, side by side, ready for whatever came next.

They didn't have to wait long for "whatever came next." Life, as it often did, had a way of delivering the unexpected when everything seemed to be moving along perfectly. Brian, who had always been strong, active, and rarely sick, had been dealing with persistent back pain for a few weeks. At first, he dismissed it as nothing more than a pulled muscle from a workout, maybe just stress from work, or even the toll of getting older. But when the pain didn't subside and started getting worse, Stacy urged him to see a doctor. It was one of those gut instincts she had, the kind that told her something was off.

Brian finally agreed and went in for a few routine tests, expecting nothing more than some physical therapy or maybe an anti-inflammatory prescription. Instead, what he received was a life-altering diagnosis—kidney cancer.

The news came like a wrecking ball. It was the kind of moment that stops time, where words on a doctor's lips seem to echo but don't fully register. Brian and Stacy sat in the small exam room, their world suddenly feeling much smaller, much darker. Cancer. The word alone was terrifying, but hearing it directed at him, seeing the look in Stacy's eyes as she tried to stay strong but was barely holding it together—it was unbearable.

Brian knew exactly who to call.

Larry.

If anyone could understand what he was going through, if anyone could help him steer through the overwhelming fear and uncertainty, it was Larry. He was a Stage III cancer survivor, someone who had fought his own battle, endured the pain, the treatments, the surgeries, and had come out on the other side. More importantly, Larry had never been just a friend—he was family.

When Brian called, his voice was steady, but Larry could hear the weight behind it. He could hear the fear that Brian was trying so hard to mask.

"Man, I need to talk," Brian said, exhaling heavily.

Larry didn't hesitate. "I'm here. Whatever it is, we'll figure it out."

There was a pause before Brian finally said it. "It's cancer. My kidney."

Larry felt his stomach drop. He knew that feeling all too well. That moment when your body feels like it's betraying you, where your life suddenly becomes measured in doctor's appointments, treatment plans, and statistics. But he also knew that cancer didn't mean the end. It meant a fight, yes, but one that could be won.

"Listen to me," Larry said firmly, his voice firm. "You are going to get through this. You are not doing this alone. I'm with you every step of the way."

And he meant it.

The first thing Larry did was make a call to the one person he trusted the most in situations like this—Dr. Matt Blum.

Dr. Blum had saved Larry's life years ago, performing the grueling surgeries that had removed the massive tumor from his chest. He was more than just a doctor; he was a hero in Larry's eyes. If there was anyone who could help Brian or at least point him in the right direction, it was Matt.

Larry didn't have to wait long. Dr. Blum called back quickly, listening carefully as Larry explained Brian's diagnosis and situation. There was no hesitation in his voice when he responded.

"I have the perfect guy for him," Dr. Blum said. "Dr. Benjamin Coons, one of my closest colleagues in Colorado Springs. He's the best in the field, and I'll make sure Brian gets in to see him immediately."

Hearing those words brought Larry a sense of relief, but he knew the real relief would come when Brian was on the other side of this fight.

When Larry told Brian and Stacy about the plan, he could see gratitude in their eyes. There was still fear—of course, there was—but knowing they had the best doctors, knowing they had a path forward, made all the difference.

FOREVER TIFFANY

For Tiffany, watching Stacy go through this was incredibly difficult. They were more than friends now; they were like sisters. Stacy had been her rock through so many things, and now it was Tiffany's turn to be hers. She had lived this nightmare before. She knew the feeling of waking up in the middle of the night, mind racing with "what ifs." She knew the helplessness, the exhaustion, the quiet panic that settled into your bones. But she also knew how to fight it.

Tiffany did what she did best—she wrapped Stacy in untiring love. She held her when she needed to cry, she listened when she needed to vent, and she reassured her when she needed strength. She cooked meals, made sure the kids were taken care of, and distracted Stacy whenever the weight of it all became too much. She reminded Stacy of what she already knew deep down—Brian was strong, and he wasn't fighting this alone.

Larry remained resolute, never uncertain in his confidence. "You'll get through this," he kept telling Brian. "And you'll be back to yourself in no time."

Before the surgery, Brian wanted to clear his mind and spend time away with Stacy—something that felt like a true reset, a fresh start. What better way than to head up to the mountains for Breckenridge's annual Oktoberfest with Tiffany and Larry?

The crisp fall air, the golden aspen trees lining the slopes, and the lively atmosphere of the festival made it the perfect destination. Breckenridge, with its charming downtown and stunning mountain views, had always been a favorite escape for Larry and Tiffany, and now, it would be a place to celebrate life, health, and friendship.

They arrived in the early afternoon, checking into a beautiful mountain lodge with sweeping balcony views of the snow-capped peaks. The warm sunlight hit the slopes just right, reflecting off the golden trees, creating a postcard-perfect scene. The weather was surprisingly warm for that time of year, making the celebration even more enjoyable.

LARRY BLAKE

Larry was already buzzing with excitement at the thought of all the craft beer they were about to consume—Colorado was known for its breweries, and Oktoberfest in Breckenridge was one of the best places to sample some of the finest brews in the country. He had been looking forward to this for weeks, making a mental list of all the local beers he wanted to try.

Tiffany, on the other hand, had an entirely different agenda. Her first priority? Shopping. She was always on the hunt for something new, something special, and this trip was no different. But before she could dive too deep into the boutiques, there was one stop she absolutely *had* to make—a sunglasses store.

Tiffany had a habit, a very strategic one at that. She always seemed to "forget" her sunglasses at home, knowing full well that Larry would never say no to replacing them. Her trick was simple: leave every pair she owned behind and casually mention her discomfort in the bright mountain sun. Of course, Larry wanted her to be comfortable—he never wanted her to have to squint all weekend—so off they went straight to the store. And just like that, another trip, another new pair of Ray-Bans.

With her shopping fix satisfied (for the moment), the group wandered through the charming streets of Breckenridge, popping into shops, grabbing a few souvenirs, and soaking in the mountain-town energy. By late afternoon, they made their way back to the hotel, eager to unwind before the big festivities began the next day.

The four of them changed into their swimsuits and headed straight for the hot tub, a steaming oasis set against the breathtaking mountain background. The warmth of the water melted away any stress, and as they leaned back, drinks in hand, they let the moment sink in.

They talked about life—how fragile it could be, how quickly things could change. Brian was going through so much, and seeing him sitting there, laughing, and enjoying this moment made everything feel even more precious. They spoke about their appreciation for each other, for the friendships that had carried them through the toughest times, and for the small joys that made life worth living.

Of course, it wasn't all deep conversation. Larry and Brian were already making plans for how much beer they were going to consume the next day, rattling off names of breweries and arguing over which ones had the best Oktoberfest selections. Tiffany and Stacy rolled their eyes, knowing full well the men were about to embark on a weekend-long drinking marathon.

As always, there were inappropriate jokes—the kind that would make most people blush, but they felt perfectly normal in this group. Nothing was off-limits; no topic was too wild. That was the beauty of their friendship—there was no judgment, no masks, just pure, unfiltered fun.

As the sun set behind the mountains, leaving a golden glow across the sky, Tiffany leaned her head back against the edge of the hot tub, eyes closed, letting the warmth of the water and the laughter of her friends surround her.

Tomorrow would be filled with beer steins, bratwurst, and endless laughter. But tonight? Tonight was about soaking in the moment, appreciating the here and now, and celebrating the simple fact that they were all together.

Life was good. And in that moment, they knew just how lucky they were.

****

Saturday morning arrived. The crisp mountain air filtered through the slightly cracked balcony door, bringing with it the distant sounds of birds and the faint hum of the town waking up. Larry stirred first, stretching beneath the warm covers before rolling over to find Tiffany nestled beside him.

She was still asleep, her golden hair splayed across the pillow, her face relaxed and peaceful. He took a moment just to watch her, something he had done countless times over the years but never got tired of. She looked so serene, her breath rising and falling in a steady rhythm, and he knew that if he could, he'd stay in this moment forever. But the day was waiting, and the festival was calling.

Slowly, he traced his fingers along her arm, his touch featherlight. Tiffany stirred, letting out a soft sigh as she shifted closer, her bare leg sliding against his beneath the sheets. She blinked her eyes open, a sleepy smile forming as she looked at him.

"Good morning, handsome," she murmured, her voice still sleepy.

Larry grinned. "Good morning, beautiful."

For a moment, neither of them moved, savoring the quiet before the chaos of the day. Then, with a playful smirk, Tiffany rolled onto her back, stretching her arms above her head. "You know," she teased, "I think we should start every morning like this."

Larry chuckled, leaning in to press a kiss to her forehead before whispering, "I couldn't agree more."

They eventually pulled themselves from the warmth of the bed, taking a long, hot shower together, partially to wake up, partially just to steal a little more time wrapped up in each other before facing the outside world. The water was soothing, the steam filling the room as they laughed and talked, their bodies brushing against each other in a way that was both familiar and exhilarating.

By the time they stepped out, the scent of soap and fresh mountain air mingled together, waking them up fully. It was time to get ready for the day ahead.

Down in the hotel lobby, they met Brian and Stacy, who were equally keen to dive into the festival's festivities. Brian, fully embracing the Oktoberfest spirit, had gone all out, decked out in full lederhosen, complete with suspenders and knee-high socks. He looked like he had just walked out of a Bavarian village, grinning from ear to ear.

Larry, on the other hand, had no intention of dressing the part. He stuck to his usual style—golf shorts, a crisp white V-neck tee, a white hat, and sunglasses. Simple, classic, effortless.

And then there was Tiffany.

She strolled into the lobby wearing tiny, barely-there jean shorts that showcased her toned, athletic legs. The fit was perfect, hugging her in all the right places, and Larry couldn't help but appreciate the view. Her long blonde hair shone over her shoulders, and her sunglasses balanced flawlessly atop her head, adding to her serene beauty. She was casual yet striking, as always.

With laughter and anticipation, the four made their way toward the heart of Breckenridge, where the Oktoberfest festivities were already in full swing. The streets were lined with long wooden picnic tables; each one crowded with festivalgoers, giant steins of beer in hand. Traditional German folk music filled the air, creating an atmosphere that was equal parts lively and intoxicating.

Then, disappointment hit.

Larry and Brian's faces fell as they reached the beer tents, scanning the taps in disbelief. They had been expecting to sample a variety of Colorado's best craft beers, eager to explore the different flavors the state had to offer. But instead, there was only *one* Colorado brewery—Breckenridge Brewery. Every other tap was German beer, imported straight from Bavaria.

Now, neither of them had anything against a solid German beer, but they had come here expecting options. *Lots* of options.

Tiffany and Stacy exchanged amused glances as they watched their husbands process the unexpected turn of events.

"You two look like someone just told you Christmas was canceled," Stacy teased, nudging Brian's arm.

Larry sighed dramatically. "I just… had a plan, you know? A beer plan."

Tiffany laughed, lacing her fingers through Larry's. "Guess you'll just have to drink what's available. Think you can manage?"

Larry squeezed her hand, giving her a smirk. "Fine. But I'm going to need *extra* bratwurst to make up for this injustice."

And so, they made the best of it. They ordered their steins of beer, choosing what sounded the most appealing, and dove into the food. The bratwursts were incredible, served on fresh rolls with a perfect balance of sauerkraut and mustard. Giant pretzels, crispy and golden, were dipped in warm cheese, and the plates of schnitzel melted in their mouths.

As they walked through the town, Larry and Tiffany strolled hand in hand, relishing the simple joy of being together in such a beautiful place. The crisp mountain air carried the scent of roasted nuts and cinnamon, and Tiffany couldn't resist stopping at a few small shops, picking up souvenirs and little trinkets.

Larry teased her about her ability to find something to buy *anywhere*, but deep down, he loved how happy it made her.

As the day wound down, they made their way back to the hotel, feeling the satisfying weight of a day well spent. But the night wasn't over yet—dinner was still on the agenda.

After freshening up, they headed to Michel's Italian Restaurant, a charming spot nestled in downtown Breckenridge. The moment they stepped inside, they were greeted by the warm aroma of garlic, fresh pasta, and simmering sauces. The ambiance was cozy, with dim lighting, exposed brick walls, and the kind of energy that made you want to settle in for hours.

They ordered rounds of appetizers—bruschetta, calamari, and a rich charcuterie board loaded with imported cheeses and cured meats. The conversation flowed, laughter filling the space between bites.

Then came the toasts.

Larry and Brian, knowing how special this weekend was, ordered Johnny Walker Blue—a drink reserved for only the most meaningful occasions.

They raised their glasses, the golden liquid catching the candlelight.

"To Brian," Larry said, his voice filled with gratitude and admiration. "To friendship, and know Brian is going to kick cancer's ass."

Brian nodded, his expression filled with emotion. "And to the people who make these great moments worth living."

The clinking of glasses felt like a promise—a promise to keep showing up for each other, to keep celebrating, and to never take a single moment for granted.

As the night stretched on, the drinks poured, the stories got funnier, and the warmth of friendship wrapped around them like a comforting hug.

They had come to Breckenridge for beer, for celebration, for a weekend away. But what they really found was another unforgettable memory—another page in the incredible story they were writing together.

****

On the morning of Brian's surgery, Larry woke up early, feeling a strange sense of calm despite the heavy day ahead. The weight of what was about to happen should have had him tossing and turning all night, but instead, there was a quiet peace within him. He stepped into the shower, letting the hot water wash over his face, clearing his mind as he reached for his phone and turned on some music.

The first song that played was Bob Marley's *Three Little Birds*.

"Don't worry about a thing, 'cause every little thing's gonna be all right..."

Larry froze. The lyrics hit him in a way they never had before, as if the universe had chosen this exact moment to send him a message. The song spoke of three little birds outside the doorstep, singing sweet songs, offering reassurance. And in that instant, Larry *knew*.

Those three little birds weren't just part of a song.

They were Stacy, Mackenzie, and Piper. Brian's girls. His most treasured people in the world.

Larry closed his eyes, letting the warmth of the water and the music sink in. It was as if something—God, fate, the universe—was speaking directly to him, telling him that Brian was going to be okay. He held onto that feeling as he stepped out of the shower, dressed, and got ready to make the hour-long drive to Colorado Springs.

As Larry pulled into the hospital parking lot, he could feel the tension before he even stepped inside. The air was heavy with unspoken fears, with the weight of waiting for news no one wanted to hear. He walked quickly through the glass doors, taking in the sight of Stacy sitting stiffly in a chair, her hands clasped tightly in her lap. Next to her was Brian's mother, Pat.

Pat was a strong woman, the kind of mother who had seen more than her fair share of loss. She had already lost her husband, Brian's father, to melanoma years before. She knew what it was like to sit in a waiting room, praying, hoping, and fearing. And now, here she was again, facing the possibility of losing her son.

Larry took a deep breath and walked over, pulling up a chair next to them. He greeted Stacy first, squeezing her hand in reassurance before turning to Pat. He could see the worry written on her face, the way her eyes darted toward the doors, waiting for an update on anything that might bring relief.

"Hi, Pat," Larry said softly, his voice calm and steady. "How are you holding up?"

She managed a small, tight-lipped smile, but the emotion in her eyes betrayed her. "I'm ok, just praying for Brian," she said, her voice barely above a whisper. "Too much waiting. Too much uncertainty."

Larry nodded, understanding more than she could know. He had been in this exact spot years before. He had felt the fear, the helplessness. But he had made it through. And Brian would, too.

He leaned forward, resting his elbows on his knees. "Listen, I know this feels impossible right now, but I promise you, he's in the best hands. Dr. Coons is the best there is. And Brian is strong. He's got too much to live for—his girls, his family, all of us. He's going to come out of this."

Stacy wiped at her eyes, nodding quickly. She wanted to believe him. She *needed* to believe him.

For the next several hours, they sat together, the silence between them broken only by the occasional small talk, the nervous laughter that tried to mask the anxiety filling the room. Every time the doors opened, they all turned their heads, waiting to see if it was a doctor coming toward them.

Minutes felt like hours. Hours felt like days.

And then, finally, Dr. Coons appeared.

They all stood at once, their hearts pounding as they waited for the news.

Dr. Coons smiled—a small, reassuring smile that made Larry's knees nearly buckle with relief. "Surgery was a success," he said. "We were able to remove the tumor completely. Brian is in recovery now, and everything went *as* well as we could have hoped."

Stacy let out a sharp breath, covering her mouth as the emotion hit her like a tidal wave. Pat closed her eyes, whispering a quiet prayer of thanks. Larry exhaled deeply, the tension finally releasing from his body.

He had known, deep down, that Brian would be okay. But hearing it, knowing it was real—there was no better feeling in the world.

Within weeks, Brian was gaining strength. By the end of the year, he was back to himself—laughing, joking, living life the way he always had.

And one night, as they all sat together—Larry, Tiffany, Brian, and Stacy—drinks in hand, reflecting on everything that had happened, the realization hit them all at once.

None of this had been by chance.

Their meeting, their friendship, it wasn't just luck.

Yes, their birthdays and anniversaries lining up had been uncanny. But this—this was something bigger.

The fact that Larry had battled cancer years before and survived. That his surgeon, Dr. Blum, had moved to Colorado, unknowingly positioning himself to help Brian years later. That Brian needed the best care possible, and Dr. Blum had led them straight to Dr. Coons—it wasn't a coincidence.

It was *fate*.

Larry had no doubt that a higher power had orchestrated it all. Some things in life couldn't be explained, and this was one of them. They were meant to be in each other's lives, meant to be there for each other in ways they never could have predicted.

As Brian healed, as life settled back into its familiar rhythm, there was a new appreciation for the bond they shared.

They had walked through fire together. And they had come out the other side.

CHAPTER 15.
Moments That Mattered

Patrick's senior basketball season had arrived, and with it came a mix of excitement, nostalgia, and the realization that this would be the last year he would step onto the court with the friends he had been playing alongside for the past four years. Every game, every practice, every moment felt just a little more significant, a little more meaningful. This was the culmination of years of hard work, early morning practices, late-night shooting sessions, sweat, dedication, and a brotherhood formed through the love of the game.

This year also brought a special twist—one that made the season even more meaningful for the family. Rylee, now a freshman, had been named the varsity team manager. It was more than just a title; it was an opportunity for her to be right there, on the sidelines, supporting her big brother and the team. She had always looked up to Patrick and admired his work ethic and the way he carried himself. Now, she would be part of his journey, part of the long road to the final buzzer of his high school career. For Larry and Tiffany, watching them share this experience was nothing short of special. It was rare for siblings to get a high school year together, let alone one where they were so closely connected through something they both loved.

As the season progressed, Tiffany and Larry took a step back from their longtime booster club duties, passing the torch to Shannon, a woman who had been a close friend of Tiffany's for years. Their relationship had its ups and downs, as friendships sometimes do, but at the core of it was love and respect. It felt good to hand the responsibility to someone who cared about the program just as much as they did. They could now focus on simply being parents, sitting in the stands, cheering for their son without the weight of running the behind-the-scenes operations.

With basketball winding down and graduation approaching, Patrick had some big decisions ahead. He had a few opportunities to continue playing at the Division III level and even the chance to play at Purdue Northwest—a school that carried deep family ties. It was where his grandfather had coached and where his father had played baseball. It would have been a full-circle moment. But Patrick had different plans. While he loved the game, he knew he wanted to focus on his studies and step into the next phase of his life with a fresh perspective.

His academic record spoke for itself. Patrick had applied to some of the most prestigious universities in the country. He even had an interview with Harvard, an accomplishment in itself. Though he was waitlisted, the fact that he had been considered was enough to make Tiffany beam with pride. It was a validation of all the hard work, the late nights, the years of discipline, and sacrifice. Offers came in from several top-tier schools, and as the family sifted through the possibilities, Tiffany couldn't help but glow with pride, knowing that no matter what path Patrick chose, his future was bright.

In the end, he made a decision that would keep him close to home, surrounded by the people who had supported him every step of the way. The University of Colorado–Boulder, with its nationally ranked physics program, was the perfect fit. It wasn't just about academics—it was about finding a place where he could thrive and grow into the person he was meant to be.

As he accepted his offer to CU Boulder, there was an overwhelming sense of excitement in the household. A new chapter was about to begin—not just for Patrick, but for the whole family. And while his days of wearing his high school jersey were coming to an end, the foundation he had built through his years of basketball, school, and family would carry him into the next phase of his journey with confidence.

The school year was a great success; it would have been nice to see the team win a title, but they made it to the second round of the state championship, losing to a very good team that featured two Division One players. Brennan wrapped up the fourth grade in a wonderful style, Rylee ended her freshman year, and Patrick was looking forward to his graduation and open house party.

May 21st, 2019, had finally arrived—graduation day. A day filled with excitement, pride, and the bittersweet realization that childhood was slipping into the past. It wasn't just any graduation; it was Patrick's, Tiffany's, and Larry's firstborn, the one who had set the standard and who had grown into a remarkable young man right before their eyes.

Family had flown in from all over to celebrate this milestone. Scott and Sandy arrived with their boys—Nathan, Christian, and Scotty—ready to cheer on their cousin as he stepped into the next chapter of his life. Amanda made the trip from Ohio, and Vicki, who had left Colorado to move in with Amanda, was back for the special day. Tiffany's uncle, Dan, and aunt Susan traveled from Florida, bringing their love and excitement for Patrick's big moment. The house was full, laughter echoing through the walls as everyone reminisced about Patrick's childhood, his successes, and the bright future ahead.

May in Castle Rock was usually mild, a perfect balance between spring and summer. Morning graduations were a tradition at the school, with families gathering early to celebrate their graduates under the warmth of the Colorado sun. But this year? This year, Mother Nature had different plans. Much like the day Tiffany and Larry had gotten married, the snow made an unexpected appearance, turning what should have been a crisp, clear morning into a winter wonderland.

The once-green turf football field was now blanketed in fresh, untouched snow. The grounds crew had worked tirelessly to carve paths for students to walk and cleared sections for families to sit. It was chaotic, cold, and completely unexpected—but somehow, it was magical. The sight of graduates in their caps and gowns, trudging through the snow, brought a unique beauty to the day, a reminder that the best moments in life often come with a twist.

Tiffany sat in the stands, bundled up in a stylish coat, her blonde hair tucked under a warm hat, her gloved hands wrapped around a steaming cup of coffee. She wasn't complaining about the cold—not today. Her heart was too full, her smile too wide. Patrick, her first baby, her little blessing, had done it. He had worked hard and stayed disciplined, and now, he was walking across the stage to receive his diploma.

As his name was called, the family erupted into cheers. Larry let out a proud whistle, and Rylee and Brennan jumped up and down, waving their arms wildly. Patrick, ever composed, shook hands with the principal, took his diploma, and flashed a small but proud smile as he glanced toward his family. In that moment, Tiffany felt her chest tighten, her eyes threatening to well with tears. Not sad tears, but the kind that come when you realize time has moved far too quickly.

For a brief moment, she saw him as a little boy again—the one who used to run into her arms after school, the one who clung to her leg when he was nervous, the one who used to fall asleep in her lap during movie nights. And now, here he was, a young man ready to take on the world.

As the ceremony ended and graduates tossed their caps into the air—white specks against the gray sky—Tiffany squeezed Larry's hand, leaning her head against his shoulder.

"We did it," she whispered.

Larry chuckled, his breath visible in the cold air. "Yeah, but I think Patrick did most of the work."

Tiffany laughed, wiping at her eyes before they could betray her emotions. "Maybe. But we were here for all of it."

FOREVER TIFFANY

And that was what mattered. Through every late-night study session, every game, every triumph, and every struggle, they had been there.

As the family gathered for photos—Patrick in his cap and gown, snowflakes still falling around them—Tiffany felt something deep in her soul. This was a moment she would never forget. The snow, the laughter, the pride—it was all part of the story.

And just like that, a new chapter was about to begin.

The day after graduation, the family gathered again, this time for Patrick's open house party. The contrast between the two days was almost unbelievable—just twenty-four hours ago, they had been bundled up in coats and blankets, watching Patrick walk across the stage in a snow-covered stadium, the cold biting at their fingers. But today? Today was summer. The sun shone brightly in a clear blue sky, the temperature climbing to a perfect 78 degrees. The last remnants of snow had melted away, leaving the yard green and the air warm and inviting. Only in Castle Rock could you experience winter and summer within the span of a single day.

The backyard was transformed into the perfect setting for a celebration. Larry had been up early, tending to the smoker, the rich scent of slow-cooked pork filling the air. Tiffany had worked her magic inside, making sure everything was set just right—the tables decorated, drinks stocked, and enough food to feed an army. There was barbecue, pizza for the kids, a spread of appetizers and desserts, and, of course, plenty of beer and wine for the adults. The sound of laughter and music carried through the neighborhood as friends and family arrived, everyone in high spirits.

Guests poured in from all over town. Patrick's teammates and coaches, friends from school, and teachers who had watched him grow over the years. Holly and Steve were there, along with Larry's parents, who wouldn't have missed this day for anything. It was a full house, a perfect mix of family and friends, all coming together to celebrate Patrick and the bright future ahead of him.

Tiffany moved through the crowd with ease, making sure everyone had what they needed. She was the heart of the party, effortlessly balancing hosting duties while still finding time to enjoy the moment. She laughed with old friends, reminisced with family, and snuck proud glances at Patrick every time she caught sight of him, surrounded by his friends, smiling and enjoying his day.

Larry was in his element as well, manning the grill, making sure the food was just right, and sharing stories with anyone who stopped by. He and other dads swapped memories from the last four years, talking about all the games, the wins, the challenges. It was a moment of reflection for everyone—how quickly time had passed, how much Patrick had grown, how proud they all were.

As the afternoon stretched on, someone suggested taking a group photo. It was one of those simple, last-minute ideas, but it felt important. Everyone gathered in the backyard, standing close together, Patrick front and center, flanked by Rylee and Brennan. Tiffany and Larry stood beside them, arms wrapped around each other; family filled in the spaces around them, everyone smiling, the sun forming a golden glow over the scene.

The camera clicked, freezing the moment in time.

At that moment, no one could have known how much this photo would come to mean. Tiffany would look back on it often, studying the faces and remembering the laughter and warmth of that day. Because within that picture was someone she cherished deeply—someone who, not long after, would be gone.

Loss has a way of arriving unannounced, slipping into life when you least expect it. It doesn't wait for the right time. It doesn't warn you. It just comes, changing everything.

But on that day, in that perfect moment, surrounded by the people she loved, Tiffany was simply happy. And for that, she would always be grateful.

FOREVER TIFFANY

To keep the celebrations going, Tiffany and Holly planned and booked a vacation for both families, returning to Mexico, to that same resort they had come to love as their home away from home. The idea of another trip to this tropical paradise filled everyone with anticipation and joy.

Brennan, always eager to make his own requests known, made a special demand for this vacation: he wanted to fly first class. He proudly told his dad that he had earned the upgrade after having a great school year. Rylee, ever the advocate for her own comforts, chimed in with a similar sentiment, insisting that if Brennan deserved first class, then why not add a little extra luxury for everyone? Larry glanced at Tiffany, and once again, he couldn't say no to her. There was something about the way Tiffany's enthusiasm made every day brighter that kept him smiling all these years. With that, Larry went ahead and booked first-class tickets on United, much to Brennan's delight—this would be his very first experience flying in the front of the plane.

The day of the vacation arrived with palpable excitement. As Brennan walked down the jetway, his eyes widened in amazement when he discovered his seat was 1A—a window seat in first class. He practically bounced with excitement, a mix of nerves and joy evident on his face as he stepped into the luxurious cabin.

Once the plane took off, cruising above the clouds, Brennan couldn't help but comment, "Dad, this is first class? I need more luxury—I thought it would be even better." His words were spoken with the earnest enthusiasm of youth, his eyes scanning the plush seats and elegant surroundings. Larry chuckled warmly at his son's remark, thinking to himself that maybe this was a valuable lesson: sometimes, even when you pay extra, there's a limit to how much more comfort you can truly receive.

For the rest of the flight, the atmosphere was filled with light-hearted banter. Brennan kept glancing around, marveling at the spacious cabin, while Larry and Tiffany exchanged knowing smiles, appreciating the little moments that made family trips so memorable. The flight, filled with laughter and the occasional playful complaint from Brennan about the "not-quite-luxurious enough" experience, became a treasured memory in itself.

Once they arrived at the resort, the familiar warmth of the Mexican sun and the gentle sound of the ocean waves welcomed them back. The resort, with its breathtaking views and relaxed atmosphere, had always been their haven. And now, with the families together, it felt like a celebration of everything that had brought them to that moment—the hard work, the sacrifices, and the steadfast love shared among them.

As the vacation stretched, the resort provided endless opportunities for fun and relaxation. There were lazy mornings by the pool, lively dinners under starry skies, and afternoons filled with laughter and adventure. Tiffany and Holly organized group outings, exploring local markets and plunging themselves into the vibrant culture of Mexico. Even as Brennan and the other kids enjoyed the resort's many amenities, Larry and Tiffany found time to savor quiet moments together, appreciating the beauty of their surroundings and the bonds that held their families together.

In every smile, every shared joke, and every heartfelt conversation, Larry was reminded once again of how lucky he was. The trip wasn't just about luxury or indulgence—it was about celebrating life, family, and the small, precious moments that made it all worthwhile. And for Larry, watching his family enjoy these moments brought a warmth to his heart that no first-class seat could ever match.

One day, both families set out for Xel Ha, an aquatic dream located in Tulum, Mexico. According to their website, *it is a wondrous park that houses an iconic natural inlet that is home to several flora and fauna species. It is also relevant to the pre-Hispanic culture of the region during its splendor times.*

Since ancient times, the native civilization discovered this magnificent natural place. Xel-Há means "where water is born" since several underground rivers flow into the inlet at this wonder of nature.

The families enjoyed time snorkeling and swimming; the water slides were amazing, and drifting on tubes through mangrove trees lined the river was relaxing and a wonderful memory. Seeing Tiffany floating in her tube, laughing as fish swam by, lit Larry's face, and seeing his children enjoying this experience made it even more so. However, after five hours, Larry and Tiffany were ready to leave; they wanted to head back to the resort. The bus was not due to pick them up for another four hours or so. Tiffany said, "Order a car service, and let's get back." Without hesitation, Larry leapt at her words, and their family got back early, relaxed, and got ready for another amazing dinner.

This trip was special—Larry, Tiffany, and their children, Patrick, Rylee, and Brennan, were joined by Holly and Steve and their kids, Dylan and Tyler. The group was excited for a full day of adventure, and from the moment they arrived, it was clear that Xel-Há was going to deliver on that promise.

The scent of saltwater mixed with the fragrance of tropical blooms, the air filled with the gentle rustling of palm trees swaying in the breeze. Vibrant fish darted beneath the crystal-clear waters, and the sound of laughter echoed as visitors took turns plunging into the pristine lagoon. It was a place that felt almost untouched by time, a preserve where nature and adventure blended seamlessly.

Eager to experience all that Xel-Há had to offer, the group wasted no time diving in—literally. Snorkeling was the first order of business, and the underwater world did not disappoint. Schools of rainbow-colored fish swirled around them, unbothered by the humans floating above. Every now and then, a stingray would glide by, its elegant form casting a shadow on the ocean floor. The kids, fearless and full of excitement, explored every nook and cranny, pointing out the most exotic creatures they could find.

Brennan, still young but eager to keep up with his older siblings, was a little hesitant at first. Tiffany held his hand, guiding him gently through the shallow parts of the lagoon, ensuring he felt safe. "Look at that one!" she whispered, pointing to a brightly colored parrotfish swimming just inches away. His eyes expanded in wonder, and soon, his hesitation turned to excitement. Larry, watching from a distance, couldn't help but smile—this was exactly the kind of moment they had come for.

Then came the waterslides—towering spirals that sent them splashing into the cool, inviting water below. Patrick and Tyler immediately challenged each other to see who could make the biggest splash, while Rylee and Dylan screamed with delight, the adrenaline rush leaving them breathless. Even Tiffany, who was usually content to watch the kids have their fun, couldn't resist taking a turn. Larry stood at the bottom, waiting, grinning as he watched his wife fly down the slide, landing in the water with a surprised squeal. She popped up, laughing, her blonde hair slicked back, and he thought, for what felt like the thousandth time, just how beautiful she was.

But perhaps the most memorable part of the day was the lazy river. They each grabbed an inner tube and let the current carry them through the lush mangrove forest, the towering trees providing a canopy of shade. The warm sun peeked through the gaps, creating dappled patterns on the water. Tiffany leaned back in her tube, her arms stretched lazily over the sides, her face turned up toward the sky, completely at peace.

Brennan and Dylan, filled with energy, kept paddling ahead, trying to race each other, while Patrick and Tyler floated effortlessly, half asleep in their tubes. Rylee drifted next to her mom, reaching out every so often to touch the water, watching as tiny fish darted beneath them.

Larry and Steve floated behind, enjoying the quiet moments between conversations. "This was a great idea," Steve said, taking a deep breath. "Nothing like this back home."

FOREVER TIFFANY

Larry nodded, watching Tiffany as she lazily dragged her fingers through the water. "Yeah," he said. "This is exactly what we needed."

The kids floated ahead, splashing each other, lost in their own world of adventure. Larry and Tiffany drifted behind, soaking in the peacefulness of the moment. It was one of those rare times when everything just felt picture-perfect—where time seemed to slow, and the only thing that mattered was being there: togetherness.

However, after five hours of non-stop fun, exhaustion began to set in. Larry and Tiffany exchanged a knowing glance—while the kids could probably keep going for hours, they were ready to head back to the resort. The only problem? Their scheduled bus wasn't set to pick them up for another four hours.

Tiffany, never one to wait when she didn't have to, turned to Larry and said, "Order a car service, and let's get back."

That was all he needed to hear. Without hesitation, Larry pulled out his phone and arranged for a private driver. Within minutes, an air-conditioned SUV was waiting for them, ready to take them back to the comfort of their resort.

As they drove along the coastline, the stunning view of the turquoise waters stretching endlessly toward the horizon filled the windows. The kids, exhausted but still buzzing from the day's adventures, dozed off in the backseat. Rylee had her head against Patrick's shoulder, and Brennan was curled up next to Tiffany, his small hands gripping her arm even in sleep.

Tiffany leaned against Larry, her head resting on his shoulder, her body warm against his.

By the time they arrived back at the resort, the energy of Xel-Há had faded into a quiet contentment. The kids scattered to their rooms for a quick rest while Larry and Tiffany stepped out onto their private balcony. The evening air was cool, the scent of the ocean mixing with the distant sound of live music playing somewhere on the resort grounds.

Tiffany leaned against the railing, closing her eyes as the breeze played with her hair. Larry stood beside her, wrapping an arm around her waist, pressing a soft kiss to her temple.

"Good call on leaving early," he murmured.

She smirked, her blue eyes twinkling. "When am I ever wrong?"

He chuckled, shaking his head. She always knew what she wanted, and he loved that about her.

As they got ready for another incredible dinner, the day's memories settled into their minds, locked away for safekeeping. These were the moments they would cherish—the small, seemingly insignificant decisions that led to unforgettable experiences.

These were the memories that would last a lifetime. The ones that, even on the hardest days to come, would find a way to surface, bringing with them a warmth that no darkness could ever truly erase.

CHAPTER 16.
The Power of Presence

The warm August sun casts golden light over the stunning CU Boulder campus. Move-in day had arrived, and with it came a mix of excitement, nervousness, and the bittersweet realization that their eldest child was officially starting his next chapter in life.

Larry and Tiffany packed up her white SUV early that morning, filling it with Patrick's belongings—bins of clothes, bedding, school supplies, and all the little touches Tiffany insisted on bringing to make his dorm feel like home. Larry marveled at how much they had packed; he was convinced Tiffany had thought of everything.

Patrick, ever the calm and collected one, sat in the front seat, quiet but eager. His roommate, Zach, was a familiar face, someone he had known from high school, which gave them all a little comfort. It made the transition a bit easier knowing Patrick wouldn't be navigating this journey completely alone.

As they pulled onto the bustling campus, the energy was electric—students moving in, parents hugging their kids a little too long, and school staff directing the controlled chaos. Move-in helpers in matching CU shirts came out with large rolling carts and were eager to assist. Without hesitation, Larry and Tiffany sprang into action, filling up the carts as fast as they could, knowing they were only given a two-hour window to move Patrick in and set everything up.

The dorm building was impressive, right across from Folsom Field, home to the Buffs football team. The massive stadium stood proudly in the distance, a constant reminder that Patrick was now a part of something much bigger than himself.

Once inside, they took the elevator up to Patrick's floor, navigating through the narrow halls filled with other families doing the exact same thing. His dorm room was small but had everything he needed.

Zach had already arrived, and the two quickly engaged in conversation while Tiffany got to work.

She was a woman on a mission. Everything needed to be placed just right—the bed perfectly made, clothes folded and put away, desk area organized, and toiletries neatly arranged. She wanted Patrick to feel as if he were still at home, to have a sense of comfort even though he was stepping into a new world.

Knowing better than to get in her way, Larry helped where he could—plugging in electronics, setting, and making sure Patrick had everything he needed. He watched as Tiffany worked with care, her maternal instincts on full display. He knew this moment was just as hard for her as it was exciting.

Patrick, ever the good sport, let her do her thing. He didn't complain or push back—he knew this was her way of showing love. He also knew this would be the last time his mom could take care of him in this way before he fully stepped into independence.

As the two-hour window ended, Tiffany stood back, surveying the room with a satisfied look. She had done it—everything was in place, and Patrick was ready.

They all stood there for a moment, taking it in. This was it—the great goodbye.

Larry clapped Patrick on the back. "You're gonna do great, bud."

Tiffany's eyes glistened slightly, but she pushed through, giving Patrick a tight hug. "Call me whenever you need, okay?" she said softly, her voice slightly quivering.

Patrick, not one for sentimental moments, simply nodded, hugging her back. "I will, Mom."

And just like that, it was time to leave.

As they walked back to the car, Tiffany turned for one last glance at the dorm, watching students and parents go through the same motions. Larry could sense the emotions bubbling beneath the surface, so he took her hand and squeezed it.

"You did good," he said, giving her a reassuring smile.

Tiffany exhaled, nodding. "I know. I just—he's really gone, isn't he?"

Larry chuckled. "Not gone. Just starting his own adventure."

She smiled, wiping a stray tear before getting into the car. As they drove away, the campus fading into the rearview mirror, they both knew that this was just the beginning of a new chapter, without Patrick.

Life was moving fast, but Larry and Tiffany had learned how to keep pace. They had built a life together that was dynamic, full of passion, ambition, and an untiring commitment to each other. They were navigating their careers, raising their children, and embracing every opportunity that came their way. They were thriving, professionally and personally, but through it all, one thing remained constant—Larry's commitment to making Tiffany feel like the world's most loved and cherished woman.

Larry had learned a powerful lesson from his father, which he considered a foundation, a pillar of their marital success. It was simple, yet often overlooked by so many couples: "Date your wife. Date her with intention. Take her out like you did before you married her. Show her how much you love her. If you do this as often as possible, your marriage will be strong."

And Larry lived by these words. He didn't just take Tiffany out occasionally or make grand romantic gestures only on anniversaries or birthdays. No, Larry *dated* his wife every single week, sometimes even twice a week. Whether it was a casual lunch together in town, a cozy evening at *The Office*—their favorite spot for whiskey and conversation—or a weekend getaway to the mountains, Larry made sure that Tiffany always knew how deeply she was loved.

No matter how busy they were or how demanding their jobs became, he never let their relationship become secondary. He never took Tiffany for granted. He would text her in the middle of the day just to say, "Thinking about you." He would leave her notes by her coffee mug, reminding her how beautiful she was. He would pick up flowers, not because it was a special occasion, but because she deserved them *just because*.

Tiffany, in turn, adored him for it. She never doubted his love, never questioned his devotion. It wasn't just about the dates or the grand gestures—it was the consistency, the little things that added up over time, the way he always *saw* her, even through their hectic lives.

Their careers were taking off in ways neither of them had imagined. Larry, now overseeing sales across the U.S. and Canada, was constantly on the move. He had mastered the art of balancing boardrooms, client meetings, and conference calls while making it home in time for a family dinner when he could. Now a program manager, Tiffany excelled in her role, managing some of the company's most prestigious accounts. She had earned the respect of her colleagues and bosses alike, proving that she could be both a powerhouse in the corporate world and the heart of their family.

Rylee had grown into a confident, driven young woman. Now a sophomore, she was no longer the quiet freshman trying to find her place. She had established herself as a leader at school, managing the basketball team with precision and organizing social events like a pro, skills she had undoubtedly inherited from her mother. She thrived in social settings, loved being surrounded by friends, and had a way of making any room she walked into feel alive.

Brennan, now in fifth grade, had found his home in Colorado. Indiana was little more than a vague childhood memory to him now. He had built a life filled with friendships, sports, and adventure. He was always outside, always moving, always filled with boundless energy. He had the carefree spirit of a child who knew he was loved, supported, and secure in his place in the world.

FOREVER TIFFANY

Their sails were wide open, catching the wind as they soared through the ocean of life. They were navigating challenges, embracing change, and growing stronger together. And at the center of it all was the love between Larry and Tiffany—a love that never wavered, never grew stale, because Larry never let it.

He *dated* his wife.

He *loved* her fiercely.

And in return, she loved him just as deeply.

It was the kind of love that only grew stronger with time, the kind that anchored a family, the kind that made every challenge, every triumph, and every moment in between truly *worth it*.

As he sat in his office, the world outside seemed almost too perfect. The way the golden sunlight stretched across the Colorado landscape, the stillness of the moment, the way the late summer breeze rustled the trees—it all felt surreal. Life had been going so well, almost *too* well. Larry leaned back in his chair, staring out the window, lost in thought.

His mind wandered back to where it all started, to his childhood, his journey through life, the battles he had fought, and the love story that had changed everything. He thought about Tiffany, the way they had met, the way she had made his life infinitely better, the way they had built something so strong, so unshakable. He thought about their three incredible children, each thriving, growing, living lives filled with happiness and possibility. It was all so… *perfect*.

And then, out of nowhere, the thought struck him like a lightning bolt: "Am I dead?"

At first, it seemed like an absurd question that shouldn't have held any weight. But as he let it settle, he realized he was serious. Could it be possible? Could he have died back in 2009 during his surgery? Could everything that had happened since then—moving to Colorado, watching his children grow, his deepening love for Tiffany—be some kind of eternal afterlife?

It *felt* real. But at the same time, he had never felt this much peace before, never experienced this kind of perfection. Eternity was supposed to be boundless, time stretching in a way that earthly minds couldn't comprehend. What if Tiffany and the kids had lived their full lives and had now joined him in whatever came after? What if *this* was heaven? The thought didn't scare him—rather, it fascinated him.

Larry turned away from the window, shaking his head at his thoughts. It was ridiculous… wasn't it? But he couldn't shake it. He needed to talk to someone. And there was only one person in the world he could ask this question to, the one person who wouldn't immediately call him crazy or send for a psychiatric evaluation.

George.

Larry picked up the phone and dialed. The call barely had time to ring before George's familiar voice answered, full of its usual energy.

"What's up, Lencho?"

Larry exhaled. "Alright, hear me out. This is going to sound insane, but I have to say it out loud."

George paused. "Okay… I'm listening."

Larry took a deep breath. "Am I dead?"

Silence.

"Wait… what?"

"I mean it, George. What if I actually *died* during my surgery back in 2009? What if everything since then—moving to Colorado, Tiffany, the kids growing up, all of it—is just… heaven?"

George let out a short laugh, then immediately stopped when he realized Larry wasn't joking. "Are you *serious*?"

"As a matter of fact, I *am*."

For the next thirty or forty minutes, they talked through the theory. Larry laid it all out—the overwhelming sense of peace he had felt lately, the way life seemed too perfect, the way he couldn't shake the feeling that something *wasn't quite right* about how good everything was. George, at first skeptical, actually started to follow along.

"Okay, but what about pain? What about struggles?" George asked. "You've had ups and downs. You've had losses. Wouldn't heaven be, like... completely free of all hurdles, all the pain?"

Larry thought about it. "Maybe it's not the way we think. Maybe heaven isn't *perfect* in the way we imagine, but more like... it just *feels* right. Like, even when something goes wrong, there's still this deep peace, this *certainty* that everything is exactly as it should be."

George was quiet for a moment. "Damn... now you've got me thinking. But... what would that mean? That your kids, Tiffany—are they real? Are they here *with you,* or are they ... part of this?"

Larry didn't have an answer to that. He rubbed his forehead, exhaling slowly.

"That's the part I can't figure out," he admitted. "But think about it—if this *was* heaven, wouldn't it make sense that the people I love the most would be here with me?"

George let out a low whistle. "You know what, man? I have no idea. But you're either dead... or you're just *really* happy."

Larry chuckled. "Yeah, well... either way, I guess I win."

They left it at that, an unanswered question hanging in the air. Larry didn't really expect an answer—at least, not yet. But one day, he would know for sure. Until then, he would keep living his life as if it *was* heaven, because he knew one thing for certain: whether he was still on Earth or somewhere beyond, he was *exactly* where he was meant to be.

As 2019 was nearing an end, Larry was in Pittsburgh for work, meeting with clients and closing out the year. It had been a long but productive trip, and he was already looking forward to heading home, seeing Tiffany, and enjoying the holiday season with his family. Then, in the middle of his meetings, his phone rang. It was his mother.

Something in the way her name flashed across the screen gave him pause. He stepped away from the table, answering in a quiet voice.

"Hey Mom, what's up?"

Her voice was soft but steady. "Larry, your grandfather has passed away."

For a moment, Larry just stood there, staring out the window at the Pittsburgh skyline. It didn't come as a complete shock—his grandfather, his mom's dad, George, had been battling a slow-growing lung cancer for years. He had chosen not to treat it, opting instead to let nature take its course. He was just a few months shy of his ninety-fourth birthday. He had lived a long, full life.

But knowing that didn't make it easier.

His grandfather had been more than just family; he had been one of the greatest role models in Larry's life. He had shown Larry what it meant to lead a family—not just in providing for them but in loving them, being present, and being strong yet gentle. More than anything, he had taught Larry how to love with intention.

There was no one in the world George had loved more than Louanne, his wife—his soulmate. They had shared a love so deep, so pure, that even after she had passed away twenty-five years earlier due to complications from a surgery gone wrong, George had never moved on. He had never even entertained the idea of loving another woman. His heart had belonged to her, and her alone.

Larry had grown up watching his grandfather speak about her with longing, with devotion that never wavered. Like clockwork, he would say every year, "I hope this is the year I get to see her again." He had said that for twenty-five years.

Now, finally, his wish had come true.

FOREVER TIFFANY

Larry's mother was flying George's body back to West Virginia, where he would be laid to rest next to Louanne. They had planned it this way years ago, selecting a side-by-side mausoleum, complete with air conditioning in the summer and heat in the winter—his grandfather's one request.

"I want to lay next to her always."

Larry had always found that romantic, but he never quite understood it, not fully. His grandfather had a deep faith, a belief that he would move on to heaven, that he and Louanne would reunite in eternity. So why the obsession with the mausoleum? Why had it mattered so much to be laid next to her physically when his soul would be with hers?

Maybe, Larry thought, it wasn't about where his body would rest but the symbolism. It was a final promise, a last gesture of love. George had been devoted to Louanne in life and would remain devoted to her in death.

Larry knew there was no question—he had to be there.

He left Pittsburgh and drove to Charleston, West Virginia, for the service. The day was filled with tears, but also with laughter. Family and friends shared stories of George—his quick wit, unwavering integrity, and always putting family first. They celebrated a life well lived, a love that had never faded, and a man who had left behind a legacy of strength, kindness, and devotion.

As Larry stood by the mausoleum, looking at his grandparents' names etched into the stone, he thought about Tiffany.

He thought about their life together, the way she had become his anchor, his greatest love. He thought about how he had never once taken her for granted and learned from his grandfather's example that true love wasn't just about feeling—it was about action, commitment, and choosing each other every day.

And he thought that, no matter what life threw at them, he and Tiffany had always found a way to push through, to hold each other up.

It seemed like every year brought some kind of life-changing event. They had faced challenges, losses, triumphs, and moments that had tested them.

But through it all, one thing remained constant.

Their love.

And as he walked away from the cemetery, back toward his mother and the rest of his family, he made a silent promise to himself.

To keep loving Tiffany the way his grandfather loved Louanne. To cherish every single moment. To never take a single day for granted.

Because in the end, love is all that truly matters.

Rylee had always been a curious and independent thinker, so when she came home from school one day and announced that she was interested in learning about the Mormon faith, Larry and Tiffany weren't entirely surprised. She had made several close friends at school who were members, and their kindness and strong sense of community had drawn her in. She wanted to understand their beliefs, their traditions, and what made their faith so important to them.

Her interest wasn't entirely out of left field. After all, her grandparents, aunt Holly, and uncle Steve had been dedicated members for years, attending nearly every Sunday. More significantly, it was in this very church where Larry and Tiffany had first met. That connection alone intrigued Rylee even more. She wanted to explore her roots, to understand the faith that had played a role in bringing her parents together.

Larry and Tiffany, always supportive of their children's desire to learn and grow, encouraged her curiosity. They saw this as an opportunity for Rylee to discover something meaningful on her own terms. Holly stepped in to help without hesitation, setting up meeting times with the local missionaries so Rylee could ask questions, learn the doctrine, and decide if this path felt right for her.

But what happened next was something Larry never saw coming.

As Rylee sat down with the missionaries, eagerly listening and asking questions, Tiffany and Brennan were drawn in. At first, they had simply been in the room, casually listening as Rylee spoke with the missionaries. But as the discussions deepened, covering topics of faith, family, eternal love, and the importance of living a good, meaningful life, something stirred inside them.

One evening, as the family sat together after dinner, Tiffany turned to Larry and said, "I think I want to join Rylee in learning more about this."

Larry looked at her, a little stunned but deeply intrigued. "Really?"

"Yeah," she said, nodding. "There's something about it that feels right. I want to understand it more. And Brennan seems interested too."

Larry turned to their youngest, who had been quietly absorbing everything around him at just ten years old. "Is that true, buddy?"

Brennan nodded enthusiastically. "I like what they're teaching. It makes sense to me."

Larry sat back in his chair, taking it all in. He had always loved and respected the church—after all, it had played a huge role in his life—but he had never pushed it on Tiffany or the kids. He had always believed faith was deeply personal, something that each person needed to discover on their own.

And now, here they were, discovering it together.

The following weeks were filled with deep conversations, study, and personal reflection. The missionaries continued to visit, answering questions, guiding them through scripture, and sharing stories of faith and perseverance. Ever the researcher, Tiffany read everything she could, wanting to fully understand what she was about to commit to. She wasn't someone who made decisions lightly—when she made a choice, she wanted to be all in.

And she was.

Within a few weeks, the decision was made. Rylee, Tiffany, and Brennan all felt strongly about wanting to be baptized. They felt a connection, a sense of belonging, and most importantly, a deeper meaning to their lives.

The baptism was a beautiful, emotional day. Family gathered to support them, including Holly, Steve, and their grandparents, who beamed with pride. Larry, already baptized when he was eight, stood beside them, holding Tiffany's hand, his heart full. He had always admired her strength, her ability to embrace new experiences with an open heart and mind. Watching Brennan, their youngest, step forward with such certainty and excitement, Larry would never forget it.

From that day forward, the church became a bigger part of their lives. It didn't replace who they were, but it added a new layer of depth and fulfillment to their already full lives. Sundays became a time to gather, reflect, and grow spiritually as a family. They felt more connected—not just to each other but to something greater.

As 2019 came to a close, Larry and Tiffany looked at their life, their children, and everything they had built together, and they couldn't help but feel incredibly blessed. Their family was strong, their love was solid, and now, with faith becoming a guiding force in their lives, they felt an even deeper sense of purpose.

The year was ending on a positive note—one filled with love, growth, and the kind of happiness that only comes from embracing life fully. Larry and Tiffany had always believed in leading with love, and now, they were doing so with an even greater sense of meaning.

And they couldn't wait to see where the journey would take them next.

CHAPTER 17.
Fighting for Forever

The holiday season of 2019 was everything it was meant to be—joyful, festive, and filled with laughter. Thanksgiving was a warm and wonderful gathering, with family and friends coming together to share the love and gratitude that had always defined their home. Tiffany, as always, created the perfect holiday atmosphere. Her attention to detail, beautifully decorated table, and ability to make everyone feel welcome made Thanksgiving more than just a meal—it was an experience. The turkey was roasted to perfection, the sides were plentiful, and the desserts, well, she had outdone herself again.

As Christmas approached, the excitement in the house grew. It was their 20th Christmas together, and Tiffany again outshined herself. No matter how busy life got, she always found a way to make the holiday season magical. The house was decorated like something out of a Hallmark movie—multiple Christmas trees adorned the home, each with its theme, garland wrapped around the staircase, lights twinkled from every room, and the smell of fresh pine and cinnamon filled the air.

When it came to gifts, Tiffany had a special talent. She always ensured the kids got exactly what they wanted, plus everything they needed, and then just a little extra—something unexpected that would surprise and delight them. She loved seeing their faces light up on Christmas morning, the pure joy in their eyes as they ran to the tree to discover what Santa had left for them. It wasn't about spoiling them, but about creating those unforgettable moments—the ones that, years from now, they would look back on with nostalgia and warmth.

New Year's Eve was always a night to remember. For Tiffany and Larry, it was more than just a party—it was a reflection of the past year and an exciting welcome to the one ahead. Their home had become the go-to place for celebrating, a tradition that had grown stronger with each passing year. Close friends gathered, drinks flowed, laughter filled every corner of the house, and music played late into the night. There was something special about ringing in the new year with the people they loved most.

Unlike many, Tiffany and Larry never set resolutions. They both believed in working to better themselves every single day, not just when the calendar flipped to January 1st. They didn't wait for a new year to make changes; they lived with the intention of always striving to be the best versions of themselves, for each other, their children, and the people around them.

Larry had picked up a saying from his great friend John, a CEO at a private equity firm. It was something that had stuck with him over the years, something he and Tiffany both embraced:

"Let's make some MAGIC today."

M—Make

A—A

G—Greater

I—Individual

C—Commitment

It wasn't about perfection; they never pretended to have it all figured out. It was about effort, about waking up every morning with the mindset that today was another chance to be better, love deeper, create memories, and make a positive impact.

As the countdown to midnight began, Tiffany stood next to Larry, her hand enveloped in his, her eyes reflecting the soft glow of the lights around them. With each second that passed, they both knew—life wasn't perfect, but theirs was. And they were making magic every single day.

As the clock struck twelve, they kissed, welcoming another year together, another chapter in the life they had built. They didn't know what 2020 would bring, but they knew one thing for certain—whatever came next, they would face it together.

As February drew to a close, Larry found himself in Houston, standing in the middle of a celebration unlike any other—the Houston Rodeo Barbecue Cook-off. It was a larger-than-life event, an annual Texas tradition where over 250 barbecue teams gathered to compete for top honors, each one boasting its unique recipes, smoking techniques, and secret seasonings. But the cook-off wasn't just about who had the best brisket or the most tender ribs—it was about the experience, the kind of weekend that brought together thousands of people to celebrate food, music, and community in the heart of Texas.

For Larry, it was a chance to step away from the routine of work and immerse himself in something he truly loved—great food, music, and company. Invitations had poured in from multiple tents, each promising a different atmosphere. Some were high-end, serving premium bourbon alongside meticulously crafted barbecue, while others had a more raucous energy, filled with laughter, live bands, and people trying their luck on mechanical bulls.

The smell of slow-smoked meat filled the air, drifting through the venue and mixing with country music blasting from every direction. Larry could hear the sizzling of ribs over open flames, the low rumble of deep conversations, and the occasional laughter from a nearby group enjoying a cold beer in the warm Texas night. This was the kind of thing that made life memorable.

As he moved from tent to tent, sampling everything from mouthwatering brisket to perfectly charred sausage links, he couldn't help but think about how much Tiffany would have loved the experience. He knew she wasn't as big a barbecue fan as he was, but she would have loved the atmosphere—the excitement, the people-watching, the energy that only a gathering of this size could create. He made a mental note to bring her with him the following year.

The music was just as unforgettable. One night, he found himself in an exclusive tent where an up-and-coming country singer performed an intimate acoustic set, her voice smooth as whiskey and twice as strong. Another night, he was in a full-blown honky-tonk scene, where cowboy boots kicked up dust on the dance floor, people swung each other around in rhythm, and the neon glow of beer signs bathed the crowd in warm, golden light.

Larry was in his element. There was something about nights like this, where time slowed down just enough to let him appreciate the moment. Between the food, the music, and the company, it was shaping up to be a weekend he wouldn't forget anytime soon.

But then, on the final night of the cook-off, something shifted.

He overheard a conversation at the next table as he stood near the bar in one of the larger tents, talking with a group of old friends. A few guys were discussing the news—something about a virus that had been spreading rapidly overseas, and now, it had officially made its way into the United States.

Larry barely gave it a second thought.

Over the years, there had been plenty of headlines about various outbreaks—bird flu, swine flu, Zika—each one sounding serious at first, only to fade into the background as life moved on. This didn't seem any different.

But as the night wore on, the talk grew louder.

People were saying someone at the event had tested positive.

At first, it was just a rumor. Some claimed it was a vendor, others said it was a guest, and a few even insisted the person had already been admitted to a hospital. Larry wasn't the type to get caught up in panic, so he shrugged it off, assuming it was just overblown gossip. He was here to enjoy himself, and he wasn't going to let an unconfirmed story ruin the night.

Still, something about the way people were talking made him uneasy.

FOREVER TIFFANY

By the next morning, the buzz around the virus was impossible to ignore. People at the airport were murmuring about it while waiting in line for their flights. He noticed a few travelers wiping their seats with disinfecting wipes before sitting down—a practice he had never seen before. Something felt different.

But even then, no one could have predicted just how much things were about to change.

In just two short weeks, the world would be completely unrecognizable.

Everything that had once felt normal—simple things like gathering with friends, eating at restaurants, traveling for work—would suddenly be thrown into uncertainty. The Houston Rodeo, which had just been filled with thousands of people celebrating and enjoying life, would soon shut down entirely.

Larry didn't know it yet, but that night at the cook-off was one of the last normal nights he would have for a very, very long time.

By Monday morning, the world felt like it was already shifting beneath everyone's feet. Larry walked into the office, and instead of the usual conversations about projects, sales numbers, and upcoming travel, all anyone could talk about was coronavirus. It was no longer just a whisper on the news—it was everywhere.

Larry sat down with Reynold, his colleague and close friend, to discuss the situation. The decision didn't take long. March 16th would be their last day in the office. The company was officially shutting down in-person operations and shifting to remote work until further notice.

The severity of it all hadn't fully sunk in yet, but as Larry packed up his laptop and essentials, he couldn't shake the feeling that something big was coming—something that no one was prepared for.

Meanwhile, Patrick was facing his own disruption. The University of Colorado, like nearly every school across the country, was sending students home. Dorms were shutting down, classes were moving online, and the college experience he had been so excited for was suddenly cut short. Larry knew what he had to do—drive to Boulder and bring his son home.

As he pulled up to Patrick's dorm, he saw the chaos unfolding. Parents and students were hurriedly packing up, some looking anxious, others just frustrated by the sudden change. Students said quick goodbyes to their friends, not knowing when—or if—they would see each other again on campus.

Patrick, while disappointed, took it all in stride. He had inherited that from Tiffany—the ability to adjust, roll with the punches, and make the best of any situation. They loaded Tiffany's SUV with his belongings, making trip after trip up and down the dorm elevator. It wasn't how he had envisioned his freshman year ending, but he knew he wasn't alone.

With Patrick safely back home, Larry turned his attention to preparation. If things were going to get bad, he wasn't going to be caught off guard.

He headed to the store, which already looked like something out of a doomsday movie. Shelves were half-empty, carts were filled to the brim, and people were rushing around, grabbing anything they could find. The usual grocery store small talk had disappeared—everyone was focused, tense, preparing for the unknown.

Larry stocked up like never before.

He filled the cart with non-perishable foods, water bottles, toiletries, and every household item he thought they might need. Then he took it a step further—he purchased six tanks of propane, ensuring that if natural gas production stopped, they could still cook outdoors. He wasn't taking any chances. He had a family to protect, and nothing would catch him off guard.

Even with all the uncertainty swirling around, Larry knew one thing: they needed one last great night out.

He picked up his phone and started making calls. Brian, Karl, and a few others were in. If everything was about to shut down, they were going to make sure they had one final night of fun before the lockdowns started.

They went all out. Downtown Castle Rock was packed. Every bar, every restaurant—overflowing with people with the same idea. It was as if the entire town had collectively decided to say goodbye to normalcy in the best way they knew—by celebrating one last time.

They bounced from place to place, ordering drinks, laughing, reminiscing about life before any of this madness started. The mood was electric, but there was a quiet understanding underneath it all. No one knew what was coming next and when—or if—they'd get to do this again.

As the night stretched on, Larry looked around at the familiar faces, the warmth of the friendships he had built, and the town he had come to love so much.

This was home.

And they would get through it no matter what the world threw at them in the coming weeks, months, or even years.

As they finally called it a night, stepping out onto the cool streets of Castle Rock one last time before everything changed, Larry took a deep breath.

Tomorrow would bring uncertainty. But tonight?

Tonight was for living.

Larry and Tiffany quickly started to embrace the lockdown in a way they never expected. Life had thrown them an unexpected pause, and instead of stressing over every little detail of the world shutting down, they leaned into the opportunity to simply be together.

March 20th marked the beginning of what would become one of their favorite quarantine traditions—Netflix binges. They had always been busy, always on the move, but now, they had nothing but time. No work commutes, running errands, or traveling—just them, in their home, with endless possibilities of what to watch.

That night, they stumbled upon what would become one of the most bizarre, yet thoroughly entertaining shows of their lives—"Tiger King." Like so many others around the country, they were glued to the screen, watching in absolute disbelief as the wild world of Joe Exotic unfolded before them.

It was eight episodes of absolute insanity—big cats, mullets, murder-for-hire plots, polygamous relationships, and a feud with a mysterious woman named Carole Baskin. Every scene left them laughing, gasping, and pausing the show just to process what they had just witnessed. Tiffany would look at Larry with wide eyes, shaking her head in amusement, saying things like, "There is no way this is real. No way." And Larry, in between sips of wine, would chuckle and reply, "Oh, but it is. And it's only getting crazier."

They spent the whole day wrapped up in blankets, propped up on pillows, and snacking on whatever they could find in the kitchen. Breakfast in bed turned into lunch in bed, which turned into dinner in bed. They laughed, they made fun of the characters, they made bets on who would betray who, and occasionally, they paused just long enough to make love, wrapped up in the warmth of their own little bubble of happiness.

There was something almost surreal about the whole experience. Outside, the world was in chaos. The news was filled with statistics, lockdown orders, and uncertainty. But inside their home and bedroom, it felt like a second honeymoon. It was as if they had pressed pause on reality and stepped into this world where nothing else mattered but each other.

The days blurred together in the best way possible. Every morning started the same—slow, lazy wake-ups with the sun peeking through the blinds, Tiffany curled up against Larry, her hair cascading across his chest as they lay there, soaking in the stillness. No alarms, no rush to get anywhere. Just soft kisses, laughter, and an unspoken agreement that they would make the most of this strange, unexpected time together.

They rediscovered old shows, found new ones, and fell into a rhythm that felt easy, effortless, and exactly what they needed. Every now and then, they would joke about how they were "thriving in quarantine" while so many others were going stir-crazy.

It was a weird time, no doubt. A time filled with uncertainty, worry, and questions about what the future would hold, but in those moments, in those long, lazy days of binge-watching, eating breakfast in bed, and being wrapped up in each other's arms, Larry and Tiffany were reminded of what mattered.

And for now, for this little pocket of time, life was simple. Life was good.

One week after settling into their unexpected quarantine routine of binge-watching shows and enjoying each other's company, life delivered a crushing blow.

Tiffany's phone rang early in the morning on March 27th. The way it rang—the urgent, unwelcome disruption of their peaceful morning—sent an immediate chill down her spine. It was never good news at this hour. She stared at the screen, her heart already pounding, before answering.

The voice on the other end was shaky, raw, and heartbreaking.

"Tiff… it's Dan… he's gone."

Her mind didn't process it at first. The words felt foreign, distant, as if meant for someone else. But as the silence stretched between her and the caller, reality set in like a crushing weight on her chest.

Her uncle Dan—the man who had been a second father to her, the man who had always been there, steady and strong, a guiding force in her life—had suffered a massive heart attack in the middle of the night. He passed away at 4:14 AM. Just like that. No warning, no time to prepare, no chance to say goodbye.

Tiffany felt like the air had been sucked out of the room. She squeezed her eyes shut, shaking her head as if she could will the words away, make them untrue. "No," she whispered, gripping the phone tighter, her knuckles turning white. "No, no, no."

Larry, sitting beside her, immediately sat up, his expression shifting from relaxed to concerned in an instant. He knew that look in her eyes, the way her body tensed, and her breath hitched as she tried to hold back the flood of emotions crashing over her. He didn't need to hear the words to know that something terrible had happened.

She felt his hand slide over hers, warm and steady, but she was already lost in a storm of emotions.

Dan wasn't just an uncle. He was so much more than that. When her father, Pat, passed away, Dan stepped in without hesitation, filling the void in ways only he could. He had always been there, watching over her like a father watches his daughter. He never had to say it out loud, but she felt it in every phone call, every conversation, every little check-in just to make sure she was okay.

And now, just like that, he was gone.

Tiffany's mind spiraled with the same agonizing question that had haunted her many times before: Why?

Why is it that every time life finally starts to feel perfect, when happiness feels within reach, the universe throws a devastating curveball? Why does loss always seem to find her just when she's starting to breathe again?

"Why can't happiness just last?" she choked out, her voice barely above a whisper. "Why can't we go a few years without death?"

Larry didn't have an answer. No one ever did. But what he did have was unwavering support. He pulled her into his arms, holding her tightly as she finally let go, sobbing into his chest.

He didn't tell her it would be okay because it wasn't right now. He didn't try to fix it because it couldn't be fixed. He just held her, letting her grieve, letting her feel the weight of yet another loss that life had cruelly handed her.

The day stretched on in a haze of phone calls and sorrow. Family members reaching out, trying to make sense of something that made no sense at all. Each conversation was laced with disbelief, with sadness, with the heavy realization that Dan, the man who had been so full of life, was gone.

Tiffany kept replaying their last conversation in her head, grasping every word, every laugh, every moment they had shared. Had she told him how much he meant to her? Had she said enough? Had he known just how much she loved him?

Larry stayed by her side the entire day, never leaving her alone for even a second. He knew she needed him, even if she didn't say it. He held her hand, brought her dinner, sat in silence when she needed it, and listened when she was ready to talk.

Losing Dan felt like losing a piece of herself. It wasn't just grief—it was exhaustion. The kind of exhaustion that comes from experiencing loss over and over again, never getting a break from the pain.

As night fell and the house grew quiet, Tiffany curled up against Larry, her body still wracked with silent sobs. He ran his fingers through her hair, pressing a soft kiss to her head.

"I'm here," he whispered. "I'll always be here."

And for now, that was the only comfort she had. The only comfort she needed.

Dan and Susan were more than just family to Larry and Tiffany; they were an example, a guiding light that shaped so much of their values. They showed them what it meant to love unconditionally, to work with profound passion, to embrace life fully, and to treat others with kindness and generosity.

Dan and Susan had a love story that felt like something out of a novel—one of those rare, enduring romances that people dream about but few ever witness firsthand. Their love was effortless, yet deeply intentional. They built a life together that was nothing short of extraordinary, and part of that life was their breathtaking home in South Florida.

Nestled within a private, gated community, their home was the kind that could be featured on the cover of a luxury lifestyle magazine. It was more than just a house; it was a sanctuary, a testament to the life they had built together. The sprawling property featured a private lake stretching over seventy acres, its waters reflecting the golden Florida sunsets in an almost magical way. In the center of the lake was a five-acre island, a hidden retreat that made their home feel like a personal paradise. They had also built a beautiful guest house where Tiffany's grandparents lived on the property, ensuring that family was always close.

Dan had recently sold his company, stepping into the long-awaited retirement he had worked so hard for. He and Susan were finally at a point where they could enjoy the fruits of their labor, travel, and slow down. Susan, one of Florida's most accomplished realtors, also planned to take a step back and enjoy more time with family. They had even built a stunning mountain retreat in North Carolina—a rustic yet elegant cabin, meant to be their getaway, their quiet escape from the fast-paced life they had led for so many years.

But life, as it so often does, had different plans.

Dan had only been retired for a few months when the unimaginable happened. His sudden passing sent shockwaves through the family. It wasn't just that he was gone—it was how it happened, so unexpectedly, in the middle of the night, without warning. One moment, they were all looking forward to a new chapter in his and Susan's life together, and the next, he was gone.

FOREVER TIFFANY

For Susan, the loss was unbearable. This wasn't just her husband—this was her best friend, her partner in everything, the man she had built a life with, the man she had planned to grow old with. And because of the lockdowns, the pandemic that was now gripping the world, she had to navigate her grief alone. There was no funeral for family to attend, no gathering where loved ones could share stories, cry together, and offer comfort. There was only silence. Loneliness.

Susan, who had always been a pillar of strength, displayed a courage that was nothing short of extraordinary. She retreated to their North Carolina cabin, where she spent months mourning the love of her life with no audience, no distraction—just the weight of grief and the quiet echoes of the life they had built together.

For Larry and Tiffany, Dan and Susan had been more than just family—they were a blueprint for the kind of love they aspired to have, the kind of life they wanted to build. Dan and Susan didn't just tell them how to love; they showed them. They led by example, demonstrating what it meant to be fully present for one another, to work hard not just for financial success but for a life well-lived, to cherish family, and to always give more than you take.

Even in Dan's absence, his influence remained strong. The lessons he had imparted, the way he had carried himself, and the way he loved Susan with his whole heart; those things didn't die with him. They lived on in Susan's resilience, in the way she carried herself through unimaginable grief. They lived on in the way Larry and Tiffany continued to nurture their own relationship, prioritizing their love and their family above all else.

And perhaps, more than anything, they lived on in the hope that their children—Patrick, Rylee, and Brennan—would one day look to them the same way they had looked to Dan and Susan. That they would follow the example that had been set, carrying forward the legacy of love, strength, and unwavering devotion that had been passed down to them.

Life in Castle Rock was shaping up differently from much of the country. While many cities were still under strict lockdowns, Castle Rock, a conservative stronghold in an otherwise left-leaning state, found ways to navigate the restrictions in its own way. Restaurants and bars were supposed to be shuttered, but for a few select regulars, there were still places to gather—quietly, discreetly, but together.

Pablo, the owner of The Office, had blacked out the windows of his beloved bar and grill. Though officially closed to the public, he allowed a handful of trusted patrons to slip in through the back door for a meal, a drink, and a few hours of normalcy. Larry and Brian quickly became two of those regulars, making their way in as often as possible. It wasn't about breaking rules—it was about holding on to something familiar, something that felt like life before the world changed. Sitting in their usual seats, whiskey glasses in hand, they talked about everything and nothing, about business, family, and the surreal state of the world. It was a small act of rebellion, but one that felt necessary.

Meanwhile, Brian and Stacy were in the middle of a major life change. They had just sold their home and were building a new one—a true dream come true for them. But while their dream home was under construction, they needed a place to stay, and fate had a way of bringing them even closer to Larry and Tiffany. Brian's mother happened to live just a street away from Larry's home, which meant the two couples were spending even more time together than before.

Stacy and Tiffany, already inseparable, were now practically living in each other's pockets. They shopped together, cooked together, worked out together, and more than anything, they leaned on each other. The friendship had deepened beyond words; they had become sisters in every way but blood. Where one went, the other followed. Whether it was a quick grocery run or a drink on the back patio, they were together, sharing laughs, venting frustrations, and savoring the bond that had become one of the strongest parts of their lives.

FOREVER TIFFANY

Patrick, meanwhile, had returned to Boulder for his sophomore year at CU, eager to live in an off-campus apartment with two of his closest friends. The university had promised a return to normal, to in-person classes and campus life. But that promise lasted less than a single day. Just as quickly as they had unpacked their things and settled in, CU announced that all learning would be virtual once again. The disappointment was heavy. Patrick had been waiting for the full college experience, but instead, he found himself staring at a computer screen in a small apartment, a world away from the bustling campus life he had imagined.

Larry and Tiffany felt for him. They knew how much he had been looking forward to this year, how much effort he had put into getting to this point. But it wasn't just Patrick who was being robbed of experiences—it was all of them. Rylee, now a junior in high school, was missing out on the social events, the in-person learning, the rites of passage that came with being an upperclassman. Brennan, having just finished sixth grade, had yet to experience what middle school was really supposed to be like.

Despite the circumstances, Brennan's school found a way to hold a small continuation ceremony for the sixth graders. It was held outside, socially distanced, but at least it was something- a moment to mark the end of elementary school and the beginning of a new chapter. Brennan had been chosen as the speaker, a role he took seriously, though he refused to let his parents read his speech beforehand.

As he walked up to the podium, Tiffany watched him with a mix of pride and nerves. Her little boy, the one who had spent years working through speech therapy, was now standing in front of over two hundred people, about to deliver a speech of his own. It was almost too much to take in. She knew Brennan's natural gift for humor—he was always cracking jokes, always looking for a way to make people laugh. Part of her feared what he might say.

But as he began to speak, any nerves melted away. His words were thoughtful, articulate, and full of gratitude. He thanked his friends, his family, and his teachers. Then, in a moment that caught Tiffany completely off guard, he specifically thanked his speech teacher.

"It was she," Brennan said, "who helped me reach this podium today."

Tiffany felt tears welling up in her eyes. For a child to recognize, at such a young age, the people who had lifted him up, the ones who had worked behind the scenes to help him succeed—it was profound. Far too many people in life take their successes for granted, failing to acknowledge those who helped along the way. But not Brennan.

Larry squeezed Tiffany's hand, both of them overcome with emotion. Their son had come so far, and this moment was a testament to all the hard work, all the patience, and all the love that had gone into getting him here.

Despite the challenges of the world around them, moments like this reminded them that life was still moving forward. Their children were still growing, still learning, still becoming the people they were meant to be. And no matter what else was happening, that was something to celebrate.

As the months passed and the world continued to learn, passing through the uncertainty of the pandemic, life for Larry and Tiffany was settling into a familiar rhythm once again. The long stretches at home allowed them to indulge in one of their preferred pastimes—binge-watching television together. They had already devoured *Tiger King* during the first phase of lockdown, and now, after years of hearing people rave about it, they finally sat down to watch *Breaking Bad*. From the very first episode, they were hooked—no pun intended.

Each night, after dinner, they would settle into their bedroom, curl up under the blankets, and dive into the world of Walter White and Jesse Pinkman. They would press "just one more episode" until it was far too late, exchanging wide-eyed glances at the show's shocking twists and turns. Tiffany, as always, had a knack for predicting what would happen next, while Larry would shake his head in disbelief at every unexpected turn.

It felt like a second honeymoon phase—a time when they were just the two of them again, lost in their own world, laughing, cuddling, and enjoying every quiet moment together. Breakfasts in bed, lazy mornings wrapped up in each other, and late-night conversations after finishing each episode made it feel like they had escaped reality, if only for a little while.

But as life often reminded them, peace was fleeting. The stillness was shattered when the phone rang once again—the kind of ring that instantly makes your stomach drop, the kind you wish you could ignore.

It was October 21st, 2020.

Tiffany answered, and in an instant, her face fell. Her grandfather, Richard "Dicky," had passed away.

Dicky was more than just a grandfather—he was a pillar of the family, a man who had taken great pride in taking care of those he loved. He was Dan's father, a man full of joy and warmth, always offering wisdom, humor, and untiring support. Losing him felt like losing another connection to the past, another reminder of how fragile life truly was.

Unlike when Uncle Dan passed, funerals were now allowed, and the family could properly say goodbye. Dicky was to be flown back to Indiana, where he would be buried next to his beloved wife, Fran. There was no question—Larry and Tiffany would be there.

Without hesitation, they booked their flights, making arrangements for Rylee to stay home and watch Brennan while they traveled. But Larry, never one to be comfortable in restrictive situations, wasn't thrilled about the idea of wearing a mask for an entire flight. He found a solution that would make the trip much more bearable—he booked their tickets on United's 787-10 Dreamliner, securing them first-class pods, ensuring they could have their own private space.

As they settled into their seats on the plane, the sleek, modern interior of the Dreamliner provided an unusual sense of calm, and they both leaned back and exhaled. It wasn't a trip they wanted to make, but it was necessary.

They quietly picked at the snacks provided by the flight attendants, stretching out in their individual pods, taking their time to enjoy every bite—after all, as long as they were eating, they didn't have to wear masks.

Tiffany glanced over at Larry, her expression a mix of exhaustion and quiet reflection. "You know, it never gets easier," she murmured, breaking the silence between them.

Larry reached over, taking her hand in his. "I know. But at least we can be there this time. We can say goodbye the right way."

She nodded, squeezing his hand tightly, her eyes glistening with emotion.

They both stared out the window as the plane soared through the sky, carrying them back to the place where they would say farewell to yet another loved one.

It was another reminder of life's unpredictability, another moment to hold onto the good times, to cherish every memory, and to never take a single second for granted.

Before they left for Chicago, Rylee had asked Tiffany if she could have a few friends over for Halloween—just four or five girls—to watch scary movies and have a fun little sleepover. Tiffany, knowing Castle Rock was a conservative town where people tended to do what they wanted despite state mandates, figured, *what's the harm?* Governor Polis had set restrictions stating that no more than two households could gather at a time, but that wasn't something they were going to enforce in their own home. Tiffany agreed without hesitation, simply reminding Rylee, "Be nice to Brennan, be safe, and don't do anything crazy."

The request seemed harmless enough—just a small group of teenage girls hanging out, enjoying Halloween, and making memories. *What could possibly go wrong?*

After arriving in Chicago, the funeral was emotional but beautiful, a perfect tribute to Richard "Dicky" and the life he had lived. The day was spent reminiscing with family, sharing old stories, and celebrating a man who had meant so much to so many. After dinner, exhausted from the day, Larry and Tiffany lay down in their room, ready to finally get some rest.

Then, at exactly 11:30 p.m., Tiffany's phone rang.

She glanced at the screen, and her heart skipped a beat when she saw "Castle Rock Police Department" flashing across it. Without hesitation, she handed the phone to Larry.

"Hello?" Larry answered, instantly alert.

On the other end, an officer spoke in a calm and measured voice. "First, let me start by saying your kids are safe, and no one is hurt."

Larry exhaled in relief but remained on edge. "Okay... so what's going on?"

The officer then asked what should have been a simple question: "Did you know Rylee was having friends over for Halloween? And how many?"

Larry, still lying in bed, rubbed his eyes and replied, "Yeah, we knew. We approved. She said maybe eight to ten girls were coming over for movies and a sleepover."

There was a brief pause on the other end of the line before the officer chuckled. "Well... I've seen about seventy-five."

Larry sat straight up in bed. "SEVENTY-FIVE?!?!"

Tiffany, who had been watching his reaction closely, raised an eyebrow. "What's going on?"

Larry put the phone on speaker so she could hear.

The officer continued, "Here's the deal. We were called because of a noise complaint. When we got there, well, let's just say your house is the *place to be* tonight." He chuckled again, almost as if he was impressed. "We have kids everywhere—front yard, backyard, basement, all over. It's a full-on Halloween party."

Larry was still in shock. "What are you going to do?"

The officer replied, "That's entirely up to you. I can make sure those who can drive get home safely, but there are a lot of kids here who don't have a way to leave. Do you want them to stay the night?"

Larry looked at Tiffany, waiting for her reaction. Surely, she would panic. Surely, she would say they needed to call the airport and get the first flight home. But Tiffany, as always, was as cool as ever. She didn't even flinch.

She smiled slightly, sat up in bed, and calmly said, "The officer said everyone is safe, right?"

The officer confirmed.

"The house isn't on fire?"

Another confirmation.

Tiffany took Larry's hand, looked him right in the eye, and said, "Then let her have fun. Let this be a party she and her friends will talk about for years—a party for the ages."

Larry, still processing the fact that their home had become the Halloween hotspot of the year, ran a hand over his face and sighed. "You're really okay with this?"

Tiffany nodded. "Rylee is having her moment. She's a good kid. Let her have it."

FOREVER TIFFANY

Larry turned back to the phone. "Alright, officer. Anyone who needs to stay, let them stay. Just make sure it's safe."

The officer chuckled. "Will do. This is going to be a story for a long time."

As Larry hung up, he stared at Tiffany in disbelief. "I don't understand how you stay this calm."

She smiled, pulling him closer. "Because, in the end, what really matters? They're safe. They're having fun. And years from now, Rylee will still be laughing about this night. What's the harm in that?"

Larry shook his head with a smirk, leaned in, and kissed her. "I don't know how you do it, but you always make everything okay."

Tiffany grinned. "That's because I'm Tiffany."

And with that, they lay back down, knowing that back in Castle Rock, their house had just gone down in teenage history.

As Larry and Tiffany returned home, they braced themselves for what they might find after Rylee's now-legendary Halloween party. They expected a disaster—trash everywhere, furniture moved out of place, maybe even a lingering smell of teenage rebellion. But to their surprise, the house was spotless. Rylee and her friends had done an incredible job cleaning up, making it almost impossible to tell that seventy-five kids had been partying there just a couple of nights before. The only evidence of the previous night's chaos was neatly tucked away in the outdoor garbage cans.

As Rylee stood in the kitchen sipping a smoothie, she looked up at her parents, gave a small shrug, and said with a sly smile, "Sorry about that."

Larry and Tiffany exchanged glances, holding back their laughter. What could they even say? The damage had been undone, no one had gotten hurt, and now Rylee had officially cemented her place in high school history. All was good.

With life settling back into its normal rhythm, Larry and Tiffany slid comfortably into their lockdown routine. They were fully immersed in Breaking Bad, watching episode after episode late into the night, wrapped up in blankets in their warm, cozy bed. There was something about these moments—just the two of them, escaping into a world of binge-worthy drama—that felt like their own little secret paradise.

One Saturday morning in November, just before Thanksgiving, they lay in bed, enjoying the laziness of the day. The cool morning air crept through the cracked window, but under the covers, everything was warm and perfect. Tiffany, in her usual fashion, was scrolling through her phone, flipping through articles, memes, and—of course—shopping pages.

Suddenly, she turned the screen toward Larry, her beautiful smile lighting up her face. "Look at this," she said, pointing to a sleek 2021 Range Rover Velar. The car had just arrived at the dealership, and it was exactly the kind of luxury SUV she had always loved.

Larry glanced at it, nodding. "Nice."

Tiffany playfully nudged him. "If you love me, you'll go buy it today."

She was mostly joking—mostly. She knew Larry adored her, and while she didn't expect him to run off and buy it on the spot, there was always that small possibility. After all, Larry had a history of spoiling her in the most unexpected ways.

Larry stretched, let out a deep sigh, and casually got out of bed. "I need a shower."

Tiffany watched him disappear into the bathroom, raising an eyebrow. Was he actually considering it?

Less than an hour later, freshly showered and dressed, Larry grabbed his keys.

"Where are you going?" Tiffany called from the kitchen.

"Out," Larry said with a smirk.

"Out where?" She narrowed her eyes.

"Oh, just running some errands." He winked.

Tiffany laughed, shaking her head. "You are something else."

Larry drove straight to the Land Rover dealership in Littleton, walking through the showroom as salespeople eyed him curiously. It was still peak pandemic protocol, and he had completely forgotten a mask. Fortunately, the dealership had extra ones on hand, and within minutes, he was masked up and ready to make his move.

He found the Velar Tiffany had fallen in love with on her phone, flagged down a salesman, and, without much back and forth, signed the paperwork.

Ninety minutes later, he was heading home, cruising down the highway in Tiffany's new car.

As he pulled into the driveway, Tiffany stood by the front door, arms crossed, shaking her head with a knowing smile. "You did not."

Larry stepped out, casually tossing her the keys. "You said if I loved you, I'd buy it today."

Tiffany let out a dramatic gasp, covering her mouth, acting shocked—even though she wasn't really shocked at all.

"You're crazy."

Larry shrugged. "Crazy in love with you."

She ran her hands over the sleek exterior of the SUV, her excitement barely contained. Larry watched as she opened the door, climbed inside, and ran her fingers over the dashboard, taking in the fresh, new car smell.

She turned to him, her blue eyes twinkling. "I love you for so many reasons… but this—this is just the icing on the cake."

Larry grinned. He knew Tiffany loved him for the right reasons—their history, their connection, their shared life. But he also knew that moments like this, little acts of spoiling her, were just another way to show how much she meant to him.

She leaned across the center console, pulling him in for a kiss. "Now... where are we taking my new car first?"

Larry laughed. "Wherever you want, beautiful. It's yours."

And with that, Tiffany's weekend had just gotten a whole lot better.

CHAPTER 18.
Sacred Promises

Another holiday season had come and gone, wrapping up the year in a familiar warmth that Larry and Tiffany cherished. Their home had been a winter wonderland once again, with multiple Christmas trees glowing in different corners of the house, garlands elegantly draped over the banisters, and the comforting scent of cinnamon and pine filling the air. Christmas morning had been magical as always—Tiffany, the master of holiday surprises, had exceeded herself again, ensuring that each of the kids received exactly what they wanted, plus a few extra surprises.

But as January settled in, the remaining warmth of the holidays was met with an underlying tension.

Larry had known for months that the company was in trouble. The energy industry had been hit hard, and the market was unstable. Oil had not only dropped to historic lows—it had, at one point, traded in the negative. There were no new projects on the horizon, no major contracts to chase. Deals were few and far between. His gut told him things were about to change, and not in a good way.

When Reynold, the president of the company, called Larry into his office, the confirmation came.

"John is flying in next week," Reynold said. "One-on-ones with each employee. It's not looking good."

Larry had seen this play out before. He'd spent enough time in corporate America to know exactly what that meant. The writing was on the wall.

He requested the first meeting, hoping to get it over with quickly. But that slot was reserved for Randy, the longest-tenured employee. Larry was scheduled second.

LARRY BLAKE

The morning of the meetings, Larry arrived early. The office was eerily silent. The usual hustle and bustle—the chatter over coffee, phones ringing, sales teams working deals—was absent. It was as if everyone knew what was coming and was simply waiting for the inevitable.

As Randy exited the conference room, he gave Larry a knowing look, the kind that said everything without saying anything at all. Larry took a deep breath, squared his shoulders, and walked in.

John sat at the head of the table, a solemn expression on his face. In front of him was a folder. A folder that Larry had handed to countless employees over the years when delivering bad news.

John exhaled heavily and leaned back in his chair. "Larry, this is the hardest day of my life. I'm sorry about this."

Larry nearly laughed. The hardest day of *your* life?

He wanted to say, *Really*, John? The hardest day of your life consists of stepping off your private jet, checking into a high-end hotel, eating at a five-star restaurant, and continuing to make millions? If that's a hard day, sign me up.

But instead, he just nodded.

John continued, explaining that Larry could stay on for another six to nine months to help shut the company down. But Larry had already made his decision. He wasn't going to sit around and watch everything crumble. He told John he would give him a departure date soon.

Surprisingly, he felt calm.

He stepped outside the office and dialed Tiffany. She answered immediately, as if she had been expecting the call.

"It's happening, isn't it?" she asked, her voice steady.

"Yeah," Larry replied.

There was a pause, but no panic. Just a deep breath before she said, "We'll be fine, babe. We always are."

Larry felt an indescribable wave of gratitude. Tiffany was unshakable, his rock, his constant. No matter the storm, she had the belief that they would make it through, and walking together, they always did.

His next call was to Bruce.

Larry had known Bruce for a few years. Their paths had crossed many times in the energy industry, and over the years, they had built a solid professional relationship that turned into a true friendship. Bruce was one of those guys who just got things done. He had an extensive network, a sharp business mind, and a reputation for being one of the best in the industry. If anyone could point Larry in the right direction, it was Bruce.

Larry laid everything out. The shutdown, the job loss, the uncertainty of what came next.

Bruce didn't hesitate.

"Give me forty-eight hours," he said. "I'll have an offer for you."

Larry hung up and took a deep breath. He wasn't out of the woods yet, but he wasn't lost either.

The energy industry, from the outside, looked massive. But inside, it was a tight-knit world. Connections mattered more than anything. Relationships built over years of trust and loyalty could open doors in moments like these. Today, those relationships were working in his favor.

As he drove home, he reflected on everything.

He had built an incredible career. He had spent years forging relationships, making deals, and working hard to provide for his family. And now, once again, he was standing at the edge of the unknown.

But one thing he knew for certain—he had been here before, and he had always found his way forward. This time would be no different.

The offer from Bruce came in just as promised, and Larry gladly accepted. He knew the moment he walked out of that meeting with John that Bruce and his team were where he wanted to be. They were true industry leaders, and more importantly, they operated with a level of integrity and expertise that Larry respected. He had always admired Bruce's business acumen and the way he built relationships, not just through deals, but through genuine trust.

There was just one small request Larry had before starting—he needed two weeks before officially stepping into his new role. Not because he wasn't eager to get to work, but because he had plans he wasn't about to cancel.

Larry was heading to Florida to play golf with his longtime best friend, Roman, and his wife, Sam. Roman and Sam weren't just golf enthusiasts—they were obsessed. The kind of people who could talk about golf for hours, wake up before sunrise to get in a round, and never turn down a chance to play. Their daughter, Alexis, was a state champion and is now playing at a Division I university. She was, without a doubt, the best female golfer Larry had ever seen in person. Watching her play was like watching magic in motion—the effortless swing, the precision, the control.

Larry had been looking forward to this trip for months, and now, it carried an even greater meaning. It was the perfect transition—a way to clear his mind, reset, and step into this next phase of his career with renewed energy.

Of course, he still hadn't officially resigned from his current position. He had made a calculated decision to wait, ensuring that there wasn't a single day without pay.

So, as he was driving to the first tee box at the course in Florida, with the ocean breeze drifting through the open window and the scent of fresh-cut grass filling the air, he made the call.

FOREVER TIFFANY

Reynold picked up on the first ring.

"Hey, Larry," he said, his voice calm, as if he already knew why the call was coming.

"Reynold, I'm making it official. I'm leaving now."

There was a pause, not of surprise, but of understanding.

"I figured," Reynold replied. "Let me guess—you're heading to Bruce's team?"

Larry laughed. "You know me too well."

Reynold wasn't bitter; he wasn't angry. If anything, he seemed relieved that Larry had found the right next step. Their professional relationship had evolved over years of working together, traveling across the country, and navigating the ups and downs of the industry. They weren't just colleagues—they were friends.

"I knew you wouldn't sit around waiting for things to fall apart," Reynold said. "Bruce is lucky to have you. And you know what? I'd probably be doing the same thing if I were in your position."

Larry appreciated that.

They exchanged a few more words, reminiscing for a moment about the good times, the successful deals, the wild stories from years on the road. There was no bad blood—only respect. Larry knew that while they wouldn't be working together anymore, he and Reynold would always stay close. Their friendship was too strong to be defined by a job.

As Larry ended the call, he felt lighter. He was free. No more uncertainty, no more waiting for the inevitable.

He stepped out of the cart, stretched his arms in the warm Florida sun, and grabbed his clubs. Roman and Sam were already on the green, waving him over with excitement.

"Alright, you ready to lose some money today?" Roman joked.

Larry smirked, grabbing his driver.

"We'll see about that."

With a deep breath, he stepped up to the tee, lined up his shot, and took a smooth, effortless swing.

The ball soared down the fairway, cutting through the crisp morning air.

For the first time in a long time, Larry felt like everything was exactly where it was meant to be.

As Larry settled into his new role at work, life at home was moving along smoothly. The family had finally found a rhythm after the unpredictability of the past year. Patrick was back to in-person classes for the second semester of his sophomore year at CU Boulder, something he was incredibly grateful for after spending far too much time in front of a computer screen. Brennan was in seventh grade, excelling in track and cross country, and proving to be a natural competitor. Meanwhile, Rylee was thriving in her junior year, juggling school and social life, and, much to her excitement, finally getting behind the wheel as an official licensed driver.

Rylee had just turned sixteen, and as they had done with Patrick before her, it was time to buy her a car. Tiffany was on a mission, and when it came to shopping, especially for big purchases, she thrived. Give her a task, set her loose, and she would come back victorious. She loved the thrill of the hunt, the comparison shopping, and the feeling of scoring the perfect deal. It didn't take long before they found exactly what they were looking for—a gently used BMW X1 35i, white with sleek black leather seats and trim. It was sporty, stylish, and just the right mix of safe and fun.

Rylee was beyond thrilled. She had envisioned this moment for years, watching Patrick get his car and dreaming about the day it would be her turn. Larry, on the other hand, was far less enthusiastic—proud, of course, but also nervous as hell. His little girl was officially on the road, out in the world, behind the wheel of a high-performance vehicle.

It didn't take long for Rylee to experience her first real taste of independent driving—getting pulled over by the Castle Rock police. She had barely been driving for a few weeks when those dreaded flashing lights appeared in her rearview mirror. But somehow, she had inherited a skill from her mother that Larry had never quite mastered—the ability to charm her way out of a ticket.

Just a year earlier, Tiffany had found herself in a similar situation. She was driving Rylee to school for a final exam, running behind schedule, and in a moment of urgency, she jumped into Larry's BMW and sped down the hill toward the high school, just a little too fast. Sure enough, red and blue lights flashed behind her, and she was pulled over. But Tiffany, being Tiffany, had a way of handling these situations with grace and ease. Dressed in nothing but a t-shirt, pajama pants, no bra, and without her purse or ID, she rolled down the window and simply said, "She's late for a final."

The officer took one look at her, nodded, and said, "Go get her to school and meet me back here."

Tiffany did exactly as instructed, dropping Rylee off before returning to the spot where the officer was waiting. He leaned in, smiled, and said, "Slow down next time and have a great day." That was Castle Rock for you—a town with an old-school, Mayberry kind of charm, where kindness and understanding were just as important as upholding the law.

So when Rylee was pulled over, she didn't panic. She was driving with her two best friends, Chloe and Lexi, all three of them blonde, giggling, and innocent-looking as ever. The officer approached the window, glanced at the trio, and asked, "What's the rush?"

Without hesitation, Rylee responded truthfully. "Heading to Dutch Bros. for a coffee."

The officer chuckled, shook his head, and simply said, "Slow down and have a nice day."

Rylee had learned something from her mother—a natural ability to remain calm and navigate any situation with confidence and a little bit of charm. Larry just shook his head when he heard the story. *Of course,* she got out of it. If it had been him, he would have had a ticket in his hand before he could even finish his sentence.

It was yet another reminder of how much Rylee had grown into a confident, strong young woman—one who was independent, quick-thinking, and just like her mother, always able to make things work in her favor.

Tiffany was excelling at work, pouring her energy and determination into her career in a way that was inspiring to watch. Larry loved seeing her thrive, seeing her build something for herself and prove, once again, that she was capable of anything she set her mind to. Even as she worked long hours and juggled the responsibilities of her demanding role, she never let it take away from what mattered most—her family. She was still deeply involved in Rylee's life, helping her grow into a strong, confident young woman, just like her mother. Though Tiffany would never admit to being powerful, she absolutely was. She always downplayed her abilities, never seeking the spotlight, always choosing to lead from behind, gently guiding those around her without demanding recognition.

The year was flying by, life was moving forward, and things felt... settled. Larry and Tiffany had found a new rhythm, one that involved long workdays and late nights together, unwinding in front of their latest binge-worthy obsession. After finishing *Breaking Bad*, they discovered *Yellowstone*, a show that became their new weekend addiction. They'd curl up on the couch together, watching the drama unfold against the stunning Montana backdrop, pausing occasionally to debate whether or not they should just pack up and move to a ranch somewhere out west. Tiffany loved the storylines, but Larry? He just wanted to be Rip Wheeler for a day.

FOREVER TIFFANY

Outside of work and family, Larry was spending a lot of time with Brian and Karl, and their friendships were stronger than ever. They had also formed a new friendship with Ben, a guy who fit right into their circle. Their weekends were filled with whiskey nights, poker nights, and long talks about work, life, and everything in between. At first, everything seemed great, but then Larry started noticing something—something subtle but persistent. Brian, Karl, and Ben, along with their wives, were spending a lot of time together as couples.

At first, Larry didn't think much of it. They were all close friends, and it wasn't unusual for them to hang out. But then, Tiffany mentioned something that made him pause.

"I've been trying to reach Stacy," she said one afternoon. "I've called her a few times, texted her, and... nothing. It's been about two weeks now."

Larry frowned. That was odd. Tiffany and Stacy had been inseparable for so long, talking almost daily, always checking in with each other. For Stacy to go silent for that long? It wasn't normal.

Larry casually brought it up to Brian the next time they were together.

"Hey, is Stacy okay? Tiffany's been trying to reach her, but she hasn't heard back."

Brian barely reacted. He shrugged and played it off, mumbling something about how things had been busy. But Larry knew his friend well enough to know when he wasn't being entirely truthful. There was something there, something unspoken.

Larry didn't push it, but in the back of his mind, it gnawed at him. He could see it in the way the dynamic was shifting. He could feel the distance growing between Tiffany and Stacy, between their families.

Tiffany, of course, never let on that it hurt her. But Larry knew.

She was tough, always had been. She had an incredibly warm, loving spirit, but she was also fiercely strong. She would never give someone the satisfaction of knowing they had hurt her, never let them see her pain. She carried it in silence, pushing forward with that quiet resilience that Larry had always admired.

But Larry knew.

He saw it in the way she stopped bringing Stacy up in conversation. In the way she busied herself with work, with Rylee, with planning their next adventure. In the way she carried herself, just a little differently, as if she was protecting her heart from further disappointment.

She wasn't one to dwell on things. She would never chase after someone who had pulled away. That just wasn't who she was.

And so, she did what she always did. She smiled, she laughed, and she made sure everyone around her felt loved. But Larry could see it—the small cracks that she refused to acknowledge. And deep down, it pissed him off.

Because if there was one person in the world who didn't deserve to be treated that way, it was Tiffany.

As 2021 neared its end, the holiday season was in full swing, bringing the usual excitement and traditions that made this time of year so special. The kids had thrown their annual Halloween parties, filling the house with laughter, costumes, and an endless supply of candy. Thanksgiving was spent at Holly's house, a warm and familiar gathering with family sharing stories, food, and gratitude. Christmas, as always, was hosted at Larry and Tiffany's home, filled with perfectly decorated trees, twinkling lights, and Tiffany's ability to make everything feel magical.

Then, of course, came New Year's Eve—their big party to close out the year and welcome the next. The house was filled with friends, drinks flowed, music played, and the energy was high. But something was missing this year.

FOREVER TIFFANY

Or rather, someone.

Stacy and Brian.

For yet another holiday, they were absent.

Tiffany had tried—over and over again—to reach out. Calls went unanswered. Texts remained unseen or, worse, left on read with no response. It was no longer a question of being busy or distracted—this was deliberate.

Larry had done his best to get to the bottom of it. He had pulled Brian aside and asked him directly.

"If Tiffany said something to upset Stacy, just tell me," Larry had pressed. "If it was me, I would want to know. I just don't get it."

Brian had dodged the conversation, brushing it off with vague responses, but Larry could see through it. There was something there, something Brian wasn't saying.

It didn't sit right.

Larry wasn't the kind of guy to dwell on drama, and Tiffany certainly wasn't one to beg for someone's time or friendship. But this was different. This was someone she had considered family. Someone she had loved like a sister. And now, without a word or explanation, Stacy had shut her out.

And yet, despite the hurt, despite the unanswered questions, it didn't stop Tiffany from having a great holiday season.

Because that's who she was.

She wouldn't let one person's absence take away from the joy of the season, from the love she felt for her family, from the warmth of the traditions she had built with so much care over the years.

She poured herself into the holidays like she always did, making everything beautiful, ensuring the kids had every little thing they wanted, wrapping gifts with the same special touch she had perfected over the years. She hosted with grace, made sure everyone felt welcome, and kept that radiant smile on her face.

But Larry knew her.

He saw the momentary glances, the flickers of sadness that crossed her face when she thought no one was watching. He noticed the way she'd glance at her phone sometimes, as if hoping—just maybe—Stacy had decided to reach out after all.

She never did.

And so, as the clock struck midnight on New Year's Eve, as the champagne glasses clinked and the house erupted into cheers, Larry pulled Tiffany close. He kissed her deeply, held her just a little tighter than usual, and whispered in her ear.

"New year, new memories. No looking back, baby."

She smiled up at him, and for the first time in weeks, he saw something real in her eyes—not just the act of moving on, but the decision to.

Whatever had happened, whatever had caused Stacy to walk away without a word—it no longer mattered.

Tiffany wasn't the type to chase ghosts.

She was ready to step into 2022 with the people who chose to be there.

CHAPTER 19.
Endings and Eternity

The weekend in Estes Park was meant to be a fresh start, a reset, and for Larry, it was one last attempt to mend the fracture between Tiffany and Stacy. The house he had rented was nothing short of perfect—a stunning cabin-style retreat nestled against the backdrop of snow-covered peaks, with massive windows that framed the breathtaking mountain views. It had four bedrooms and four bathrooms, ensuring everyone had their own space, but with a cozy living room and an oversized dining table designed for long nights filled with laughter, stories, and plenty of drinks.

Larry and Tiffany had claimed the luxurious main-level suite, with a private fireplace and a soaking tub that Tiffany had already declared she'd be using at least twice before they left. Karl and Jessica took the downstairs walkout basement, enjoying the added privacy, while Brian and Stacy, along with Ben and Stephanie, occupied the two upstairs bedrooms.

The drive up had been smooth. Larry and Tiffany opted to take the scenic route alone, enjoying the rare quiet time together. Karl and Jessica had done the same, while Brian, Stacy, Ben, and Stephanie had all carpooled in Stacy's SUV, a choice that Larry hoped would encourage some reflection and conversation between Brian and his wife.

By the time everyone arrived, the kitchen island was overflowing with an absurd amount of food—freshly baked bread, cheeses, charcuterie boards, enough steak and seafood for a feast, and desserts that no one really needed but would certainly devour. The liquor selection was even more excessive—bottles of aged whiskey, fine wines, and enough craft beer to keep them going through an entire Colorado winter.

The first night set the tone. They gathered around the large dining table for a game night, diving into Cards Against Humanity and a few other party games that promised inappropriate jokes and uncontrollable laughter. It didn't take long before Larry and Brian, having indulged in a few too many Colorado gummies, found themselves in absolute hysterics. Every card played seemed funnier than the last, and before long, the entire table was roaring with laughter.

For the first time in months, Tiffany and Stacy were talking like old times—smiling, whispering inside jokes, leaning into each other as they laughed. It was effortless, like the months of silence had never happened.

Larry watched carefully, sipping his whiskey as he observed the two of them. Was this real? Was this just the alcohol, the relaxed atmosphere, the mountain air? Or had they truly let go of whatever had come between them? He wasn't sure.

Would one of them bring it up? Would they address the unspoken tension, the months of unanswered calls, and awkward avoidance? Or would they let it all slide, pretending as if it had never happened?

He hoped—prayed—that this weekend would be the turning point, that whatever had fractured their friendship could be left in the past. But he also knew that time would tell.

For now, at least, the night was perfect.

As the fire crackled in the background and the mountains stood silent outside, Larry clinked glasses with Brian, Karl, and Ben, raising a quiet toast to friendship, to fresh starts, and to the hope that some things, no matter how broken they may seem, could still be put back together.

The morning started slowly, with the soft glow of sunlight peeking through the mountain cabin's massive windows. The air was crisp, fresh, carrying that distinctive scent of pine and woodsmoke from the surrounding forests. As everyone began to stir, Karl and Brian took charge in the kitchen, their voices echoing through the open space as they worked over the stove.

The aroma of sizzling bacon filled the house, soon followed by the comforting crackle of eggs hitting the pan. Hashbrowns were crisped up in a cast-iron skillet, while Karl poured fresh orange juice into champagne flutes, creating the perfect morning mimosas.

Larry sat back, watching the scene unfold. These were the moments he lived for—good friends, good food, and Tiffany moving about the kitchen, her blonde hair still slightly tousled from sleep, her laughter carrying through the air as she leaned against the counter, sipping her mimosa and stealing a piece of bacon off Brian's plate when he wasn't looking.

After breakfast, they all decided to head into downtown Estes Park. The sun had climbed higher into the sky, casting a golden glow over the quaint mountain town. The temperature was unseasonably mild for February, making for the perfect day to stroll through the shops, visit local artisans, and take in the charming energy of the town.

As they walked, the river that cut through downtown rushed beside them, the snowmelt from the mountains creating a steady, peaceful hum. People were everywhere—locals enjoying their weekend, tourists taking in the views, families sipping hot cocoa and carrying bags filled with souvenirs.

Larry noticed that Tiffany and Stacy had drifted off on their own, walking side by side, deep in conversation. It wasn't forced. It wasn't awkward. It was easy, natural, the way it used to be. They popped into shops together, picking up little trinkets, laughing as they tried on ridiculous mountain-themed hats, and stopping for coffee at a small café along the riverwalk.

Larry felt something he hadn't felt in months—hope.

Maybe things really could go back to the way they were.

By the time the sun began its descent behind the peaks, the group was ready for their evening plans—a visit to the legendary Stanley Hotel.

The grand, historic hotel stood tall against the backdrop of the Rocky Mountains, its white facade glowing in the fading light. It was famous for inspiring Stephen King's The Shining, and the ghost stories surrounding it were the stuff of legend.

They started the night in The Whiskey Lodge, an elegant yet rustic bar within the hotel, where they indulged in craft cocktails and shared appetizers. The space had a warm, inviting atmosphere—soft lighting, rich wood decor, and a selection of top-shelf whiskeys displayed behind the bar.

The guys ordered an Old Fashioned, while Stacy, Tiffany, and Jessica opted for a Huckleberry Mule. Karl and Ben, still recovering from the previous night's excess, kept it simple with bourbon neat.

The drinks flowed, the conversation was effortless, and everything felt… normal.

Then came the ghost tour. Their tour guide was young, maybe mid-twenties, but spoke about the hotel's history with a level of detail that was almost eerie. He led them through dimly lit corridors, up grand staircases, and into rooms that were supposedly the most haunted in the building.

Everyone was hoping for something—a flicker of a light, a whisper from beyond, maybe even a shadow passing through the hall.

But nothing happened.

No ghosts, no apparitions—just a well-done tour filled with fascinating history, a few well-placed jump scares, and a deeper appreciation for the hotel's rich past. Still, it was a great experience, one that had them buzzing with excitement as they made their way to their final stop of the night—The Post Chicken & Beer.

FOREVER TIFFANY

The restaurant, located in the renovated 1909 Carriage House of the Stanley Hotel, had been featured on Diners, Drive-Ins, and Dives and was known for its motto: Hot Chicken Loves Cold Beer.

The group was seated at a long wooden table, large enough to fit them all comfortably. Tiffany and Stacy took the seats along the window, sitting side by side, their heads occasionally leaning in close as they whispered and giggled.

The guys had gone hard the night before, and tonight, it was the girls' turn.

Tiffany and Stacy indulged in a few Colorado gummies, and Larry sat back, watching them with amusement.

They were completely in sync, arm in arm, sharing cocktails, stealing bites off each other's plates, their laughter ringing through the restaurant. It wasn't just a chuckle here and there—it was the kind of laughter that turned heads, the kind that made everyone around them smile, even if they didn't know why.

Larry stole glances at Brian, who was watching too, a grin on his face. They both knew this was a moment. A moment where everything felt like it was back to normal. A moment where the months of tension, unanswered calls, and unspoken words seemed to fade into the background.

But was it real? Or was it just the magic of the moment—the drinks, the high spirits, the escape of a weekend in the mountains?

Only time would tell.

For now, Larry didn't care. He was just happy to see his wife smiling again. Happy to hear that laughter, to feel the warmth of their friendship, reigniting.

He reached across the table, took Tiffany's hand in his, and gave it a squeeze. Whatever happened after this weekend, at least for tonight, everything was exactly as it should be.

LARRY BLAKE

As Larry and Tiffany basked in the warmth of rekindled friendships and the simple joy of being surrounded by their closest people, they had no idea that this weekend wasn't just a spontaneous getaway, a fun escape into the mountains. It wasn't just a stroke of good luck that had brought Tiffany and Stacy back together.

It was something greater. What they couldn't see—what none of them could see—was that this moment, this reunion, had been orchestrated by something far beyond their own plans. It wasn't Larry's persistence, it wasn't Brian's silent hopes, and it wasn't just a coincidence that Stacy and Tiffany found themselves laughing together again, arms linked as if no time had passed.

It was the work of God.

Because He knew something they didn't.

He knew what was coming.

He knew that Tiffany would need Stacy more than anyone could have possibly guessed. That in a short amount of time, Tiffany's world would be turned upside down, shaken to its very core. That she would need Stacy in a way no friend had ever been needed before.

God knew that when the storm came, Tiffany couldn't weather it alone. She would need a sister, a confidante, someone who could hold her up when she felt like she was falling. She would need someone to sit with her in the darkness, to cry with her, to fight for her when she didn't have the strength to fight for herself.

And so, He worked in ways that none of them could see at the time. He softened hearts. He guided their steps. He made a way where, just weeks ago, it seemed impossible.

And as Tiffany sat there, laughing with Stacy in that cozy mountain restaurant, sipping her cocktail, feeling the warmth of the moment, she had no idea that this was a gift, a lifeline she would soon cling to with everything she had.

Because the hardest chapter of her life was just around the corner.

FOREVER TIFFANY

And when it came—when everything changed—she wouldn't have to face it alone.

The celebrations didn't slow down once they returned from their mountain getaway—if anything, they picked up speed. Life at home moved forward in a whirlwind of milestone birthdays, heartfelt decisions, and the kind of days that become the building blocks of lifelong memories.

Brennan was the first to step into the spotlight, turning fourteen in early spring. Fourteen. A number that somehow felt both impossibly young and startlingly grown. His birthday party was everything a teenage boy could want—his favorite foods grilled and served with love, laughter echoing from the basement where he and his closest friends played ping pong and video games, and that unmistakable energy of youth hanging in the air. These boys weren't just his friends anymore. They were brothers. A chosen family built from years of classroom projects, weekend practices, and sleepovers filled with whispered jokes long past bedtime.

Larry and Tiffany stood together, watching Brennan from across the yard as he laughed, really laughed, at something one of his buddies said. Larry wrapped an arm around Tiffany's waist and whispered, "When did he get so tall?"

She smiled, eyes soft with nostalgia. "Feels like just yesterday he was running through the house in footie pajamas with cereal stuck to his face."

Brennan's party was followed just one week later by another major celebration—Rylee's eighteenth birthday. Eighteen. Adulthood. A legal marker of independence. It felt surreal to Tiffany, who had spent months watching her daughter transform from a girl into a young woman before her eyes. This wasn't just a birthday—it was a threshold. One step away from high school and one step closer to the unknown future.

There was a quiet heaviness in Tiffany's heart that she carried alongside the pride. She had helped Rylee through scraped knees and middle school heartbreaks, late-night study sessions, and impossible social drama. And now, suddenly, her daughter was ready to step into the world on her own. The emotions swirled like a storm—joy, love, pride, and that bittersweet ache that only a mother truly understands.

The college decision had been a journey in itself. For months, Tiffany sat beside Rylee at the kitchen island, laptops open, applications sprawled across the countertop, cups of coffee cooling between them. They researched, debated, and dreamed. Rylee's friends had already chosen their paths—Chloe, off to Lynn University in Florida with her volleyball scholarship; Lexi, bound for the University of South Carolina; and another close friend heading to Kansas to cheer in the Big 12.

But Rylee's heart was different. She didn't want to follow someone else's story. Even though CU Boulder, where Patrick was now a senior, would have been the easy choice—comfortable, familiar—she wanted her own space, her own adventure.

It wasn't until they visited the University of Colorado at Colorado Springs that everything clicked into place. The moment she set foot on campus, something settled in her chest. The campus was nestled in the foothills of the Rocky Mountains, with Pikes Peak rising like a guardian in the distance. It felt right. Not too far from home, but far enough to stretch her wings.

That night, over dinner, with the late-spring sun still spilling golden light across the dining room table, Rylee announced her decision with a confident smile.

"I'm officially a Mountain Lion."

Larry raised his glass with a proud grin. "To Rylee—the first UCCS Mountain Lion in the family."

Tiffany squeezed her daughter's hand, her eyes misty. "You're going to do amazing things, baby girl."

FOREVER TIFFANY

They clinked their glasses together. It was one of those simple family moments that somehow felt like a ceremony, small in scale, but immense in heart.

And then came graduation.

The weather couldn't have been more perfect. Not a single cloud dotted the Colorado sky, and a warm breeze danced through the football stadium, carrying the scent of spring flowers and fresh-cut grass. The bleachers were filled with proud parents, smiling siblings, and teary-eyed grandparents. Families held signs, cheered names, and took more photos than their phones could handle.

Rylee walked with grace across the stage, her cap tilted just right, her gown catching the sunlight. Her long blonde hair flowed down her back, her makeup flawless, her eyes shining with the thrill of this long-awaited moment. She didn't just look beautiful—she radiated confidence and joy. The little girl who once twirled in the living room in princess dresses was now a high school graduate, ready to step boldly into adulthood.

Tiffany and Larry were beaming from the stands, their cheers echoing through the stadium. Brennan clapped louder than anyone, proud of his big sister.

Later that weekend, the celebration continued at home with a stunning open house party.

Larry did what he did best—smoked pork shoulders to perfection, slow-cooked and seasoned with love. The aroma filled the neighborhood, drawing in neighbors and friends alike. Tiffany, true to form, made sure everything was flawless. Food overflowed from every counter. Dips, desserts, charcuterie, cupcakes, custom cookies—all themed in Rylee's school colors. Purple and white adorned every inch of their home. From streamers to balloons, from napkins to the flowers that Larry had planted in every pot and patio planter—each bloom a testament to their pride in her.

The back deck was buzzing with laughter and music, while the lower patio hosted drinks and heartfelt conversations. At the firepit patio, guests gathered as the sun dipped behind the mountains, casting a golden light over the celebration.

This wasn't just a party. It was a moment—a bookmark in the story of their lives. A chapter closed. A new one just—beginning.

And as Tiffany watched her daughter laugh with friends, pose for pictures, and receive endless hugs of congratulations, she felt a peace settle over her.

Yes, the house would be quieter soon.

But the memories made here- the laughter, the love, the milestones—they would never fade.

They were stitched into the fabric of their family forever.

CHAPTER 20.
Through It All

As the golden days of summer 2022 began to slip away, Tiffany felt a tug on her heart—a quiet whisper from home. After a swift series of celebrations, transitions, and nonstop movement, she knew what her soul needed most: time with family. Real, unhurried, heart-filling time. So, with a smile and a determined spark, she began planning a trip back to the place where it all began—Northwest Indiana.

It was a journey she'd been craving. A chance to return to her roots, to walk familiar streets, to laugh with the people who knew her best. This trip wouldn't be just for her. She gathered her crew—Rylee, Brennan, and Rylee's new boyfriend, Landon—and pitched the idea with the kind of excitement that made it impossible to say no. And then she called Amanda.

Her sister didn't hesitate. Amanda agreed to make the journey too, bringing along her three boys—Jacob, John, and Josh. Seven kids. Two sisters. One shared mission: to reconnect, recharge, and relive the magic of the past.

They all crammed into Vicky's cozy new home at the marina. It wasn't spacious, and it certainly wasn't quiet, but it was perfect. The air was thick with laughter, the kind that comes easily when you're surrounded by the people you love most. Tiffany was glowing. Her heart swelled every time she looked around and saw her family, her kids, her sister, all under one roof. She didn't need anything more.

Days were spent down by the water's edge, where memories bloomed like wildflowers. The cousins raced across the sand, barefoot and free, just as Tiffany and Amanda had once done in their own youth. Jet skis zipped across the lake, with Brennan whooping as he took the throttle and Rylee squealing behind him, arms wrapped tightly around Landon. Tiffany watched from the beach, feet in the water, her sunglasses hiding misty eyes. This—this was everything.

Every night brought something different, something delicious, and something nostalgic.

One evening, Tiffany took them to Dairy Dip, the tiny local ice cream shop tucked into the corner of town like a sweet secret. It was nothing flashy—just a simple walk-up window and a few faded benches out front—but for Tiffany, it was sacred. She grinned as she introduced Landon to her favorite order: an upside-down banana split, all chocolate ice cream, extra fudge drizzle. The kids ordered sundaes and shakes, eyes wide as they took their first bites. Tiffany laughed as Brennan's cone began melting faster than he could eat it, a chocolate river running down his wrist.

"See?" she said, bumping Landon's shoulder. "It's not summer in Indiana without Dairy Dip."

Another night, they gathered around the dining table, greasy boxes from JJ's Pizza Shack spread open like treasure chests. The smell alone was enough to send Tiffany back in time—golden crusts, spicy sausage, gooey cheese that stretched with every slice. JJ's had been her favorite since she was a little girl, and now she was passing it on to the next generation.

"This," she said, holding up a slice, "is the best pizza in the state. Maybe the country. Maybe the world."

No one disagreed.

On yet another evening, they picked up dinner from Ma Johnson's—a hole-in-the-wall joint that had no seating, no decor, and no pretense. Just incredible food. The battered cod was massive, crispy, and flaking with every bite, and the jumbo shrimp were like little golden pillows of heaven. Ma Johnson's wasn't just a restaurant. It was tradition. One of those places where the smell alone brought back decades of memories, where the taste stayed long after the last bite.

Tiffany sat outside on the marina deck that night, a plate of fish in her lap, and the breeze off the lake warm against her face. Amanda sat beside her, and for a long while, they didn't say anything at all. They didn't have to.

The kids played below, their laughter echoing across the water, while Vicky stood at the window watching her daughters, her grandkids, her legacy. And Tiffany, her heart full and still, leaned into that moment. It was the kind of moment she knew she'd carry with her for years—the kind that would come back to her on a hard day, when life felt too heavy. The kind of moment that reminded her what really mattered.

Family. Home. And the joy of simply being together.

This trip wasn't a vacation. It was a return. A recharge. A reconnection to the people and the places that had made her who she was. And she would treasure it always.

On the final day of their Indiana getaway, Tiffany had something special planned—a perfect send-off to cap a week filled with nostalgia, laughter, and family bonding. She gathered Rylee, Brennan, Landon, and her nephews for a full day in the heart of the city she had always loved so deeply. There was, after all, no place like Chicago in the summer.

The drive into the city was filled with music and conversation, the skyline growing larger as they approached. Tiffany's heart fluttered at the sight—those iconic buildings stretching into the sky, Lake Michigan shimmering in the sunlight. She had spent so many days here growing up, wandering the Magnificent Mile, snapping photos at Navy Pier, window-shopping along Michigan Avenue. Today, she was determined to pass that magic on.

Their first stop was the museum—a timeless, marble giant that had always felt like walking into a different world. The kids marveled at the dinosaur skeletons and ancient Egyptian artifacts, moving from exhibit to exhibit with wide eyes. Tiffany loved watching them explore, loved how their curiosity bloomed with every new hallway.

She wasn't just showing them a museum. She was showing them a piece of her childhood, the wonder she remembered so clearly.

Afterward, they made their way to Ed Debevic's—a classic, kitschy diner with a reputation for playful rudeness and over-the-top antics. Sure, it was touristy. Sure, the waiters wore paper hats and called you names. But Tiffany loved it. The chaos, the dancing servers, the oversized burgers—it was part of the experience. Part of what made it fun. She laughed with the kids as the waiter rolled his eyes at their order and called Landon "pretty boy" before dropping a plate of fries on the table with dramatic flair.

They ate like they hadn't all week, ordering milkshakes piled high with whipped cream, onion rings the size of bracelets, and towering burgers slathered in sauce. For Tiffany, it wasn't about the food—it was about the joy. About letting loose. About giving these kids a day they'd never forget.

By the time they left the restaurant, their feet were sore, their arms heavy with souvenir bags, and the sun had begun its golden descent over the city skyline. The car was parked nearly a mile away—an easy walk under normal circumstances, but they were worn out. Tiffany flagged down two rickshaws, laughing as she handed out seats and gave the drivers the destination.

"$150 for two rickshaws to ride a mile?" Larry would have raised his eyebrows and chuckled, calling it "Tiffany Style" without missing a beat.

But that was Tiffany.

She didn't think twice about those things, not when it came to making memories. She didn't worry about what things cost when the payoff was joy. She lived for these moments, where her people were smiling, carefree, and living in the now. She was a free spirit, but not in the kind of way that chased whims. No, Tiffany's freedom came from the way she loved. Fiercely. Fully. Fearlessly.

She wasn't wild. She was intentional.

FOREVER TIFFANY

She loved action—planning days like this, knowing it would become one of those memories they'd carry with them forever. She put her family first in every way, but she did it with the joy and spark of someone who was completely, unshakably herself. That rickshaw ride through downtown Chicago, wind in their hair, laughter echoing down the sidewalk, wasn't just a ride—it was a statement.

Life was meant to be lived, and Tiffany knew how to live it better than anyone.

As they climbed into the car and pulled away from the glittering skyline, Tiffany looked in the rearview mirror, watching her kids' tired, happy faces.

This was her joy.

This was her freedom.

And this was her love, wrapped in laughter, set to the rhythm of a Chicago summer, and tucked into the heart of a day no one would ever forget.

As the golden days of summer slowly slipped away, the air in Castle Rock began to shift. The mornings turned crisp, the leaves hinted at change, and the rhythm of the household began to follow the familiar drumbeat of back-to-school season. For the family, this year's transition carried a special weight—one of endings, of beginnings, and of that bittersweet in-between space where memories and milestones collide.

Brennan was stepping into eighth grade, his final year before high school. He'd grown taller over the summer, his once-boyish frame starting to fill out with the promise of adolescence. He was busy with basketball, crushing it on the track, and had one eye already fixed on what came next—high school, with its louder gyms, faster races, and the dreams he kept tucked behind his signature grin. Tiffany saw it in his stride—he was moving forward with purpose, just like his big brother before him.

But it was Rylee's move-in day that really marked the changing of the seasons in the household.

The morning air in Colorado Springs was unusually still as Larry and Tiffany pulled into the University of Colorado, Colorado Springs campus, the SUV packed tight with storage bins, rolled-up rugs, laundry hampers, and the nervous excitement that always accompanied sending a child out into the world.

Tiffany had planned every inch of Rylee's dorm room for weeks. This wasn't just decorating—it was an art form, a love language, a way to leave a piece of herself behind. As they hauled the final cart into Rylee's suite-style dorm, Tiffany immediately took charge like a designer stepping into a blank canvas.

The centerpiece was a soft, white shag rug that transformed the sterile tile floor into something warm and welcoming. Dreamcatchers, delicate and whimsical, were hung with perfect symmetry above Rylee's bed—hand-selected, not only for their style but for the energy they brought. They represented protection, dreams, and comfort. Tiffany wanted Rylee to feel wrapped in magic and meaning each night as she lay down to rest.

Rylee matched her mother's energy, unpacking and organizing with the same attention to detail. Together, they folded throw blankets, stacked notebooks, and arranged framed photos of friends and family. Larry, meanwhile, played the role of supportive bystander, perched in the corner chair, watching the women in his life create something beautiful.

He leaned back with a quiet smile, resisting the urge to ask the one question burning in his stomach: "When can we eat?"

After what felt like a full renovation project, Tiffany declared the room complete. It was "Tiffany Style"—part boho chic, part mother's love, part sanctuary—and Rylee lit up with gratitude.

They headed out for dinner to commemorate the occasion. Of all the culinary options in town, Rylee and Tiffany chose Olive Garden.

FOREVER TIFFANY

Larry tried not to look pained as he opened the door to the familiar chain restaurant, thinking longingly of the little mom-and-pop Italian place they'd passed earlier. Still, he smiled. Tonight wasn't about him.

They settled into their booth, the scent of garlic bread sticks filling the air, and ordered with the kind of laughter that only comes from shared history. The conversation wasn't deep or heavy—it was light and full of joy. Rylee was out in the world now, a college freshman ready to chase dreams of her own, and she radiated excitement for what lay ahead.

As the sun dipped below the horizon and painted the sky in hues of lavender and gold, Larry sat across from his two girls and felt the quiet shift of life again. Another child launched, another chapter opened. The pride swelled in his chest.

Meanwhile, up in Boulder, Patrick was already waist-deep in his senior year at CU. He had fully settled into life on his own, living in a four-bedroom apartment just off campus with his closest friends—Bryce, Cole, and Evan. The four of them were like brothers. They cooked together (albeit with more takeout than recipes), worked out together, and celebrated every small victory with the kind of passion only college seniors could muster.

Patrick was thriving. His mind, always sharp and curious, was focused on the road ahead. Whether he was studying, working a part-time job, or talking about what came next, his eyes always seemed to look forward, not with anxiety, but with purpose. Larry and Tiffany often gaped at his maturity. He was still their goofy, quick-witted Patrick, but he had grown into a man who carried himself with intention.

He didn't talk much about what lay after graduation—at least not in specifics—but his actions showed he was preparing. Whether it was research internships or graduate school possibilities, he was laying bricks for the road ahead.

LARRY BLAKE

For Larry and Tiffany, it was a beautiful, surreal season. One child had launched. Another was just leaving the dock. And Brennan, their youngest, was already stretching his wings.

They were proud—so deeply proud—and yet, in those quiet moments when the house felt too still, they missed the chaos. The door slamming. The sibling arguments. The dinners with all five chairs full.

But they knew this was the point.

This was what they had raised them for—to go, to grow, and to chase the lives they were meant to live.

And as they sat on the back deck that evening, the lights of Castle Rock beginning to twinkle in the distance, Tiffany reached for Larry's hand and smiled. "Two down," she whispered. "One to go."

Larry squeezed her hand and nodded, a lump forming in his throat.

But tonight, they would celebrate.

Because this chapter wasn't about endings—it was about beginnings. And the best stories always start right here.

The year was winding down, and with the arrival of December came Tiffany's favorite season—the holidays. As soon as the first snowflakes touched the ground and the temperatures dipped just enough to justify extra throws on the couch, Tiffany came to life in a way only she could. For her, Christmas wasn't just a holiday—it was a season of enchantment, and their home became a reflection of that joy.

The transformation began the moment Thanksgiving leftovers were packed away. Tiffany dove headfirst into her Christmas decorating ritual with a joyful intensity that had become legendary among friends and family. She approached it like an artist preparing for her biggest exhibition of the year. By now, her nutcracker collection had grown to nearly 150 unique pieces—each one with its own story, its own charm, its own perfect little spot.

FOREVER TIFFANY

Two large soldier nutcrackers stood proudly in the living room's built-in cutouts, guarding the fireplace like loyal sentinels. Smaller nutcrackers lined windowsills, countertops, the tops of cabinets—even sneaking their way into the bathrooms and bedrooms. Some were classic wooden soldiers, others were decked out in glittering holiday uniforms or dressed as ballerinas, kings, and drummers. There were chef nutcrackers in the kitchen, skiing nutcrackers by the back door, and a stunning white-and-gold nutcracker that Tiffany insisted had a "queen's energy" and belonged on the mantle.

In the center of it all stood the Christmas tree—tall and elegant, every branch draped with care. Ornaments collected over decades sparkled under soft white lights, each one placed deliberately, no space too empty, no branch too crowded. Beneath the tree, gifts were already arranged well before Christmas Eve—each one wrapped with ribbons that curled just so, tags handwritten with a graceful touch that felt personal, special.

It was a magical Christmas, not just because of the decorations or the twinkling lights, but because Tiffany had that rare gift: she made the season feel like something out of a movie. Warm, welcoming, and filled with wonder.

As New Year's approached, the magic didn't fade. Hosting their annual New Year's Eve celebration had become one of Tiffany and Larry's favorite traditions—an evening full of laughter, music, champagne, and a house bursting at the seams with friends who had become family. The main level was glowing with soft lights, music poured from the speakers, and the bar was fully stocked. Larry had prepped his signature drinks, and the smell of Tiffany's appetizers filled the air—sweet and spicy, made with the same love she put into everything.

Everyone gathered for the countdown, huddled in the living room, glasses raised, eyes on the clock. And as midnight hit, the cheers and kisses and hugs rang in another new year, another chapter.

Patrick and Rylee were home for the holiday stretch, and it was comforting to have the family all under one roof again. The energy was different now—older, more mature—but no less sweet. They were preparing to return to campus for their spring semesters, and Patrick was now just six credits away from graduating from the University of Colorado Boulder. Larry looked at him and saw a man ready to take on the world, and he couldn't help but feel a swelling sense of pride.

Rylee, too, was growing into her own. Confident, thoughtful, and grounded. Watching her and Patrick together—teasing, laughing, reconnecting. It was like time had folded in on itself, giving Larry and Tiffany a glimpse of who their children had become while still holding the echoes of who they used to be.

It was a beautiful end to another beautiful year. One that came with growth, change, and the ever-deepening love that filled their home—a home that, in every season, but especially at Christmas, Tiffany had turned into an enchanting world of magic.

Autumn had blanketed Colorado in golden hues, and with the crisp air came a sense of momentum. The kids were thriving—Brennan charging through eighth grade with a mix of teenage curiosity and middle-school swagger, Rylee settling confidently into her college life at UCCS, and Patrick, well, Patrick was standing at the edge of one chapter and the start of something extraordinary.

Tiffany, in her usual fashion, was juggling everything with grace and tenacity—managing her team, mentoring younger professionals, showing up for her kids, and still finding the time to breathe life into the smallest moments. A few months earlier, during a rare quiet evening, she had nudged Larry with one of her signature ideas—part suggestion, part gentle command.

"You should take Patrick somewhere special," she had said, her voice light, but purposeful. "Something to celebrate all he's done. He's earned it."

She was right. Patrick had just wrapped up a remarkable internship at Arrow Electronics, working at the company's world headquarters in Denver. It had been an experience that gave him a real taste of the future, and now it was time for a reward.

Larry had known immediately where to go.

Mexico City. Formula 1. A weekend of roaring engines, rich culture, and a memory neither of them would ever forget.

****

They touched down in Mexico City on Thursday, October 27th. The descent into the sprawling metropolis revealed a sea of colors and movement—a city pulsing with life in every direction. Patrick leaned toward the airplane window, wide-eyed, as if trying to drink it all in. From above, it was chaos and order, beauty and grit, all woven into one.

Once they emerged from customs, the weight and warmth of the city wrapped around them like a living thing. The air buzzed with motion—cars honking in a melodic rhythm, vendors calling out their wares, people weaving through streets like a constant, flowing river.

Their driver wound his way through the historic Reforma district, finally pulling up in front of the Marquis Reforma Hotel & Spa—a polished gem nestled between the elegance of the St. Regis and the timeless class of the Four Seasons. Inside, the marble floors gleamed, and the chandeliers sparkled. It was the perfect balance of comfort and sophistication.

That night, they dined at Bartola Steak & Grill, a hidden culinary treasure tucked into a quiet block off the main boulevard. The meat was rich and expertly charred, the sides flavorful and surprising, and the cocktails… dangerously smooth. They talked and laughed, and somewhere between the second round of drinks and the final bite of dessert, Larry paused.

He looked across the table at Patrick—his son, now a man. With his slightly shaggy hair and neatly trimmed beard, he looked like the world was ready for him, and more importantly, he was ready for the world. But in that moment, Larry didn't just see the man—he caught a flash of the boy he once carried on his shoulders, the boy who used to sit cross-legged in footie pajamas at the kitchen table, asking about planets and basketball stats.

The boy who changed his life.

Charleston. San Diego. Boulder. Countless road trips, locker rooms, airports, and sideline chats. And now, Mexico City.

This trip, Larry knew, was the exclamation point at the end of their shared chapter of childhood. Something bigger was coming next—for Patrick, for all of them.

The next morning, they were up early and headed to the Autódromo Hermanos Rodríguez. The racetrack was only three miles away, but in the sea of traffic, it might as well have been thirty. What should've been a short drive took nearly an hour, but neither of them minded. The anticipation crackled in the air like static. This was Formula 1. This was speed, precision, and legacy.

Practice sessions filled the day with roaring engines, pit crews hustling like clockwork, and the energy of a crowd that lived for the moment. Patrick absorbed every detail. Larry watched the way he moved through the crowd, equal parts fan and analyst, soaking it all in like it might disappear tomorrow.

That night, instead of hailing a cab, they wandered down the street from the hotel and stumbled upon a small, tucked-away restaurant where the aroma of cumin and lime drifted out onto the sidewalk. The walls were adorned with mismatched art, the kitchen half-open to the dining room. The food came fast and hot, and the margaritas were strong and salty. They ordered enough for six people, laughed until their stomachs hurt, and toasted to the life they were building.

FOREVER TIFFANY

Later that night, back in their room, they FaceTimed Tiffany. She smiled as they recapped the day, laughing at Patrick's impression of a frantic pit crew and Larry's story about nearly walking into a street vendor's flaming grill. She was back home, but her presence was felt with every beat of their adventure. After all, she had planted the seed. This was her gift to them, as so many things had been.

Saturday's qualifying was everything they had hoped for—thrilling, loud, and filled with anticipation. Lando Norris, Patrick's favorite driver, only managed to secure eighth on the grid, but it didn't dampen the spirit. They knew the real show would come on Sunday.

As they exited the racetrack and headed back to the city, they heard the music first—the unmistakable rhythm of drums and trumpets echoing off the buildings.

The Day of the Dead parade was underway.

The streets of Mexico City had transformed into a living dream. Dancers moved in hypnotic waves, their faces painted in intricate skull patterns, their costumes bright as the morning sun. Floats rolled by like works of art—marigold petals, flickering candles, enormous puppets honoring ancestors and lost souls. The crowd pressed together, united by reverence and celebration.

Larry and Patrick stood still for a moment, shoulder to shoulder, watching the swirl of culture and color pass in front of them. There were moments in life that felt like a painting, where everything aligned in texture and tone. This was one of them.

In the middle of that street, in one of the largest cities in the world, they felt something that couldn't be measured in laps or trophies. They felt alive.

They didn't say it aloud, but they both knew: this trip had been more than racing. It was about time. About moments. About the quiet realization that the baton was slowly, surely, passing from one hand to another.

And it had all begun with her—Tiffany, the soul behind the scenes, the woman whose love never needed a spotlight to shine. The one who, once again, had given her family something they would carry forever.

****

Race day had finally arrived, and the city of Mexico was humming with anticipation. The streets buzzed with energy as fans draped in team colors and national flags made their pilgrimage toward the Autódromo Hermanos Rodríguez. Larry and Patrick moved with the crowd, their credentials in hand and excitement written all over their faces. This wasn't just another sporting event—this was Formula 1, on the grandest of scales, in a city that knew how to celebrate every second of it.

Their seats were in the heart of the action—the stadium section, where the track wound directly through the old baseball arena, now converted into the most electric part of the course. The layout created an amphitheater effect, and the crowd didn't just watch the race—they roared through it.

It was the party zone, where chants erupted before the cars ever made it to the turn, where drums pounded and horns blew, where painted faces and foam fingers mingled with $800 sunglasses and team-issued polos. When the cars whipped by, the sound was deafening, but the fans only got louder. This wasn't a polite golf clap type of crowd—this was a wall of sound, a pulse of passion that bled into the track itself.

Patrick was on his feet, caught in the euphoria of it all. His phone was raised high, capturing clips of the drivers flashing past in streaks of color and speed. Larry stood beside him, his arm occasionally slung around his son's shoulder, grinning with the quiet satisfaction that only a father can know—this was the good stuff.

Max Verstappen, dominant as ever, was untouchable. Just as he had been the year before in Austin, he commanded the race from start to finish, carving through turns with surgical precision. Lando Norris, Patrick's guy, battled hard but settled for ninth. Still, Patrick never stopped cheering. His loyalty was unquestionable.

As the race wound down and the final laps ticked away, the crowd's intensity never waned. Streamers flew, flags waved high, and the smell of street tacos and gasoline circulated in the warm air. The checkered flag dropped, and though the race was over, the memory would only begin to set in.

That night, Larry and Patrick went out one last time. Their steps were slower now, not from exhaustion, but from the deep satisfaction that came after something unforgettable. They wandered into a lively restaurant with open windows and music spilling onto the street, the kind of place where the laughter never really stopped.

They didn't rush dinner. They ordered too much food, too many margaritas, and let the night stretch out around them like a familiar blanket. They replayed every moment—Max's dominance, the sea of orange-clad Dutch fans, the way the cars screamed down the straight, the perfect weather, the parade, the people. All of it.

And maybe it was the tequila, or maybe it was just the realization that time doesn't stop for anyone, but Larry looked across the table at Patrick and smiled—not with his mouth, but with his eyes.

"This," he thought, "this was the kind of weekend that makes a life."

The trip had been more than either of them had hoped for. More than racing. More than bonding. It had been a magical pocket in time—a capsule of joy, of pride, of love between a father and son who had been through everything together.

Early Monday morning, they boarded their flight back to Denver. As the plane lifted off, Patrick leaned his head against the window, earbuds in, already dozing off. Larry sat back in his seat, hands folded, his thoughts drifting.

He thought of Tiffany. He thought of her gift, her love language that always came in the form of experiences, thoughtfulness, and putting others before herself. She had orchestrated this trip in spirit, and he would never forget that.

As the clouds parted below and the sun streamed in through the tiny oval window, Larry closed his eyes and whispered a silent prayer of thanks—for the race, for the city, for the memories.

But most of all, for the boy who had become a man sitting beside him.

CHAPTER 21.
A Mother's Way

2023 was off to a promising start. The chill of January had barely lifted when Rylee came home from college for a quiet weekend. Her energy was different—thoughtful, maybe even a bit restless. After dinner, as the three of them lounged in the family room, she looked up and said what had clearly been on her mind for a while.

"I think I want to transfer," she said gently.

Larry and Tiffany both turned toward her, surprised but not shocked. They listened as she explained, not out of dissatisfaction, but a longing for something more. More energy. More excitement. She wanted the big games, the electric buzz of campus-wide events, the tailgates, the student section roaring in the stands. She wanted the life Patrick had built for himself at CU Boulder.

She wasn't unhappy. She was simply ready for a new chapter—one where she could plant herself in the middle of it all, not just orbit around the edges. And as she laid it all out, Tiffany's eyes glistened with pride. It was a brave thing to admit that your path wasn't quite the right fit and to have the courage to adjust the sails.

Rylee explored her options carefully. There were visits, late-night discussions, lists, and pros-and-cons scribbled in notebooks. In the end, she made her decision: Utah State University in Logan, Utah. It had the atmosphere she was looking for, nestled in the mountains, buzzing with spirit, and full of opportunities. It felt like a fresh beginning, and she was ready.

As spring crept in and the school year began winding down, another monumental day loomed ahead—Patrick's graduation from the University of Colorado Boulder.

Thursday, May 11th, arrived with gray skies and steady rain, the kind of weather that tests your optimism. But it didn't matter. The family wasn't going to let a little cold or wet dampen a day this significant.

The CU football stadium was packed with students and families from every corner of the state and beyond. Ponchos fluttered like flags in the wind, umbrellas danced among the seats, and yet the crowd buzzed with energy and pride. Vicki had flown in for the occasion, bundled in layers, determined not to miss this moment for anything.

Patrick, ever calm and composed, stood tall among his classmates. His black gown fluttered in the breeze, the white tassel on his cap catching in the wind as he scanned the sea of cheering faces.

Governor Jared Polis took to the stage to deliver the commencement address, his words offering encouragement, humor, and a challenge to the graduates to lead with courage and integrity. Despite the cold, the crowd listened intently, inspired by the energy of the day.

After the main ceremony, families broke off and followed their graduates to department-specific celebrations. Patrick's was in the economics department—a tight-knit group of students who had worked through pandemic lockdowns, virtual classrooms, and the uncertainty of a shifting world.

As Patrick walked across the stage, receiving his degree in economics, Tiffany held back tears. Larry clapped with pride, feeling the weight of every tutoring session, every long night of study, every hurdle his son had overcome. This moment was the culmination of not just four years at CU, but a lifetime of quiet effort and determination.

And for Patrick, it wasn't just a piece of paper—it was proof. Proof that even through the uncertainty of COVID and the struggles of early adulthood, he'd made it. His freshman year, which began in the isolation of lockdown, was now a distant memory. What lay ahead was a world of opportunity.

That day, wrapped in rain and celebration, was a turning point for the family—a bridge from all they had worked toward to all that was still to come. It was a moment of triumph. A moment of gratitude. And like everything else in their lives, it was shared together.

A couple of weeks after celebrating Patrick's graduation from CU, it was time for another milestone—Brennan's eighth-grade continuation ceremony. This was the final step before high school, and it carried all the pride and emotion of a major transition.

Larry and Tiffany arrived early, holding hands as they walked through the school's familiar halls, knowing it would soon be Brennan's past. They found seats near the front of the auditorium, which was buzzing with anticipation. Family members filled the room, snapping photos and chatting excitedly, the atmosphere warm with nostalgia and hope.

They were proud of Brennan—more than proud, really. He'd thrived in middle school, managing the often-awkward journey of adolescence with confidence and a sharp sense of humor. He was a kid who could make anyone laugh, often turning simple conversations into full-blown comedy sketches.

So when the school announced he had been selected as one of four student speakers, Larry and Tiffany were thrilled... and just a little terrified. After all, Brennan was unpredictable with a microphone in his hand. They had gently tried—more than once—to get a preview of what he had planned.

"Just let us take a peek," Tiffany had coaxed.

"It's fine," Brennan had said, grinning. "I got this."

Those three words— "I got this"—didn't do much to ease their nerves.

The ceremony began with cheerful music, applause, and a welcome from the school principal. The first two speakers, both young women, delivered sweet, heartfelt speeches. They thanked teachers and classmates, offering short reflections that lasted just under two minutes each. It was exactly what you'd expect at a continuation ceremony.

Then, Brennan approached the microphone. No notecards. No neatly folded speech. No phone in hand.

Just Brennan, standing there with his trademark confidence, grinning at the crowd of roughly 350 people like he was about to host a comedy special on Netflix. Tiffany leaned toward Larry and whispered, "Oh no." Her hand found his and squeezed—not a squeeze of affection, but a panic grip that said, brace yourself.

Brennan started off with a joke—something about how surviving eighth-grade deserved a trophy and maybe hazard pay. The audience laughed. Then another joke. More laughter. Then, there was a story about a teacher who had to threaten to confiscate his phone three times in one week. The teachers in the room chuckled knowingly. Brennan thanked classmates, calling out a few by name and dropping inside jokes and one-liners with flawless timing.

Four minutes passed… then six… then ten.

Larry was now slouched low in his seat, one arm across his chest and the other hiding his face, peeking through his fingers like he was watching a horror film. Tiffany kept shifting in her chair, her smile frozen in place as she silently prayed that her son didn't cross any invisible line.

But Brennan wasn't inappropriate. On the contrary, he was brilliant.

He spoke from the heart without a script, blending humor, gratitude, and wisdom in a way that felt completely natural. Somehow, in the middle of the jokes, he'd brought in reflections about friendship, growth, and perseverance. He even tossed in a few sentimental notes about his parents and teachers, earning a soft "aww" from the crowd.

Fifteen minutes in, he was still going strong. Tiffany leaned in, whispering through clenched teeth, "Is he… still going?!"

Larry didn't answer. He just shook his head, somewhere between dazed and proud.

Finally, after just shy of twenty minutes, Brennan wrapped it up. His final words were a clever callback to one of his opening jokes—perfect timing. He dropped the mic (figuratively) and walked off stage to thunderous applause. The crowd erupted. Even some of the staff members were on their feet, clapping and laughing.

Brennan had absolutely killed it.

And then... came the final speaker.

A sweet, quiet girl stepped up to the podium, holding a carefully folded paper in both hands. Tiffany and Larry exchanged a glance that said it all: Bless her heart.

How do you follow that?

You don't.

But she gave her speech with grace, and the audience respectfully applauded.

As they walked out after the ceremony, parents came up to Larry and Tiffany, offering congratulations—not just for Brennan's academic success, but for raising a kid who could command a stage like a seasoned performer. One mom said, "He should run for mayor someday." Another whispered, "He should be doing stand-up."

Tiffany just smiled, finally releasing that breath she'd been holding for twenty minutes.

Later that night, over dinner, Larry raised a glass.

"To Brennan," he said, "for being the only eighth grader in history to give a TED Talk at continuation."

The family laughed.

And in that moment, surrounded by pride, joy, and just the right amount of embarrassment, they knew Brennan's future—whatever it held—was going to be anything but ordinary.

In 2020, Holly and Steve had done something bold and beautiful—they built a vacation home in Arizona, a sun-washed oasis that looked like it had leapt straight from the pages of a luxury travel magazine. The house was stunning in every possible way: wide, open spaces flooded with natural light, a gourmet kitchen made for gathering, and a backyard that felt more like a private resort than a residential patio. A sparkling pool stretched out in the center, complete with a built-in swim-up bar, tall palms swaying overhead, and the kind of sunsets that stopped conversations mid-sentence. It was the kind of place that whispered, "You've arrived."

At first, they insisted it was just a vacation home—somewhere for quick getaways, warm winters, and a little golf therapy when the Colorado cold became too much. It was never meant to replace home. Not then.

But by spring of 2023, the tides had shifted in ways no one could ignore.

Dylan, their youngest, was graduating high school—a milestone that always tugs on a parent's heart—but she wasn't just moving out; she was heading to the University of Arizona. And that changed everything. Holly and Steve looked at each other and, without needing to say much at all, they knew it was time. It wasn't just about a house anymore. It was about being close to their little girl, about leaning into this new chapter of life, about choosing sunshine and simplicity.

They decided to sell their beautiful Castle Rock home—the home that had been filled with laughter, sleepovers, birthdays, and late-night talks on the patio. The home that had been just minutes away from Larry and Tiffany for the past eight years. A place that had witnessed so much life, so many milestones. That chapter was closing.

And they weren't the only ones flipping the page.

FOREVER TIFFANY

Larry's parents, Diana and Larry Sr., were next to make the call. A coaching opportunity had opened up for Larry Sr. in Arizona, and with half of their family heading south, the decision was clear. They were going too.

They waited for Dylan's graduation to wrap up, let the open house celebrations wind down, and then—just like that—they packed up a lifetime of memories and drove toward the desert, toward a brand-new beginning.

For Larry and Tiffany, it was a moment of deep, aching stillness. The kind of goodbye that doesn't come with a party or a cake or a toast. It was quieter. Heavier. More personal.

Tiffany stood in the middle of her kitchen one afternoon, looking out the window toward the neighborhood that now felt just a little emptier. She was losing more than just a sister-in-law. More than a best friend. She was losing her person. Holly wasn't just the friend who had known her since childhood. She wasn't just her ride-or-die. She was the keeper of secrets, the one who could finish her sentences, the one who had held her hand through every stage of life. And now she was going to be hundreds of miles away.

But it didn't stop there.

Tiffany was also losing Diana—her second mom, her steady place to land. Diana had been there through everything. From the first time Tiffany ever met Larry, through births, heartbreaks, soccer games, school concerts, and the quiet, everyday moments that make up a life. She had become more than a mother-in-law—she was an anchor. A mentor. A soft voice of wisdom who always seemed to know what to say without ever saying too much.

And now?

No more Wednesday trivia nights at The Hideaway, where the fun happened, and the laughter was as loud as the jukebox. No more last-minute lunches at The Office, sliding into their usual booth like they owned the place. No more Sunday dinners where they all crowded into the kitchen, stories overlapping, kids running up and down the stairs, Diana sneaking extra helpings onto everyone's plates.

Everything was shifting.

The holidays were going to feel different. The town was going to feel different. Life… was already different.

For Larry, the weight of the change came crashing in during a quiet drive one evening. He and Tiffany had lived near Holly and Steve since 2005. That was nearly two decades of proximity. Of impromptu plans and late-night text threads and "you home? We're stopping by." They'd grown up together as adults—watched each other's kids become teenagers, become drivers, become themselves. They had taken that first road trip to Indianapolis long before there was ever a them. Before Larry and Tiffany had even fallen in love, Holly and Steve had already been part of the story. It was impossible to imagine a version of life without them just a few minutes away.

But now, that part of the story was ending.

They were all moving forward—Holly and Steve to Arizona, Diana and Larry Sr. to a new chapter of purpose and sunshine. It was beautiful in its own way, but painful too.

And while the goodbye felt monumental, what none of them could possibly know—what Tiffany certainly didn't know—was that this was just the beginning.

Because the hardest part of the year hadn't come yet.

In the months ahead, their world would tilt. And Tiffany… she would need her people more than ever before.

But for now, there were boxes to pack. There were hugs to give. And there were tears Tiffany wouldn't let herself cry.

Not yet.

FOREVER TIFFANY

She hugged Holly a little tighter that last day. Laughed a little louder at one more trivia night. Savored one more shared plate of nachos at The Office.

By mid-2023, Holly had reached a place in life that many only dreamed of. She had built a beautiful home, raised a close-knit, loving family, and was now leading an impressive career that had taken her to the highest levels of corporate success. Earlier in the year, she had received the call—an offer to become the CEO of a tech company based on the East Coast. She had broken through the proverbial glass ceiling, not just stepping into the room but owning it, commanding it with grace and power.

She was, without a doubt, a force.

But Holly knew leadership wasn't a solo act. She needed someone by her side—someone brilliant, loyal, strategic, and grounded. She needed someone who had walked the path with her, who knew how to balance ambition with empathy. She needed Tiffany.

The calls started not long after Holly had settled into her new role. Late-night conversations, mid-day check-ins, texts that read, "Just think about it…" and "We'd make a hell of a team." At first, Tiffany smiled and brushed them off, but the wheels were already turning. Holly wasn't offering a job—she was offering a chance to build something extraordinary together.

But before any decisions could be made, Tiffany shifted her focus to something more immediate: a family trip back to Indiana.

This time, Larry went along. The summer air was heavy with nostalgia even before they touched down. It had become something of a tradition now—these warm-weather pilgrimages back to the Midwest, back to where it all began. Vicki welcomed them into her home once again, and Amanda joined too, bringing her boys and her energy and her laugh that always filled the room.

Some of the family stayed at Scott and Sandy's lakefront property—a peaceful slice of Indiana paradise where the sun danced on the water each morning and the sound of laughter drifted over the dock until well after sunset. The days were filled with easy joy. They wandered through local festivals, picked up funnel cakes and kettle corn, and strolled streets lined with handmade crafts and vintage booths. Tiffany took Landon and the kids to all her favorite childhood haunts—Dairy Dip for upside-down banana splits, JJ's Pizza Shack for greasy slices loaded with cheese, and Ma Johnson's for fried cod and jumbo shrimp, still wrapped in white butcher paper and just as delicious as ever.

The pace of life was different here—slower, gentler. But the undercurrent of change was unmistakable.

Patrick had landed his first "real job," a business analyst position that came with a title, a salary, and a seat at the grown-up table. He was already back in Colorado, stepping into his career with purpose and maturity that made both Larry and Tiffany beam with pride. Rylee, too, was on the brink of her next chapter—preparing to leave for Utah State and all the independence that came with it. It was clear now: their kids weren't kids anymore. Life was moving. Fast.

One evening, as the golden light of sunset spilled across Vicki's back patio, the family gathered outside around a long table, drinks in hand, conversation flowing as easily as the warm summer breeze. Vicki's neighbor, Nikola, joined them—a woman in her late forties with a magnetic smile and a quiet strength that made an impression from the moment she sat down.

But behind her smile, there was pain.

Nikola was battling cancer—an aggressive, unrelenting kind. She was single, living in a beautiful home along the water with a boat built for Lake Michigan's unpredictable waves. Her life, once vibrant and full of promise, now felt quieter, lonelier. The fatigue showed in her eyes, even as she tried to mask it with warmth and good humor.

Larry and Tiffany could feel it. They recognized the invisible weight she carried—the shadow that hung over every sentence, every

FOREVER TIFFANY

moment. And then, in the stillness of that summer evening, Larry began to share his story. Not to preach. Not to inspire. Just to connect. He spoke of the diagnosis, of the fear, of the surgeries, and the slow climb back to life. Of faith. Of grace. Of how he never expected to be here, yet here he was.

Nikola listened quietly, her eyes brimming with something that wasn't quite tears but carried all the emotion of them. For just a few minutes, the darkness receded. For just a while, she didn't feel so alone.

That night, bathed in the warm glow of string lights, surrounded by clinking glasses, the scent of lake water in the air, and the sound of laughter echoing off the shoreline, felt like something sacred. A pause. A breath. A memory absorbed into the soul.

Because even though they didn't know it then, cancer was not finished with their story. It was waiting, just ahead, ready to step into their lives again. But on that night, in that place, there was only gratitude. There was only family.

There were bare feet in the sand, fireflies dancing in the distance, and the quiet comfort of being together.

And for Tiffany, who had been pouring herself into everyone else for so long, it was a rare gift—those summer nights on the water's edge. A moment of peace before the storm. A memory that would shine like a lighthouse when everything around her turned dark.

****

August arrived in the blink of an eye, ushering in another chapter of change for the family. The sun still hung high in the Colorado sky, but there was a shift in the air—one that came with suitcases, Target runs, and the bittersweet buzz of college move-in season. Tiffany and Larry had done this before, but this time, it felt different.

They rented a black Ford Expedition, spacious enough to carry everything Rylee needed to start her sophomore year in style. Rylee followed behind in her brand new Jaguar F-Pace, a sleek and elegant machine that reflected just how far she had come—and how much of her mother's influence now lived inside her.

Tiffany rode with Rylee, music playing softly, the two of them singing along to old road trip favorites, laughing, and sharing that rare magic that only mothers and daughters can conjure. Larry drove solo, watching the mountains roll by through the windshield, his thoughts drifting like the clouds above them. The trip to Logan, Utah, was beautiful—miles of open road framed by rolling hills and a vast sky. Larry couldn't help but feel the weight pressing gently on his chest.

This was no longer just a drive to drop off his little girl at college.

She wasn't a Mountain Lion anymore. That chapter had closed. She had traded her view of Pikes Peak for the Cache Valley, her small dorm for a new space inside Millennial Towers. She was now an Aggie, ready to start fresh at Utah State University.

And this time, it felt real.

They arrived in Logan and pulled into the lot outside Millennial Towers, a modern student living community tucked into the scenic Utah hills. Tiffany had, of course, already arranged everything. Rylee wouldn't just be moving into a college apartment—she was moving into her space. A space that Tiffany had mentally mapped out weeks before. Rylee's room was the largest in the apartment, complete with a king-sized bed dressed in plush white bedding and layers of throw pillows in soft, soothing colors. The bathroom featured double sinks just for her, and every drawer and cabinet was already imagined with purpose and care.

Tiffany got to work, unboxing, folding, fluffing, arranging. She placed dream catchers above the bed and added twinkling lights near the windows. She organized drawers, set up the mini coffee station, and styled the bookshelf with photos, quotes, and candles. Larry watched from a distance, amused, proud, and just a little in awe.

FOREVER TIFFANY

He smiled to himself, thinking about how what he once called "Tiffany Style" had now become "Rylee Style," too. The attention to detail. The deep care. The joy of making something beautiful. Rylee had grown up watching her mom pour love into the little things, into every room, every birthday, every lunch packed just right. And now, here she was—her own version of that same spirit.

A mini Tiffany, without a question.

By the time the last box was unpacked, the room was magazine-worthy, glowing with comfort and personal charm. Rylee stood in the center, hands on her hips, soaking it all in. Tiffany wrapped an arm around her and smiled.

"You ready?" she asked gently.

Rylee nodded. "Yeah. I think I am."

They went out for dinner that evening, the three of them sharing plates, laughter, and the quiet knowing that something had shifted. Rylee wasn't just going to school—she was stepping fully into her next chapter. There would be homesickness, there would be new friendships, and there would be long nights of studying and self-discovery. But more than anything, there would be growth.

And as they said their goodbyes the next morning, Tiffany hugged her daughter just a little tighter, holding on for one last second before letting go. Larry placed a hand on Rylee's shoulder and gave her that steady, proud smile she had always relied on.

The road home would feel a little longer this time.

But their hearts were full.

Their daughter was ready.

And the world—well, the world better get ready for Rylee.

After returning home from moving Rylee into her new apartment, Tiffany did what Holly had been waiting for her to do all along—she picked up the phone and called.

"I'm in," she said.

Holly didn't even need to ask what she meant. She smiled, calm and unsurprised, as if the universe had finally corrected itself. "I knew you would be," she said with a soft laugh. And of course she did. Holly had always known Tiffany better than anyone—had known how her mind worked, how her heart processed things, how even when she said "let me think about it," she already knew the answer deep down.

This wasn't just a job offer. It was the offer—an opportunity tailor-made for Tiffany. It came with a high-level position at a company poised for massive success. It came with ownership shares and real equity, meaning that if the company sold or went public, Tiffany would have a payday that would mark a new chapter entirely. But more than the financial upside, it was the challenge. The excitement. The thrill of building something.

And Holly knew… Tiffany was always meant to lead.

To Larry, watching it all disclose was like watching someone you love step fully into their power. He had always known who she was. From the moment they met, Tiffany had never done anything halfway. She was a dreamer and a doer. A planner and a force of nature. And while her dream job for many years had been the most sacred and important one—full-time mother—Larry was in awe of the way she had evolved. She had once lovingly traded financial gain and professional advancement for the irreplaceable role of being home with Patrick, Rylee, and Brennan. She had sacrificed without ever calling it that. She had been there for every scraped knee, every school project, every late-night talk, and every early morning drop-off.

And now… now she was something else entirely.

Still that mom—still the glue, the heart of the home—but also a leader in the tech world, guiding teams, mentoring others, helping shape a company's direction while juggling meetings, strategies, growth plans, and deadlines.

FOREVER TIFFANY

Larry often found himself just... staring. In wonder. How could someone do it all and make it all look so effortless?

They were both working from home now—an unspoken gift of the times. Larry's office was tucked just off the main level of the house, a warm space where his routine and rhythms played out in quiet confidence. Directly above him, at the top of the stairs, sat Tiffany's office. Same square footage. Same light streaming in through tall windows that overlooked the greenbelt behind their home. On good-weather days, they both worked with the windows cracked open, Colorado breezes drifting in, and the sound of birdsong floating between them.

Every now and then, Larry would lean back in his chair, peer out the window, and call up toward the sky, "Hey! Lunch date?"

It was their little thing.

Sometimes she'd laugh and call back, "Give me five minutes." Other times, she'd appear at the top of the stairs like a vision, ready for their midday escape to The Office or wherever the day took them.

They weren't just working. They were living together. In rhythm. In sync. A marriage built on twenty-plus years of love, growth, sacrifice, joy, and an unshakable friendship that kept them tied through all of life's seasons.

There was harmony in their days. Music in the way their lives blended—one floor above the other, one shared purpose at a time.

And while they didn't know it then, this chapter—the one filled with laughter, afternoon lunches, and open windows—would become one they would hold onto tightly in the months to come. Because sometimes, life gives you a little stretch of magic... before it changes everything.

Just one month into her new role, Tiffany was already shining.

She had found her rhythm quickly, balancing high-stakes meetings, strategic planning sessions, and mentoring her team with the grace and precision only she could deliver. She was thriving—no question about it—and everyone around her could see it. There was a new energy in her, a radiance that came not from external success, but from the deep, inner knowing that she was exactly where she was meant to be.

So, when Stacy suggested a girls' day—lunch, the mall, a little retail therapy—Tiffany didn't hesitate. It felt like the perfect reward for her hectic first few weeks. They laughed their way through lunch, caught up like sisters, wandered store to store like they used to in their early twenties. But the day had a Tiffany-style twist, and it was always more than just window shopping.

Because when Tiffany was really happy, she glowed in ways that made everything feel possible.

And on this day, she was ready to finally give herself something she had dreamed about for years.

After lunch, they pulled into the dealership. She hadn't made an appointment. She didn't call ahead. She just knew. There, on the lot, gleaming in the afternoon sun, was the one—a pristine white Range Rover, black panoramic roof, buttery tan leather interior that looked like it belonged on the pages of a luxury lifestyle magazine. Every feature imaginable. It was perfect.

Tiffany didn't hesitate.

She slid into the driver's seat, adjusted the mirror, ran her hand across the soft-stitched leather, and took it for a quick spin around the block. Like her, the ride was smooth, quiet, and self-assured.

Before she even got back to the lot, she was on the phone.

"Hey babe," she said sweetly. "I found something..."

Larry had heard that tone before. It was the "I just found something that will bring me joy" tone. It was the "I know you're going to say yes because you love to see me light up" tone.

And he did.

He didn't ask about the price. He didn't ask if it was the right time. He didn't need to.

Because Tiffany had earned this—not just through her new role or the long hours she was putting in, but through years of selfless love, untiring care, and the quiet sacrifices that had built the beautiful life they now breathed.

So, when she asked, "Should I do it?" all he said was, "Go get it, angel."

Moments later, she was sliding behind the wheel of her dream car—not just another Range Rover, but *the* Range Rover. The one she had envisioned for years. It was the finishing touch on a chapter of her life that had finally arrived.

Back at home, Larry stood in the driveway, watching her pull up with that wide, contagious Tiffany smile that made his heart race just like it had on their very first date.

She stepped out, sunglasses on, a confident glow about her as the afternoon sun bounced off the bright white paint of the car.

He didn't say a word.

He just walked over, wrapped his arms around her, and whispered, "God, I love seeing you happy."

Because for Larry, that was everything.

Her joy was his joy. Her smile—the one that made the whole world feel lighter—was his greatest reward.

And on that day, as she climbed into her dream car with Stacy riding shotgun and the sound of her laughter echoing through the neighborhood, Larry knew what he had always known: He was the luckiest man in the world.

September 22nd, 2023.

The sun had just begun to climb over the horizon as Larry and Tiffany boarded their flight to Salt Lake City, a crispness in the early fall air and a quiet excitement between them. It wasn't just another weekend getaway—it was Parents Weekend at Utah State University, and they were headed to Logan to spend time with their daughter, Rylee.

The flight was smooth, the sky stretched wide and cloudless as they descended into Utah. Once they landed, they made their way to the National Rental Car counter, where luck had a bit of fun in store. Tiffany, smiling like a kid on Christmas morning, gave Larry a playful nudge as the attendant handed over the keys to a sporty white Ford Mustang. "We're going to do this trip in style," she laughed, tossing her bag into the backseat.

The Mustang hugged the mountain roads with ease as they drove north, sunlight pouring through the windshield, painting the rolling hills and golden foliage in warm tones. The ninety-minute drive was breathtaking—miles of open landscape, towering peaks in the distance, and the kind of conversation between husband and wife that only seems to happen on long drives: a little reflection, a lot of laughter, and a few quiet pauses to simply be.

By the time they arrived on campus, the energy in Logan was intense—football weekend buzzed in the air, families filled the sidewalks, and the entire town seemed wrapped in the kind of fall magic that only college towns seem to know. They met up with Rylee at a softball game. She waved from the stands with her signature glow—her long hair tied back, eyes lit with joy. She had quickly formed a close bond with Kya, a sophomore on the women's softball team, and the two had become inseparable.

Watching Rylee cheer her friend on, hugging them and chatting with ease, both Larry and Tiffany felt a quiet pride that settled deep in their bones. Their girl wasn't just surviving in her new chapter—she was thriving. She had found her place.

FOREVER TIFFANY

That evening, they took her to dinner in town. The three of them sat close in a cozy booth at a local favorite spot—laughing, swapping stories, catching up on everything from classes to new friends to apartment mishaps. Tiffany reached across the table to brush Rylee's hair behind her ear and smiled. That smile. The one that only a mother who knows she's done her job right can wear.

Saturday came early, the Utah sun climbing over the Wasatch Range as they grabbed coffee and wandered the beautiful, sprawling campus. Tiffany and Rylee ducked in and out of shops while Larry, carrying bags and nodding politely, mostly wondered when lunch would happen. But he didn't complain. Watching the two of them together—laughing in dressing rooms, swapping stories over lattes—was worth every moment.

That night, the town pulsed with anticipation. The Utah State Aggies were set to take on James Madison University at Merlin Olsen Field. The stadium lights beamed into the night sky like spotlights announcing something grand, something unforgettable.

Larry and Tiffany found their seats, nestled in the heart of the parent section. The student section pulsed with energy across the field, and that's when they saw her.

Rylee.

Front and center. On her feet. Leading the chant like she was born to do it.

"Nothing like a Scotsman…"

Her voice rang out, her hands raised in the air, and her energy was electric. She wasn't just part of the crowd—she was leading it. Larry wrapped his arm around Tiffany, who was watching in silence, eyes shimmering, heart filled with admiration and pride.

She smiled, but there was a trace of something else, too—pride, yes, but also the quiet ache of a mother whose little girl wasn't so little anymore. Tiffany leaned into Larry, and he kissed her forehead.

"She's gonna be just fine," he whispered.

"I know," Tiffany replied softly. "But what would I do without her?"

Sunday came far too quickly. They met Kya and her mom for breakfast at a local gem tucked into the near downtown. The line wrapped around the corner—longer than Texas, Larry joked—but the food was worth every second of the wait. Pancakes stacked like mountains, omelets the size of footballs, and laughter that never once left the table.

They talked about everything, about the girls' future plans, about how Kya and Rylee had hit it off so quickly, and about how proud they all were to watch their daughters stepping confidently into the world.

As the weekend came to a close, hugs were exchanged, goodbyes said, and tears held tightly behind grateful smiles. Driving back to the airport, Tiffany stared out the window at the winding roads, the campus fading behind them.

"She's really doing it," she said.

Larry nodded. "Yeah. And so are we."

It had been a weekend of joy, of reflection, of watching the next chapter reveal. But what they didn't know then—what neither of them could have predicted—was that this weekend would be one of the final moments of life as they knew it.

But for now, it was simply a perfect memory—imprinted into their hearts, sealed by laughter, lit by stadium lights, and held together by the kind of love that only a parent can understand.

They returned home from Logan with that familiar hope that life might settle back into rhythm again—the kind of rhythm that feels comforting, like a favorite song on a lazy Sunday afternoon. The bags were unpacked, the weekend memories still warm in their hearts, and the cool Colorado air hinted at the holidays soon to come. But what they didn't realize—what no one ever does in these moments—is that the ground beneath them had already begun to shift. Subtle at first. Almost imperceptible. But change, true and lasting change, had already set its course.

****

Patrick, newly graduated and standing on the edge of adulthood, was starting to feel unsettled. He had taken a job in his field, a logical first step for an economics major with a sharp mind and a polished résumé, but something was off. He would sit at his desk, go through the motions, but his heart wasn't with it. Each passing day felt heavier than the last. It wasn't fear—it was intuition. A quiet, persistent whisper inside him was telling him that this wasn't it. That his passion, his purpose, was waiting for him somewhere else.

He started quietly looking, sending out résumés, taking interviews, and hoping—really hoping—that he would find his place. Larry and Tiffany watched closely, supporting him the way parents do when their children are discovering their path. They were proud of his ambition, but quietly pained to see them away..

Meanwhile, across town, another shift was happening. For months now, Stacy had been dreaming out loud about the possibility of something more—more freedom, more flexibility, more financial security. She'd say it casually over coffee or mention it in passing while walking the aisles of Target with Tiffany, but the longing was real. She wanted to work from home. She wanted to be more present, to feel more in control of her time, of her life.

And of course, she said it to the one person who could actually make that happen.

Her best friend.

Tiffany.

It didn't take long.

The stars aligned—just like they always seemed to when Tiffany was involved—and before anyone could blink, Stacy was officially part of the company. She joined the same team where Tiffany was already booming, alongside Holly, creating a circle of trust and talent that was as rare as it was beautiful. There was excitement, of course, but also nerves. The kind that comes with stepping into something new, something unknown.

Stacy found herself in the very position Tiffany had been in years earlier—stepping into a fast-paced world of tech and leadership, guided not just by a job description, but a best friend who believed in her. Tiffany became her mentor, her coach, her biggest fan. And Brian? Brian was beaming. His wife was flourishing. His daughters, Piper and Mackenzi, looked at their mom with admiration in their eyes. She was setting an example—of strength, of reinvention, of not being afraid to start something new.

But as one part of life fell into place, another began to fall apart.

It happened in the simplest, most unassuming of ways—on an otherwise ordinary morning.

Larry and Tiffany had always shared the mornings. It was part of their rhythm. Their routine. She would soak in her oversized tub, steam curling up the windows, and he would step into the adjacent shower, the glass walls between them making it feel like one warm, intimate space. It was during these quiet early hours that they would talk about their day, share ideas, laugh at something silly, or sometimes say nothing at all and just relish being near each other.

Sometimes, when the timing felt right—and it often did—Tiffany would step into the shower with Larry, wrapping her arms around him, bringing warmth and closeness that few couples ever hold onto through the years. It was sacred, it was playful, it was them.

But that day—this day—was different.

Tiffany was perched on the edge of the tub, her wet hair swept over one shoulder, and she reached for her robe before pausing. She looked down at her inner forearm, just near the elbow crease.

"Huh," she said casually. "Looks like I got bitten by something last night."

Larry, half-lathered and peering through the fogged glass, leaned out slightly to get a better look.

It was small. About the size of a nail head. Deep maroon with a reddish hue at the edges.

"Yeah," he said. "Looks like a spider bite or something. Weird."

Tiffany shrugged. "It doesn't hurt. Just kind of... there."

And that was it.

Just a tiny red dot. A blemish no bigger than a freckle. Easily dismissed, easily forgotten.

But they would remember it.

They would remember exactly where it was. What it looked like. The way it didn't seem like anything... at first.

Because that was the moment. The moment the story began to change.

That small red dot—one that didn't hurt, didn't itch, didn't do anything at all—was the start of something that would shake the very earth beneath their feet.

It would test their faith, their strength, their love.

They didn't know it yet. Couldn't possibly imagine.

But everything they thought they understood about life, about time, about what truly mattered—was about to be rewritten.

Forever.

The year was drawing to a close, the days growing shorter as the glow of Christmas lights began to dance on rooftops across Castle Rock. It was the time of year Tiffany loved most—when the world felt a little softer, a little kinder, wrapped in warm sweaters and peppermint-scented air. The tree was up, the stockings were hung, and the familiar nutcrackers had once again claimed their usual posts throughout the house, each one a quiet guardian of the holiday magic Tiffany had curated so beautifully over the years.

The kids were blossoming. Brennan, now officially a teenager, had made a big decision—he was going to play high school lacrosse. He wanted to follow in Landon's footsteps, who had become more than just Rylee's boyfriend over the last year—he was family. Landon was flourishing as well, playing lacrosse at Canisius University in Buffalo, New York. His commitment and drive were inspiring, especially to Brennan, who looked up to him with wide eyes and quiet admiration.

Patrick, on the other hand, had recently closed one chapter and was eagerly seeking his next. His first job after college hadn't quite stirred the passion he was hoping for. He knew there had to be more—something that would make him feel alive when he opened his laptop each morning. He had begun interviewing with a company in the energy sector down in Houston, and for the first time in a long while, he felt hopeful. Confident. Maybe this was the start of something big.

Rylee had settled comfortably into life at Utah State. She was doing well, and her calls home were often jam-packed with laughter and stories of campus life, football games, and deep conversations with new friends. Tiffany smiled every time she heard her daughter's voice. Her baby girl was growing.

And through it all, Tiffany herself was pouring everything into her new role, guiding her company forward with the same elegance and forte she had always carried—quiet, modest, but undeniably powerful.

But underneath the surface, something was stirring.

****

It had started weeks earlier, right after they'd returned from Utah. The tiny red mark on the inside of Tiffany's right forearm—nothing dramatic, just a small dot. They both brushed it off at first. Larry thought it looked like a spider bite. Tiffany barely noticed it, much consumed with work, family, and the holiday rush.

Over the next few weeks, it began to change. It darkened. It thickened. And eventually, it morphed into something that resembled more of a skin tag. Still, Tiffany shrugged it off, more annoyed than alarmed. She wasn't one for doctors. Never had been. Her threshold for pain, for discomfort, was notoriously high—perhaps too high. She told Larry, again and again, "I'll go in after the holidays. Just let me get through this season."

Looking at the slight concern on Larry's face, "First of the year," she promised.

Larry didn't press—he knew Tiffany. Once she made a promise, she would follow through. But still, something inside him tugged, quietly unsettled.

Then, just a few days after Rylee returned home for winter break, everything changed.

The house was full again, just the way Tiffany loved it. The sounds of laughter and footsteps, the rustling of wrapping paper, and the smell of cookies in the oven—it all felt flawless. For a moment, everything seemed right.

Until it wasn't.

It was early one morning, their usual routine just beginning. Larry had stepped into his office for a moment, the soft hum of holiday music coming from the speaker in their bedroom. Tiffany was a few steps behind, moving slower than usual.

Then came the call.

"Larry!" she yelled—his name not spoken, but cried out in a voice he hadn't heard before. A voice that cut through the still morning air like glass.

He dropped everything and rushed into the bathroom.

LARRY BLAKE

And there she was—standing in front of the bathroom mirror, her shirt off, her eyes wide and swimming with tears. Her hand was raised to her side, and Larry could see the tremble in her fingers.

"I found a lump," she said, her voice barely holding together.

"In your breast?" he asked, already feeling his chest tighten.

She shook her head.

"No... look."

Her hand raised, revealing the area under her right arm.

Larry's heart almost stopped.

There, where smooth skin had once been, was a large, hard mass—bigger than an orange, not quite the size of a softball. It had come out of nowhere. It wasn't there yesterday. It hadn't even hinted at its existence. But now, it sat ominously beneath the skin, angry and unnatural.

He stepped forward, slowly, carefully, as though even breathing too loudly might make the moment worse. Tiffany's eyes locked on his. They were full of fear—raw, unfiltered fear.

"I'm sure it's nothing," she whispered. "I'll get it looked at."

But even as she said it, they both knew.

This wasn't nothing.

This wasn't just a spider bite, or a swollen lymph node, or some strange allergic reaction.

This was something. Something big.

Larry wrapped his arms around her, burying his face in her neck, trying to will back time to undo whatever this was before it took hold. But he couldn't. All he could do was hold her. Steady her.

Neither of them said a word, but both felt it.

The promise of a peaceful holiday had vanished. And the quiet hope that the new year would bring rest and renewal had been replaced with an unspoken, haunting question.

What now?

And so, on that cold December morning, with the tree glowing in the living room and the stockings still hung with care. Slowly but surely, their world started to tilt.

They would look back on that moment–the day everything began to change.

CHAPTER 22.
Hope in Her Eyes

The day after Tiffany discovered the lump, Larry transformed into a man on a mission.

There was no waiting. No hesitation. No room for "let's see how this plays out." Not when it came to her. Not when it came to the woman who was the center of his world.

He picked up the phone and called the University of Colorado Anschutz Medical Campus—one of the top medical facilities in the country. He demanded urgency. This couldn't wait. But the voice on the other end of the line, calm and clinical, shattered his hope with one word.

"June."

"June?" Larry barked back into the phone, disbelief converting into fury. "That's six months from now! She found a mass the size of a baseball. June won't work."

His voice echoed through the house, bouncing off the walls like a warning siren. Tiffany heard it from the other room but didn't flinch. She knew Larry was doing what he always did—fighting for her.

When Anschutz failed them, Larry pivoted. He called their family physician, refusing to take no for an answer. He explained everything—every detail, every symptom—and finally, finally, they got a bite. There was an opening in early February. It wasn't immediate, but it was something.

He booked it.

Still, it wasn't enough. Larry couldn't sit still. He continued dialing every top-tier cancer facility within driving distance, trying to bypass the bureaucracy, hoping someone would hear the desperation in his voice and understand this wasn't just about an appointment—it was about time. And every day they waited felt like a risk too great to take.

And yet, through it all—through the calls, the panic, the waiting—Tiffany never once let the fear take center stage. Her eyes never went hopeless.

She didn't retreat. She didn't curl into bed or dwell on the "what ifs." No, not Tiffany. She embraced the season with the same joyful energy she always did. With Christmas just around the corner, she doubled down on creating joy, not just for her family, but for everyone around her.

Friends came and went from their homes in the days leading up to the holiday, arms full of gifts, laughter satisfying the halls. And there was Tiffany—effortlessly beautiful in her winter sweaters, smiling with her usual glow, offering cookies and cocktails, and hosting as if nothing was wrong. No one would have guessed the weight she carried beneath that warm exterior. No one would have seen the silent storm that was taking shape just beneath her skin.

She made it look easy. Graceful. Seamless.

But then, that's who Tiffany was.

Even as her mind contested with unanswered questions, even as her body whispered its warning signs, she never let anyone see her break. Not Larry. Not the kids. Not even her closest friends.

She carried it the way she carried everything in life—with elegance, with fire, and with the fierce determination to protect the people she loved from fear.

And that Christmas, though filled with sparkle and tradition, held a different kind of feel. It was the kind that forms when love stands strong in the face of uncertainty. When a woman, facing the unknown, chooses to rise anyway.

Larry watched her move through the season with amazement. She wrapped gifts like everything was normal. She laughed at jokes, posed for pictures, and filled the house with music and light.

But he knew.

He knew what lay under her soft sweater and gentle smile. He knew what she didn't say out loud. And every time he looked at her, really looked, he felt heartbreak and overwhelming love.

Because Tiffany wasn't pretending; she was protecting.

And she was doing it the only way she knew how—by loving bigger, brighter, louder.

As snow dusted the rooftops and the world paused to celebrate, Larry clung to every second, memorizing the shape of her laugh, the curve of her smile, the warmth of her hand in his.

Because deep down, he knew the fight hadn't even begun yet.

****

February 10th, 2024, arrived with the kind of chill that sunk deep into the bones—a sharp Midwestern winter day that greeted Tiffany and Rylee the moment they stepped off the plane in Chicago. The air was brittle, the sky grey, and snow clung to the edges of the runway like lace. But inside that terminal, warmth emitted—not just from the heating vents above, but from the joy of being together, mother and daughter, on another one of their signature adventures.

Their plan was simple: spend a weekend in Chicago visiting family, then head north to Ann Arbor, Michigan, to watch Canisius College take on the University of Michigan in a highly anticipated lacrosse match. The Wolverines, ranked 13th in the country, were a powerhouse. But for Tiffany and Rylee, it wasn't about rankings. It was about him—Landon. It was his first collegiate game, and they weren't going to miss it.

FOREVER TIFFANY

Bundled in layers, scarves wrapped high and coats zipped tight, the two made their way into the massive stadium. The air was freezing, their breath visible with every cheer, but the cold didn't dull their spirits. They clapped, they shouted, they huddled together, and watched with pride as Landon sprinted onto the field in his Canisius gold and navy. Even though the game ended in a crushing 21-5 defeat, it didn't matter to Rylee. Her eyes followed Landon's every move like he was the star of the show. And Tiffany, always watching her daughter first, saw it in her eyes—the longing, the pride, the love.

Tiffany didn't need to hear the words to know what Rylee was feeling. She felt it, too. She knew what it meant to love someone deeply and miss them even more deeply. So she did what she always did when love was involved—she acted. Before they'd even boarded their return flight, Tiffany had pulled out her phone, opened her travel app, and started booking flights. Buffalo wasn't exactly down the street, but that didn't matter. If her daughter needed to be there for someone she loved, Tiffany would make it happen. She arranged several trips for Rylee to fly east and catch Landon's games, because that's what love looked like in their family. It wasn't about grand gestures or perfect words. It was about *showing up*.

What Tiffany didn't realize at the time was that her quiet, generous decision—one rooted in compassion—would soon lead to a moment that would alter their family's destiny forever.

When Tiffany returned from Chicago, the calendar turned its page toward something familiar, something cherished—Estes Park. It was time once again for their annual mountain retreat, the trip that marked both Tiffany and Larry's wedding anniversary and Brian's birthday. It had become a tradition, a sacred pause in their busy lives—a weekend to escape, to reconnect, and to celebrate the simple blessing of friendship.

Larry, the planner of the group, had reserved a cozy townhome nestled just off the main strip in downtown Estes Park. It wasn't grand or flashy, but it was perfect—three bedrooms, warm wood finishes, a stone fireplace that sparkled with life, and windows that presented a gentle view of the snowy rooftops and distant mountain peaks. It was intimate, just enough room for the six of them: Larry and Tiffany, Brian and Stacy, Karl and Jessica.

Unlike the year before, when the weather had been mild and the skies clear, this time the roads leading up the mountain were slick with ice and fresh snow. The sky hung low with thick gray clouds, and flakes drifted down like whispers. Still, no one complained. They knew the warmth that waited at the top, not just inside the townhome, but in the laughter, the memories, and the love that always came overflowing with this weekend.

Tiffany was quieter this time. She tried her best not to let it show—the discomfort in her arm, the swirl of unknowns that clouded her thoughts. But Larry saw. He saw it in the way she moved, the way her hand subtly rubbed the area beneath her sleeve when she thought no one was looking. He caught her drifting off in thought now and then, her eyes not focused on the conversation but somewhere far away, somewhere none of them would want to be.

Still, she was present. She made herself be. Tiffany had always known how to set aside her own pain for the sake of everyone's joy, and she did it again this weekend. She smiled, she laughed, and she leaned into the little moments like they were lifelines because, in a way, they were.

Friday night was spent in the way it always did—familiar and effortless. The snow continued to fall softly outside as the six of them circled around the dining table, wine glasses and whiskey tumblers in hand. They played games, swapped stories that had been told a dozen times before, but still made them laugh, and relished in the comfort of each other's company.

There was something about that table, about those six chairs and those six hearts. It wasn't just friendship. It was much more. They had become family—true family, the kind that doesn't come from blood, but from time and truth and showing up for one another when it really

FOREVER TIFFANY

matters. In a world that so often delivers counterfeit connections, they had found the real thing.

And what they had was rare.

On Saturday morning, Brian and Karl took their usual post at the stove, humming along to a playlist of old favorites as the smell of sizzling bacon and fresh coffee filled the air. Karl whisked eggs like a pro while Brian poured mimosas and buttered toast. It wasn't a fancy breakfast—it never was—but it was perfect in every way that mattered.

Tiffany wandered in wearing her softest sweater, hair loosely pulled back, and a sleepy smile on her face. She stole a piece of bacon from the pan before Larry could pretend to stop her, and then wrapped her hands around a hot mug of coffee. Larry watched her as she tilted her head back in laughter at something Jessica had said, and in that moment, all he could think was how lucky he was to be standing in that room, with her.

No one said a word about the tumor under her arm.

Yes, they all knew. Tiffany had shared the news with their closest friends shortly after the diagnosis, trusting them the way only someone with a bond that deep could. But this weekend wasn't for fear or sadness. It wasn't about treatments or appointments or what might lie ahead.

This weekend was about now.

It was about hot breakfasts and snowy sidewalks and inside jokes whispered over cocktails. It was about leaning into joy with both arms and letting the weight of worry take a back seat. Tiffany never asked them to ignore what was happening—she didn't need to. They understood her heart. She didn't want to be treated like a patient. She wanted to be herself. She wanted to live, not linger in what-ifs.

And so they honored her unspoken wish.

No tears. No quiet stares. Just presence. Just love.

They shopped, strolled through the quaint shops of downtown Estes, loitered over cups of cocoa, and returned each night to a house that glowed with laughter and warmth. They talked about everything and nothing. They made memories that, unbeknownst to them, would one day become sacred.

Time is funny like that. When you're in it, it can feel so casual, so routine. But later, when you're looking back, you realize those were the golden days. The ones you'd give anything to return to.

On that weekend, no one knew how much would change in the months to come.

But Tiffany knew one thing for sure—this weekend mattered.

And for Larry, watching her move through each moment with grace and strength and quiet courage, he knew something too.

She was the bravest woman he had ever known.

Upon returning home to Castle Rock, Tiffany kept her promise and finally went in to have the strange growth removed from her arm. What had started months ago as a small, maroon-colored dot had now grown to resemble a skin tag nearly the size of a half-dollar. She had brushed it off for too long—work was too busy, the holidays had come and gone in a blur, and there was always something else that needed her attention. But now, it was time.

The doctor numbed her arm and began the excision, careful and methodical with every movement. But Tiffany, true to form, wasn't lying still with idle hands. As the scalpel moved, so did her voice—confident and calm as she led a Teams meeting with her staff, her phone propped carefully on a sterile counter nearby. Her arm might have been getting stitched, but her mind was still racing with timelines, deliverables, and strategy.

"Wait," a man on the screen said mid-call, squinting. "Tiffany... are you having surgery right now?"

She smiled without missing a beat. "Sorry, I thought I had the angle just right so no one would have to see this," she replied with a laugh, brushing it off like it was a papercut.

That was Tiffany. Always in motion. Always pushing forward. If there was ever a defense mechanism more uniquely hers, it was that relentless pursuit of normalcy, even in the most anomalous of moments. She refused to let anyone worry. It wasn't in her nature to ask for help. She was the helper. She was the one people leaned on.

A few days later, the call came.

Larry watched her expression shift the moment the word landed: melanoma.

It punched through the air like a bullet, invisible but heavy enough to drop the breath from her lungs. Larry didn't say anything at first. He just looked at her, trying to read past her brave face. She was nodding as the voice on the phone continued, taking notes and staying calm—so Tiffany. But he saw the trace in her eyes. He felt the ripple under the surface.

Later that day, Larry was sitting at The Office with Brian, a beer sweating in his hand but untouched. He told Brian the news, still trying to make sense of it. *Melanoma.* It sounded... mild. At least that's what Larry had always assumed. Sunburns and moles. Outpatient procedures. Quick fixes.

But when Brian's face changed—when his eyes darkened with something that looked an awful lot like grief—Larry's stomach twisted. Brian had lost his father to melanoma years ago. He rarely spoke of it. But now, in that dimly lit bar, his silence said more than any words could.

Larry stared into the foam of his untouched beer and felt the walls shift.

This wasn't minor.

This wasn't nothing.

And though Tiffany hadn't said it out loud, he knew deep down... they were standing at the edge of something immense.

Something scary.

Something that would test everything they knew.

Tiffany had always lived by one sacred rule—no matter what storm brewed inside her, the people she loved would *never* feel its weight. She refused to let her illness cast a shadow on their lives, especially not on moments that deserved to shine. Life was moving forward, whether or not she was ready for it, and "the show," as she often said with a smile, "must go on."

And so, with Brennan's sixteenth birthday just around the corner, Tiffany did what she always did best—she planned something unforgettable.

Brennan wasn't just turning sixteen. He was stepping into manhood, that delicate but powerful shift from childhood into a world where everything began to matter just a little more. And Tiffany wanted to mark the occasion the only way she knew—with elegance, laughter, love, and, of course, impeccable food.

The reservations were made at Flemings Prime Steakhouse in the Denver Tech Center—a family favorite that had become their go-to for the most meaningful moments. It had hosted their Mother's Days, Easters, milestone birthdays, and countless cherished date nights over the years. This night would be no different—only now it carried a heavier meaning for Tiffany, who, with every step into that restaurant, was making a quiet vow to continue showing up for her family in every way she could.

The guests that night were a reflection of the village that raised Brennan and wrapped him in love—Larry, Patrick, Rylee, Brian, Stacy, Mackenzie, and Piper all gathered around the large, elegantly set table that Flemings had prepared with exceptional care. A crisp white tablecloth stretched across the table, sprinkled tastefully with sparkling "Happy Birthday" confetti. The lights were soft, the ambiance rich and warm, and the staff greeted them like royalty—each server seemingly aware of just how much this family meant to one another.

They started with a round of celebratory drinks—sparkling waters for the teens, cocktails for the adults, and a chilled bottle of wine that glowed amber in the low lighting. The seafood towers arrived shortly after, cascading with oysters, shrimp, lobster tails, and chilled crab—an edible sculpture of indulgence and celebration. The laughter began to build, rising softly like the flame of a candle slowly being fed.

Next came the soup and salads—perfectly prepared, passed across the table with compliments and shared bites. Then the entrées—thick, buttery steaks cooked to perfection, plated with roasted vegetables, truffle mashed potatoes, and sides that seemed to melt under the fork.

Tiffany sat glowing, her signature blonde waves falling gently against the neckline of her sweater. No one could see the discomfort beneath, the invisible weight she carried. Tonight, she was as radiant as ever, her eyes never straying too far from Brennan's smile. For that night, for those few hours, her cancer didn't exist. It had no seat at this table.

Brennan, always humble, always witty, took it all in stride—but even he couldn't hide the gratitude in his grin. He looked around the table, knowing what this night meant, not just for him but for his mom. She had pulled this together like she always did, with grace and intention.

When the chocolate cake arrived, thick with ganache and dusted with cocoa, it carried sixteen candles burning bright. The restaurant quieted just enough for the melody of "Happy Birthday" to rise from their corner. Patrons turned to smile, staff peeked around the corners, and Tiffany sang the loudest of all—her voice clear, unfaltering.

Larry watched her carefully from across the table, memorizing every detail of her—her smile, the way she leaned into Rylee as they laughed, the glow in her cheeks from the wine, the strength hidden in her laughter. And for a brief, beautiful moment, he allowed himself to believe she had forgotten about the monster inside her.

Just for tonight.

Just for this one perfect evening.

He reached beneath the table, gently took her hand in his, and gave it a light squeeze.

She looked at him, smiled with her eyes, and he knew... she still had fight left in her. Still standing. Still giving them all the magic they had always known her for.

It was more than a birthday.

It was a memory—a living, breathing moment in time that would be replayed over and over in the hearts of everyone who sat at that table.

Because Tiffany had made it happen.

And no matter what came next, that magic would live forever.

Later that week, Patrick greeted them with a smile that could've lit the entire front room.

He had news—big news.

He had landed the job in Houston. The one he had been quietly chasing for weeks, hoping, waiting, willing it into existence. And now, it was his. He would be starting on March 18th, and the move was scheduled for just a few days earlier, on the 12th. For Tiffany and Larry, it was the kind of news that brought joy and pride—the kind of milestone moment every parent holds close.

Larry wasted no time. Having worked in the energy sector since the early '90s, he knew Houston well. The names of neighborhoods rolled off his tongue like a local—Midtown, Montrose, West U—but it was The Heights that had always stood out. Historic charm, leafy streets, boutique shops, and restaurants lining the sidewalks—it had

FOREVER TIFFANY

everything. It felt right. Patrick found a beautiful place there, and move-in day was set for March 14th.

Tiffany and Larry, true to form, wanted it to be perfect for him. His first place, his first step into real adult independence—he needed to feel supported, grounded, and surrounded by love. That was always Tiffany's style.

At the same time, another door that had long been stuck had finally cracked open. After what felt like an exhausting barrage of phone calls, messages, and polite persistence, Larry finally got through to UC Health. Dr. Luke Mantle's office had called back. Tiffany had an appointment on the books—March 7th. It was the relief they desperately needed. For the first time in weeks, there was structure. There was a plan. There was hope.

But as it so often does in life, hope was quickly tested.

Just days before the lacrosse season opener, Brennan called from practice, his voice tight, strained. He had gone down during drills, and something was wrong—he felt it. Larry and Tiffany rushed him to the ER. The news was heavy, crushing. A torn ACL, MCL, and meniscus. A full reconstruction. Their hearts sank. It was the kind of injury that steals an entire season, maybe more. The Steadman Hawkins Clinic confirmed it: surgery would be required, and it was scheduled for late March.

Another battle. Another weight.

Still, they clung to the plan. They had to. Tiffany's appointment on March 7th came fast. She walked in wearing confidence like a coat, hiding the unease bubbling just under the surface. Dr. Mantle examined her carefully, his expression serious, measured. He ordered a biopsy of the underarm tumor. Within days, the results came back. As suspected—melanoma.

But it wasn't just that. A PET scan. A brain scan. Layers of concern unfolding.

The diagnosis didn't shatter Tiffany—it lit her on fire. If the cancer thought it had chosen the wrong woman, it had no idea what was coming. Dr. Mantle outlined a treatment plan with military precision: two rounds of immunotherapy to shrink the tumors, followed by surgery to remove them. It was aggressive, it was fast, and it was hope. There was a shot. And Tiffany wasn't just going to fight—she was going to obliterate it.

Larry never doubted her. Not once. She was a spitfire, a goddess of grit, and the biggest badass he had ever known. She was ready to beat the ever-living shit out of this disease. It would not win.

Just a few days later, Larry and Patrick loaded up the car and set out for Houston. Father and son, two men driving down long highways and quiet stretches of thought. Patrick tried not to bring up his mom—maybe it hurt too much, maybe it made it too real. But Larry, always knowing when to break the silence, reassured him with a simple truth.

"She's going to be okay, son. You know who your mom is. She's a goddamn warrior."

Patrick nodded, his eyes holding the weight of both hope and fear. Tiffany was his everything—the guiding light of his life—and he didn't want to imagine a world where she wasn't invincible.

Before the trip, Tiffany had insisted they stop by American Furniture Warehouse in Denver. She may not have been able to join them in Houston, but she could still play her role—and oh, how she played it.

She and Larry had let Patrick pick out everything—his first grown-up furniture set, a full home's worth. Couches, a dining table, bedroom pieces, all handpicked with care. The delivery was scheduled for the 14th, and Tiffany made sure Larry had a long list of all the extras that would make the place feel like a real home.

From afar, she orchestrated the entire thing. Dishes, pots and pans, silverware, bath towels, bedding—it all had to be just right. And though she wasn't physically there, her fingerprints were on every item in that apartment. Larry and Patrick did their best to arrange it the way she would have. And when it was done—when the last pillow was fluffed and the final dish placed in the cabinet—it was nearly perfect.

Almost.

But Tiffany could never truly be replicated.

They had tried. God, they tried.

And when Patrick stood in the middle of his new place, looking around with quiet satisfaction, he smiled, because it felt like she was there anyway.

And in some small way, she always would be.

As Patrick and Larry stood in the middle of the freshly furnished living room in Patrick's new Houston apartment, they took a moment to admire what they'd pulled off. The sunlight streamed in through the tall windows, casting a warm glow over the perfectly placed furniture, the gleaming new kitchenware, and the cozy touches that made it feel more like home than just a place to live.

They were proud—not just of the setup, but of the journey. It was a quiet moment between father and son, filled with reflection and pride.

Then Larry's phone buzzed.

It was Tiffany.

He smiled, assuming she wanted a video tour to inspect the final product and to give her signature "Tiffany Style" stamp of approval. He answered casually, "Hey, babe. Want to see how we did?"

But her voice carried a tone he hadn't quite expected—soft, almost excited.

"Hey, how's it going?" she said. "I have Rylee on the phone too... she has something to tell you."

Larry's gut tensed. His mind, perhaps too weathered by recent months of fear and uncertainty, immediately went into defense mode.

What now? he thought. *Another surgery? More news?*

And then he heard the words.

"Dad... I'm pregnant. You're going to be a grandfather."

The world stopped rotating for a moment.

Larry froze.

A beat of silence.

His eyes locked with Patrick's, who stood there waiting, confused by the sudden shift in his father's expression. Larry's mind raced. What did she just say? A baby? My little girl?

He couldn't speak. He couldn't think.

Grandfather?

Tiffany's voice chimed in, full of joy. "Isn't it amazing? Can you believe it?"

She was beaming—he could hear it in her voice. She was already in full-blown grandma mode, her mind likely racing through nursery designs, baby clothes, and which stroller was the safest. She loved babies—always had. And now her very own daughter was going to become a mother.

Larry sat back on the arm of the couch, still trying to process it. Rylee... his little girl, his witty, bold, stubborn free spirit. The one who used to curl up in his lap to watch cartoons and always insisted on taking charge of the remote. She was going to be a mom?

It made sense now—all those surprise visits to Buffalo to see Landon, all the weekends packed with flights and cheering from the stands. Those trips had come with a surprise souvenir, one that neither of them had quite planned, but one that was already changing everything.

And yet... as the news settled into his bones, Larry began to feel something he hadn't expected.

Calm.

A deep, grounding calm.

Because he knew Rylee. And more importantly, he knew who she'd learned from. She had been raised by the G.O.A.T.—the greatest of all time—her mom. Rylee had grown up watching Tiffany handle life with strength, grit, and grace. She had been loved hard, raised right, and shown every day what it meant to fight for family.

She'll be just fine.

Of course, with news like this, came a thousand questions—and at the top of that list: What about next school year?

But Rylee and Landon had already beaten them to it. Without missing a beat, they shared their plan.

They would transfer together to the University of Colorado Boulder. Landon would play for the Buffs, and together, they would raise their baby in the town they both now considered home.

It was bold. It was brave. And it was theirs.

Larry looked around at Patrick's apartment—his son standing tall in his new life—and felt a wave of gratitude. One child was flying the nest, the other was preparing to build one of her own.

And he? He was going to be a grandfather.

It wasn't the life he planned... but it was the life he loved.

Immunotherapy began swiftly.

Tiffany sat quietly in the stiff recliner, the hospital lights dull against her pale skin. The slow, steady drip of the IV was like a metronome, counting out time in a room where hope and fear lived in equal measure. Larry sat beside her, his hand resting gently on her knee, his heart pounding silently in his chest. He didn't show his fear. Not to her. Not to anyone. He was the rock. The steady hand. But inside, he was praying—harder than he had ever prayed before—that this treatment would work. That it would be the beginning of a miracle.

The infusion took its toll quickly.

The fatigue hit first. Tiffany barely made it from the car to their bed when they got home. Then came the fevers, the body aches, the chills that burrowed into her bones like winter winds. The sparkle in her eye—the one that lit up rooms, that made people feel seen, feel loved—it dulled. But only just.

The doctors had warned them. If her temperature ever rose above 100.1, they were to go straight to the hospital. No questions asked. Larry monitored her like a hawk—thermometer at the ready, watching for signs, hoping each long day of side effects was still a step in the right direction. They were in this fight together, and neither of them was backing down.

Then, a glimmer of hope.

The PET scan results came in, followed closely by the brain MRI. The cancer had not spread beyond her right arm. Her brain—beautiful, brilliant, fiercely determined—was clean. Larry exhaled for what felt like the first time in weeks. For Tiffany, it was the first real victory in a battle that had only just begun.

But as they were trying to find strength in that small piece of good news, another wave of pain swept in—this one emotional, not physical.

Word came from Indiana. Chastadie—Patrick's friend Nick's mother—had passed away. Melanoma. The same cruel disease. She was young, full of fire and fight, just like Tiffany. And it had taken her. Fast.

FOREVER TIFFANY

She had been diagnosed only months earlier. It spread to her brain and, with barely enough time to process what was happening, she was gone. February 16th, 2024. Just like that.

She was born in 1982, the same decade as Tiffany. A mother, a friend, a woman with decades still ahead of her. Her passing was more than heartbreaking—it was terrifying.

Tiffany sat silently after hearing the news, her mind racing. She knew Chastadie had been strong. She worked out. She ate clean. She was vibrant. And still, it wasn't enough. Tiffany's heart ached for her family—for Nick, for all the people left in the wake of such a sudden, brutal loss. But beneath that ache was something deeper.

Fear.

Tiffany didn't let many people see it, but that night, Larry saw it in her eyes. Not fear for herself, not entirely. Fear of what could come if things didn't go the way they hoped. Fear for her children, for Larry, for the life they had built so lovingly together.

But then came something else—something stronger than fear.

Resolve.

She knew now what she had to do. She had to keep fighting. Keep the cancer out of her brain. Keep it contained. Keep it from stealing her light.

She would push through every fever, every wave of exhaustion, every jab of pain from the medication that coursed through her veins. Because she wasn't just anyone.

She was Tiffany.

She had always defied expectations. She always chose strength, even when the world begged her to break. And now, more than ever, she was ready for war.

Melanoma had picked the wrong woman.

CHAPTER 23.
Tiffany's Touch

Hours felt like days.

Days dragged into weeks.

And weeks? They stretched endlessly, like a slow-moving storm cloud hovering just overhead.

For Larry, time had warped into something cruel and unrelenting. He was nervous. Anxious. Restless. Hopeful one moment, hollow the next. Every emotion a person could feel, he felt it. Every worst-case scenario whispered in the back of his mind, and though he fought to quiet it, it was always there, lurking.

But Tiffany?

She was calm.

Not numb, not in denial—just grounded. Present.

Her face glowed with life. Her energy, though dimmed slightly by the effects of immunotherapy, still sparkled. She still smiled with that same radiant fire. Her determination was unwavering, like a soldier marching through the storm, eyes on the sunrise just beyond the horizon. She wasn't rattled. She wasn't shaken. She had made a decision: she was going to beat this, no matter what it took.

The plan was in motion. Tiffany had just completed her second PET scan—an important post-treatment image that her surgical oncologist needed before proceeding. The scans would reveal the progress after two rounds of immunotherapy. The hope was that everything would be clean, that the internal battlefield was calm, and that the surgeon could safely begin his work. Just one more step toward healing. Just one more hurdle to clear.

FOREVER TIFFANY

The day after the scan, Tiffany and Larry returned to UC Health to meet with Dr. Luke Mantle, their trusted anchor in this swirling storm. He had been more than a doctor—he had become a coach, a steady voice, a believer in Tiffany's resilience. He had seen something in her from the beginning: fire. Fight. Faith. And he believed, with everything he had, that she would overcome.

But that day, as he entered the room, his expression betrayed something different.

A pause.

A breath.

A look that Larry would never forget.

Dr. Mantle sat down slowly, his hands folded as if bracing himself for the weight of the words he had to speak. Tiffany looked directly at him, her back straight, her shoulders square.

"I'm so sorry, Tiffany," he said gently. "Your scans show progression of the disease."

The air left the room. It wasn't loud. It wasn't dramatic. Just quiet devastation. The kind that wraps around you like a fog and settles deep in your chest.

The cancer had spread. It had moved to her lungs, her liver, and her thyroid. Not large amounts—not yet—but enough. Enough to halt the surgery. Enough to change the plan.

Dr. Mantle's face mirrored the grief in his voice. He wasn't just reporting a medical update—he was delivering something personal. His eyes said it all: I wanted this to go differently. I believed it would. He looked at Tiffany not as a patient, but as a fighter he had been rooting for, someone he truly believed in.

But Tiffany didn't flinch.

She nodded slowly, calmly absorbing the words, then met Dr. Mantle's gaze with the same steady fire she'd shown since day one.

"Okay," she said. "Then what's next?"

That's who Tiffany was.

To her, this wasn't defeat. It was a plot twist. A detour. A setback, yes—but not the end of the road. She didn't crumble, didn't spiral. Her strength didn't waver for a second.

Dr. Mantle laid out the revised plan. Chemotherapy pills would begin immediately—an oral form of treatment designed to attack the cancer cells spreading through her body. It wasn't the ideal next step, but it was a step. A new strategy in the war. And Tiffany was ready for it.

Larry sat beside her, nodding, listening. But inside, he was falling apart.

He had been doing everything he could to remain strong, to carry the weight without letting her see how heavy it truly was. But the words hit him like a truck: lungs, liver, thyroid. It was spreading. It was real. And for the first time, the whisper in the back of his mind became a roar.

What if he lost her?

The thought was unbearable. He pushed it away, shoved it deep down where it couldn't touch the surface. But it was there. It was real.

She was his everything.

She wasn't just his wife—she was his compass, his light, his calm in every storm. His partner. His person. The one he shared every morning coffee with, every evening walk, every late-night laugh. Their love was not ordinary—it was blessed. It was the kind of love people spend their whole lives chasing, and he had it. *She* was it.

He didn't just love her. He needed her. And the idea that she could be taken from him?

He couldn't breathe.

But as he looked over at her, sitting upright, eyes focused, already asking what came next, he felt something stronger than fear.

Pride.

Tiffany wasn't just fighting. She was leading the charge. Brave. Fierce. Determined. She was facing the darkest news yet with the same unshakeable grace she'd shown from the beginning.

And Larry?

He would follow her into battle.

Every step. Every breath. Every moment.

Because she was his heart.

And she was still fighting.

The waiting room at Steadman Hawkins was still, the kind of sterile quiet that feels odd—too calm for the storm that rages in your heart. Larry sat with his hands clasped together, elbows resting on his knees, his head bowed slightly as he watched the second hand tick around the face of the wall clock. Every tick was a heartbeat, every minute a lifetime.

Brennan was in surgery.

It was the kind of moment no parent ever prepares for, no matter how many times you tell yourself everything is going to be okay. But there was comfort in knowing that Dr. Jason Dragoo—renowned in the world of orthopedic surgery, a specialist with a reputation built on skill, precision, and remarkable outcomes—was the one overseeing Brennan's operation. The Steadman Hawkins Clinic was world-class, and Brennan was in the best hands possible.

Still, nothing ever truly settles the ache of watching your child endure pain. Larry knew Brennan had torn his ACL, MCL, and meniscus. He had watched his son limp through their front door, eyes down, hope shaken. He remembered how crushed Brennan had been to miss his freshman lacrosse season—the one he had dreamed of for years. The one he had watched Landon chase with passion and promise. Brennan wanted that path too, and in a blink, it had been taken from him.

The surgery had gone beautifully. Brennan had come through it like a champ—strong, calm, even a little brave in the way only a sixteen-year-old boy can be when he knows his mom and dad are just outside the door. Dr. Dragoo walked into the recovery room with a confident smile, giving Larry the kind of look every father needs in moments like these. "It went exactly as we hoped. He did great."

Larry smiled, nodded, and thanked him sincerely, but inside, something much heavier was stirring.

He sat there beside Brennan's hospital bed, watching the slow rise and fall of his son's chest. And in that quiet room filled with white noise and beeping monitors, Larry's mind drifted. Not to fear, not to panic—but to the weight of emptiness.

It wasn't just Brennan.

Just a few weeks ago, he and Patrick were standing in an apartment in Houston, celebrating his son's first steps into the real world. A life far away from Colorado, far away from home. Rylee, now on the brink of motherhood, had whispered words through the phone that had shifted the earth beneath him: "Dad, I'm pregnant."

And Tiffany... sweet, beautiful, strong-as-steel Tiffany. She was fighting a monster. A disease that threatened everything. Cancer had come crashing through their doors like a thief in the night, and it wasn't just taking—it was haunting, lingering in every breath, every thought, every unspoken fear. Larry knew what they were up against. He saw it every time Tiffany reached for his hand a little tighter than usual. He heard it in her laugh, still joyful, but tinged with something heavier now. He felt it when she looked into his eyes and didn't have to say a word.

This was real. This was happening.

FOREVER TIFFANY

And for the first time in a long time, Larry felt something he wasn't used to: the mass of helplessness.

He thought back to that strange conversation with George years ago—the one that had started as a joke, then turned into something deeper, something spiritual. "Am I already dead?" he had asked. Life had seemed too perfect back then. Everything was going so well; it felt like a dream. Could heaven look like this?

Now, sitting in the recovery room beside his son, with the gravity of everything that had shifted in the past few months, Larry realized something else. Maybe he wasn't in heaven anymore. Maybe he was back in the real world—the one that breaks and bends you, the one that tests everything you believe about love, purpose, and strength.

But Larry also knew this:

He had never been alone.

Every step of his life had been guided by a higher power. God had been there from the beginning—through the good and the bad, the laughter and the pain. And in this moment, this heart-wrenching chapter of life, Larry knew it was time to do the only thing he could.

He bowed his head, closed his eyes, and turned it all over.

All of it.

The surgery, the cancer, the uncertainty about Patrick's future, the new life growing inside his daughter, the woman he loved more than life itself...

He placed it all in God's hands.

Because God had given him this family. God had written this story. And now, more than ever, Larry needed Him to help write the next chapter.

With a quiet breath and tears glistening in the corners of his eyes, Larry reached for Brennan's hand and held it gently. His boy was going to be okay.

And somehow, someway… so would they.

The days seemed to move in strange patterns now—rushing past like a river in flood, yet dragging at the same time like molasses in the winter cold. It was a cruel contradiction. The minutes felt endless, the weeks vanished in a blink. And through it all, Tiffany kept moving.

She never stopped.

Tiffany poured herself into her work with the same passion, drive, and sophistication that had always defined her. Even now, battling through treatment, her strength never vacillated. She led a growing team at the tech firm with a grace that inspired those around her. It was clear to everyone, from the entry-level associates to the executive suite, that Tiffany wasn't just a director anymore. She was the heart of the company, the steady voice on every call, the leader people leaned on when things got tough. The truth was, she was already doing the work of a Chief Operating Officer.

Holly knew it. They had talked about it—about making it official. But Holly, ever the protective best friend, also knew Tiffany was fighting the biggest battle of her life. She wanted her to focus on her health, not on client deliverables, quarterly growth, or the endless tangle of operational concerns. "Titles can wait," Holly had told her one afternoon. "Your life can't."

But Tiffany had simply smiled that knowing smile of hers, the one that could calm a storm or shift the mood in a room. "I want to keep pushing," she said. "It keeps me going. It makes me feel like me."

And so she did. She showed up to every meeting. She coached team members through challenges. She strategized, negotiated, and delivered—just like she always had. No one who worked with her could tell that beneath her beautiful sweaters and jackets, beneath the calm voice and perfectly organized calendar, she was fighting a brutal, invisible war inside her own body.

As spring melted into summer, and the air grew light with the scent of blooming lilacs and fresh-cut grass, Tiffany began to look for signs of hope—tiny victories in a fight that often felt crushing. She clung to them like treasures.

Rylee was staying on top of her prenatal checkups, glowing in her own quiet way as she prepared for motherhood. Brennan, though still working through the disappointment of a torn-up knee and a missed lacrosse season, was showing remarkable dedication in his physical therapy. Larry took him to the clinic three times a week to watch him build strength and discipline with every session.

And for the first time in weeks, Tiffany had a glimmer of good news to hold onto.

The tumor under her arm—the one that had first signaled the arrival of the storm—was shrinking.

It wasn't gone. Not yet. But it was smaller, noticeably so. The maroon-and-purple mass that once sat beneath her skin like a warning bell had softened, its edges less defined, its size reduced. She could feel the difference, and so could Larry. When she showed him one morning, he gently ran his fingers across the fading swell, and for the first time in a while, he permitted himself to exhale in relief.

Hope.

It wasn't a cure, but it was a way forward to hope. And in a battle like this, even something small could mean everything.

Tiffany was eager to share the update with Dr. Mantle at their next appointment. She knew not to celebrate too soon—knew this fight was far from over—but it was a step in the right direction. A crack in the darkness where light could begin to pour in.

She didn't say it out loud, but deep down, she allowed herself to believe.

Maybe… just maybe… she was winning.

By the time Tiffany and Larry returned to see Dr. Mantle, the quiet optimism they had begun to feel had started to fade. Tiffany had noticed the change herself first—she could feel it in her body, a subtle but distinct shift. The tumor beneath her arm, the one that had shrunk after her first rounds of chemotherapy, had grown again. Not to the size it had once been, not quite—but it was larger than it had been just weeks before, and Tiffany knew her body well enough to trust the signal.

Dr. Mantle, ever meticulous, pulled out his measurements from the last visit and confirmed what Tiffany already suspected. There had been progress, but it had stalled, and now, they were seeing signs of movement in the wrong direction.

Without hesitation, he ordered a new PET scan and a follow-up brain MRI.

But Tiffany—headstrong, resilient, fiercely independent Tiffany—shook her head at the latter.

"No brain MRI," she said, calmly but firmly.

Both Larry and Dr. Mantle looked at her, their concern immediate and unspoken.

"Tiff," Larry said gently, "I think we should just—"

"I don't want to know," she interrupted, her voice clear but not sharp. "If it's there, it's there. I remember what happened to Chastadie… and if that's what's coming for me, I don't need to see it on a screen first. I'm not afraid. I just don't want to spend my days worrying about every little dot on an image."

She wasn't being reckless. She was being Tiffany.

Dr. Mantle tried once more, explaining the value and the insight it could provide for treatment options. Larry backed him up. But in the end, they both knew—it was her choice. Always her choice. Larry didn't like it. Not even close. But he respected it. Because she wasn't coming from a place of fear—she was coming from strength. From resolve.

FOREVER TIFFANY

When the PET scan results came in a few days later, they were a mixture of relief and fresh concern.

The good news—astonishing news, in fact—was that all of Tiffany's major organs were clear. Her liver, her lungs, her thyroid, all of it. The disease had retreated from the places it had once begun to creep toward.

But.

There were now two small lesions on her spine—new arrivals, tiny but unmistakable. The scan lit up just enough to give them pause.

It wasn't the worst news. But it wasn't the best either. Still, there was something different in the room that day—something that had been missing in recent weeks.

A plan.

Dr. Mantle referred Tiffany to one of the best radiation oncologists at UC Health, Dr. Lanning. From the moment they met him, both Tiffany and Larry knew he was exactly what they needed. He was calm and compassionate, and perhaps most importantly, he explained things not with complicated jargon or cold detachment but in real, human terms. He had a warmth that immediately put Tiffany at ease. And Larry, always the silent guardian, breathed a little easier knowing this man was now in their corner.

Dr. Lanning outlined the next phase of treatment with confidence and clarity. "We'll target both lesions," he said. "Two treatments per day, every other day, for the next ten days. Then we'll rescan and see where we are."

Tiffany nodded, already locked in.

She wasn't done fighting. Not by a long shot.

They left the appointment hand in hand, stepping out into the late spring air. The world looked the same, but everything inside them had shifted again. The path forward wouldn't be easy, but at least now, it was visible. There were steps to take, plans to follow, and a team that believed in her fight just as much as she did.

And if Tiffany had proven anything to the world by now, it was this: you never count her out.

During their consultation with Dr. Lanning, something entirely unexpected—and oddly hopeful—caught his attention. As Tiffany leaned back in the chair, legs crossed with casual confidence, Dr. Lanning paused mid-sentence, his eyes narrowing—not out of concern, but out of curiosity.

He tilted his head slightly and said, almost offhandedly, "Tiffany... have you always had those pigmentation spots on your legs?"

Tiffany glanced down, then back up at him, her expression casual, as if it was no big deal. "No," she replied. "They showed up a couple weeks after my second round of immunotherapy. Right around the time they were taking me off the drug."

Dr. Lanning smiled—really smiled. It was the kind of smile doctors give when something clicks, when an unexpected clue fits into the puzzle just right.

"That," he said, "might be one of the best signs we've seen so far."

Larry straightened up in his chair. Tiffany's eyebrows lifted. "What do you mean?"

He leaned forward, his tone turning animated with just a hint of excitement. "When the immune system is truly activated by immunotherapy—especially checkpoint inhibitors—it sometimes begins attacking melanoma cells because of their pigmentation. Those cells come from melanocytes, the pigment-producing cells in your body. When that happens, it can create what we call vitiligo-like patches. It's rare. But when we see it, it often means the immune system is responding aggressively—and correctly—to the cancer."

FOREVER TIFFANY

Tiffany looked at Larry, a flicker of cautious hope flashing behind her blue eyes.

Dr. Lanning sat back in his chair and added, "I'm going to call Dr. Mantle immediately. This could be a big deal. It could change things."

Larry could feel his heart lift, if only just a little.

Maybe, just maybe, the PET scan from earlier hadn't shown a spread at all. Maybe it had shown what doctors sometimes call hyper-flaring—the appearance of progression, when in fact, the immune system is lighting up the affected areas like a Christmas tree just before obliterating the cancer cells.

It was possible. More than possible. It was hope in disguise.

And while Larry was thrilled at the idea, the strategist in him couldn't help but keep one foot on the ground. He knew they couldn't go back in time. They couldn't change what had already happened—the fear, the confusion, the tears behind closed doors. But they could move forward. With new information. New resolve.

Maybe, just maybe, Tiffany could go back on immunotherapy. Maybe the storm they were in was the sign that the medicine had worked, and all that remained now was to push harder, to finish the fight.

Larry looked over at Tiffany, who sat as she always did—with grace, confidence, and just the right touch of excitement. She wore the tiniest pair of jean shorts Dr. Lanning had probably ever seen in a clinical setting, but that was Tiffany. She could turn heads and command a room while never once losing her class. Paired with one of her signature hoodies and her white baseball cap, her golden ponytail perfectly looped through the back, she was larger than life—poised, sexy, strong, and unshakably herself.

And in that moment, Larry didn't see cancer. He didn't see chemo, or PET scans, or radiation schedules. He just saw Tiffany—the woman who had always known how to light up a room, who never let anyone around her fall, and who wasn't about to fall herself.

They had more battles ahead. But maybe, just maybe, the tide was starting to turn.

And if so, Tiffany was ready—hoodie, ponytail, fire, and all.

It was early June, and the air in Castle Rock hung with that hopeful stillness only summer could bring. The kind of day where the windows stayed open late and the scent of cut grass drifted through the rooms like a slow dance. Tiffany had just wrapped up her final round of radiation treatments. Her strength was returning in pieces—never all at once, but enough to make her feel like herself again. She was curled up on the couch, her legs tucked beneath her, eyes fixed on the television but not really watching. Larry was in his favorite chair, just a few feet away, sipping from a glass of water and listening to the quiet rhythm of the moment.

And then, Tiffany spoke.

"You know," she began softly, her voice almost blending into the quiet hum of the room, "Dr. Mantle said it was okay for me to travel for work… and I have. And everything went just fine."

Larry looked over, curious. "Yeah, I remember. Are you thinking about another work trip?"

She shook her head gently, and a different kind of light flickered in her eyes—the kind of glow Larry had seen before, right before she'd spring one of her grand ideas.

"No," she said, her smile creeping in, small but unmistakable. "I want to take the family to Mexico. I want to sit on the beach, listen to the waves, and watch the sunset with everyone we love."

Larry leaned forward. His answer was instant and firm. "Nope. Not gonna happen. We'll go as soon as you beat this disease, and Rylee has the baby in November. We'll plan for next summer."

FOREVER TIFFANY

He said it with certainty. With love. With protection.

But Tiffany didn't budge.

Instead, she turned to him fully, folding her hands in her lap. Her bright blue eyes locked onto his, and that magical smile—one that could soften him with a single glance—grew a little sadder, a little deeper. Her next words landed like a thunderclap in Larry's chest.

"What if I don't have next summer?" she asked gently. "What if I'm really dying?"

The room went still. The kind of still that made the world outside feel like it had stopped moving.

Larry didn't respond right away. He couldn't. He just stared at her, stunned by the brutal honesty, by the truth wrapped in those seven simple words. It was everything he'd refused to let his mind consider—until now. Tiffany had never said anything like that before. She was always the strong one, always the fighter, always putting on her armor and refusing to let the fear show. But this time, she was raw. Open. Vulnerable.

Without saying a word, Larry stood up. He didn't hesitate. He didn't argue. He simply walked out of the room, tears already forming behind his eyes. He stepped into his home office, closed the door behind him, and sat down at his computer.

With his heart pounding in his chest and his hands shaking, he opened the browser and searched for it—their place. The resort.. The one they had returned to time and time again, the one where their children laughed in the pools, where Tiffany floated in pools, smiling at fish darting beneath the surface while snorkeling. The one where memories weren't just made—they were engraved into their souls like carvings in stone.

He didn't think. He just booked it.

The flights. The rooms. Everything.

And as the confirmation page flashed across the screen, Larry broke down. The tears came fast, unrelenting, like a storm finally breaking after days of pressure. He wasn't crying out of fear—though it was there—or anger, though that too had started to bubble beneath the surface. He cried because he loved her more than he could ever explain. Because he would move mountains for her. And if there was even the slightest chance that this would be their last vacation together, it wouldn't be missed. Not for anything.

Yes, Dr. Mantle had said to stay close to home. Stay within reach of major hospitals. No international travel. Not now.

But none of that mattered anymore.

They were doing everything he'd advised against—but for all the right reasons.

This wasn't about ignoring protocol. It was about honoring life. Love. Time.

Tiffany wasn't just his wife. She was his soul. His heart in human form. And if there was only one last trip left to take, it would be spent beside the ocean, her feet buried in the sand, her laughter drifting through the air like a song only Larry could hear.

They were going back to their place. Their Mexico.

And no matter what happened afterward, they would have this moment—this stretch of days suspended in sunshine and surf—forever.

Because sometimes, when you love someone enough, next summer just can't wait.

Patrick had found his rhythm in Houston. The towering skyline and inexorable humidity were a far cry from the familiar serenity of Colorado's front range, but something about the constant buzz of the city—the energy, the diversity, the opportunity—suited him. He had embraced the concrete jungle. The crowded freeways, the bustling coffee shops, the sprawling neighborhoods—it was all new, all different, and he was thriving. The new job was more than a paycheck—it was a launchpad, and Patrick had leapt with both feet, already making a name for himself in the energy world.

Meanwhile, back in Colorado, life continued to shift in all the ways that families did when the seasons changed. Rylee and Landon had officially found their place. Tiffany had gone with them for the tour, and the moment she stepped inside the bright, modern two-bedroom, two-bath apartment just off the CU Boulder campus, she smiled widely. It was clean, new, full of light, and full of promise. More than anything, it felt like stability. Like the beginning of something beautiful. Rylee glowed with excitement, and Tiffany, despite all she was going through, felt proud, fulfilled, and just plain happy.

June rolled in like a warm breeze, and Tiffany did what Tiffany always did—she indulged in the moment, no matter how hard the days were. They celebrated Larry's birthday and Brian and Stacy's anniversary, which happened to fall on the same day, a double celebration that gave everyone reason to smile and toast to love, life, and friendship.

But there was one holiday Tiffany held especially close to her heart: the Fourth of July.

It was her second favorite day of the year, right after Christmas, and she treated it like a sacred event. She loved everything about it—the simplicity of being outdoors, the smell of barbecue in the air, the sound of laughter floating through the neighborhood. It wasn't about patriotism or fireworks to her; it was about connection. Togetherness. Family.

The morning started with the comforting crackle of the smoker out back. Larry had started the fire early, slow-cooking pork and ribs while Tiffany prepped side dishes inside. The kitchen smelled like summer—baked beans, cornbread, and coleslaw. Brennan and Larry tossed a football in the yard, while Rylee helped set the patio table, her laugh echoing through the house. Tiffany moved between them all like she always had—directing, laughing, loving—wearing one of her signature pairs of shorts and a sweatshirt just baggy enough to hide the tumor beneath her arm. Her white hat sat perfectly atop her blonde ponytail, a small detail that Larry had come to associate with comfort.

Later in the afternoon, they made their way to Kris and Celeste's house. Their home sat just across the street from Karl and Jessica's, and the four families had built a rhythm over the years that felt like an extension of home. Rylee, Brennan, and Landon joined Brooklyn and Kris's kids in a game of cornhole while the adults gathered around the firepit with drinks in hand.

As the sun sank behind the Rockies, casting a golden glow across the horizon, the laughter slowed, and the anticipation for the fireworks grew. Though they were illegal in Colorado, Rylee and Landon had made the classic trek north into Wyoming a few days earlier to pick up the good stuff—the kind of fireworks that didn't just light up the sky, but shook the ground beneath your feet.

And when they lit them, they did not disappoint.

Sparks exploded in every direction, brilliant whites and blues and reds bursting into the night sky. Everyone stood in the driveway, heads tilted up, cheers and gasps echoing into the warm summer air.

Larry glanced at Tiffany.

She was seated just off to the side, arms wrapped around her knees, eyes lifted to the sky. The glow of the fireworks lit her face in flickers, each burst reflecting in her eyes like glittering stars. He watched her jump slightly as one exploded too close, and she laughed—really laughed—the kind of laugh that shook her shoulders and made her eyes squint.

And in that moment, Larry saw their entire life together. He saw her at 20, behind the wheel of that red Ford Escort. He saw her in the delivery room with Patrick. He saw her holding Brennan's tiny hand in the school parking lot. He saw her dancing in the kitchen, barefoot, with a wine glass in hand. He saw her strength, her fire, her fierce love for their family—and he saw the fear, buried deep behind her brilliant eyes.

She caught him staring again.

She always did.

"Stop looking at me like I'm dying," she whispered, her voice soft but firm.

Larry swallowed the lump in his throat, forcing a smile. "I'm not looking at you like you're dying," he replied, his voice thick with emotion. "I'm looking at you like I'm seeing you for the very first time. I'm just... drinking in every moment."

Tiffany rolled her eyes, but her lips curled into a smile, and she reached for his hand.

Larry gripped it tightly. What he didn't say—what he couldn't say—was that yes, part of him was staring at her like she might slip away. Because he was terrified. If there was any way to take the cancer from her body and put it into his own, he would do it without a second's hesitation. He would suffer every treatment, endure every pain, just to give her one more day of freedom from it all.

But he couldn't.

All he could do was love her.

Hold her.

Watch her, and remember.

The fireworks finale lit up the sky like a thousand stars breaking loose from heaven, and for a moment, time stood still. The porch. The laughter. The smell of barbecue persistent in the air. Tiffany's hand in his.

It was a night none of them would ever forget.

And deep down, they knew it.

Because moments like that—golden, glowing, and wrapped in love—don't come twice.

They're the kind you hold on to *forever*.

The trip had finally arrived—the one Tiffany had dreamt about since the very first day she'd asked Larry, with tears in her eyes, "What if I don't have next summer?" It wasn't just a getaway; it was a declaration. A defiant, beautiful, soul-igniting declaration that despite the diagnosis, despite the fear and fatigue and constant appointments, life was still worth celebrating. It was a trip to reclaim joy. To breathe. To feel the ocean breeze on their skin and remember what it meant to just be a family.

There was electricity in the air the morning they left. The bags were packed, passports checked, and smiles—some real, some forced—were on every face. Tiffany, wrapped in one of her soft hoodies with her white baseball cap pulled low, sat next to Larry at the gate, her fingers gently laced in his. She was quiet but calm, her spirit carrying that same steady resolve that had been her foundation from the moment the red dot appeared.

The flight from Denver was smooth. As the wheels touched down and the plane taxied toward the terminal, Tiffany looked out the window and smiled. The lush greenery, the swaying palm trees, the hazy warmth of the afternoon sun—it was like the universe had painted this arrival just for her.

The air was thick with heat and humidity as they walked out of the airport. A man held a sign with their name on it, just like always, and before they knew it, they were loaded into the SUV and heading toward their beloved resort. This wasn't just any resort—it was their sacred place, their spiritual reset button. It was the same place where they'd spent birthdays, anniversaries, and the lazy days of summers gone by. A place where memories lived in the gentle crash of waves and the sparkle of poolside drinks.

FOREVER TIFFANY

When they arrived, the staff greeted them like royalty. "Welcome back," one of them said, placing a cold towel in Tiffany's hand, just the way she liked it. Their rooms were perfect—three spacious suites with ocean views, arranged with care. Larry had made sure of it. Patrick and Brennan would share one suite, a boys' retreat where they could unwind, joke, and reconnect. Rylee and Landon had their own quiet oasis—a space that symbolized their growing love and the new chapter waiting for them back home. And then there was Larry and Tiffany's room—a sanctuary with the kind of bed you sink into and never want to leave, with wide sliding doors that opened to the ocean's heartbeat.

Patrick's flight out of Houston had been delayed, but that didn't matter. When his car finally pulled up to the resort later that evening, Tiffany ran—yes, ran—to greet him in the lobby, her arms wrapping around him like it had been years since they'd last seen each other. It didn't matter that it had only been weeks. This moment was different. This was family, reunited on sacred ground.

They stood in the glow of the moonlight that night, the warm breeze blowing softly as the waves whispered in the distance. No talk of scans or medicine, no mention of hospitals or what came next. This was their time. And as Larry looked around the dinner table, filled with laughter and stories and candlelight, he felt something powerful.

They were living.

Not surviving, not hiding, not bracing for the worst—but truly living. And that, above all else, was Tiffany's gift to them.

Most days at the resort unfolded like pages in a dream—slow, sun-drenched, and filled with the kind of joy that doesn't ask questions, only invites you to stay a while. From the moment the morning sun crept across the sky and bathed the pools in golden light, the family would find their way to their favorite spot—lounged up as close to the swim-up bar as humanly possible.

LARRY BLAKE

It was a rhythm they knew well. The soft splash of water. The occasional laughter from kids playing in the distance. And those frozen daiquiris—oh, those daiquiris. The resort's signature specialty. Tiffany, never much of a drinker back home, found something special in those bright, frosty creations. Beer was a no-go, and wine had never been her thing—but in Mexico, with the ocean breeze wrapping around her and the sun kissing her skin, daiquiris were more than just a drink—they were a symbol of escape, of joy, of this beautiful, sacred pause in their story.

Patrick and Landon? Well, they did exactly what you'd expect from two young men on vacation in paradise. They soaked up the sun and tossed back their fair share of tequila cocktails and cervezas. Brennan, never one to be left out, tagged along like a little brother on a mission, soaking in every moment with his heroes, idolizing their confidence, their ease, their laughter.

Rylee, just weeks into her pregnancy, moved at a different pace—soft and slow. She lounged in the shade under palm trees with her mom, feet dangling in the cool water, hands resting gently on the beginnings of new life. They whispered. They laughed. They planned. And sometimes they just sat in silence, letting the breeze carry their thoughts out to sea.

And Larry? Larry didn't need to be doing anything grand. He simply watched. Watched Tiffany smile with her eyes closed, feeling the sun on her face. Watched Patrick and Landon cracking jokes, drinks in hand, already talking about what to do for dinner. Watched Brennan floating lazily with a grin that wouldn't quit. Watched Rylee, his baby girl, glowing and content beside the woman who taught her everything she knew about love. For Larry, this was it. Heaven on earth. Just sitting back, heart full, drinking in the magic of his people being happy. That was always his favorite view.

Then came Friday.

Not just any Friday. In their world, Friday night at the resort meant one thing: White Party Night.

FOREVER TIFFANY

It wasn't optional—it was a sacred ritual. The entire resort transformed. The palapas were lit up with strings of twinkling white lights. The beach glowed with lanterns. The music shifted from chill daytime acoustics to pulsing live beats. Everyone dressed in white. And not just any white, crisp, beautiful, tropical whites. Linen pants, flowy dresses, pressed shirts, bare shoulders, glowing skin.

It was, hands down, Tiffany's favorite night of any vacation.

Larry had taken care of everything in advance. Their butler—a man named Daniel who now seemed more like a family friend—had secured their table. Not just any table, but the table. Front and center, just off the edge of the beach, closest to the stage. On the table sat a silver bucket filled with ice, cradling a bottle of chilled champagne, waiting to be popped the moment they arrived.

But when the family walked up, the scene wasn't quite what they expected.

Two women were seated at their reserved table, clearly unaware—or perhaps pretending not to notice—the elegantly displayed "Reserved" sign perched in front of them. The butler gently approached, explaining the situation with a smile. The women didn't take it well. Voices raised slightly, annoyance written across their faces, arms crossed in defiance.

Rylee just laughed.

This wasn't her first rodeo. She'd been coming to this resort long enough to know the ins and outs. Most guests didn't realize you could reserve front-row tables with bottle service, but Tiffany did. Oh, Tiffany always knew. She had long since cracked the resort's secret code, and it always worked in their favor.

The women were kindly escorted elsewhere, and the family took their rightful place at the edge of the party's heartbeat.

Tiffany was radiant. Her white dress hugged her frame in all the right places, soft and flowing, with delicate details at the sleeves. Her sun-kissed skin shimmered under the lights, and her hair, let down across her shoulders, flowing in the ocean breeze, looked like something out of a magazine. Larry couldn't take his eyes off her.

He leaned back in his chair, the Caribbean breeze brushing past him, and looked at her through a blur of tears he refused to let fall. She was everything—his reason, his rhythm, his heartbeat.

And in that moment, with the music swelling, glasses clinking, the sky overhead painted with stars, and his angel beside him glowing in white, Larry made a wish.

Not a wish for a miracle. Not even for more time.

He simply wished that this night would never end.

Because this wasn't about the past or the future.

It was about now.

It was about the sparkle in Tiffany's eyes, the laughter in her voice, the joy on their children's faces. It was about living—really living. And that, more than anything, is what she had always taught him.

To love big. To live loud. And to never take a single heartbeat for granted.

Saturday morning arrived with a soft ocean breeze and a sky so blue it looked like it had been painted just for them. It was a day Tiffany had circled in her mind for weeks—a day to leave worries on the shore and let the sea carry them away. Larry, always looking to create something special for his family, had arranged for something unforgettable: a private charter on a forty-eight-foot catamaran, gliding across the warm turquoise waters of the Caribbean.

The marina buzzed with life as the family made their way down the dock, passing rows of sleek boats before arriving at their vessel—a gleaming white catamaran bobbing gently in the water. A barefoot crew, all smiles and charm, welcomed them aboard with chilled drinks and island music drifting from hidden speakers. The atmosphere was light, festive, and exactly what Tiffany needed.

As the boat pulled away from the shore, Tiffany made her way to the front deck, where soft cushions and netted lounges stretched over the bow. She picked the perfect seat—sun-drenched with an unobstructed view of the endless sea. With her legs tucked beneath her, a wide-brimmed hat shielding her eyes, and a smile that could melt the horizon, she looked totally at peace.

The family gathered around her, basking in the moment, the waves dancing below them, the catamaran cutting smoothly through the surf. About thirty minutes into their journey, the boat slowed. They had reached the perfect snorkeling spot, the water as clear as glass, revealing glimpses of coral and shadowy shapes of fish flitting below the surface.

Landon and Patrick wasted no time. With laughter echoing across the water, they leapt in, disappearing below the surface like two adventurers on a quest. Armed with snorkels and boundless energy, they explored a vibrant underwater world—tropical fish of every color darted through coral gardens, and sunken statues stood silently like ancient relics, waiting to be rediscovered. They popped up now and then, calling out about what they saw, eyes wide and smiles even wider.

Brennan, still healing from his recent knee surgery, sat nearby with a grin, offering commentary and jokes. He understood why he couldn't join in, but there wasn't a trace of disappointment—he was happy just to be there, surrounded by the people he loved most.

Rylee, now visibly pregnant, stayed aboard with Tiffany, the two of them nestled together in the shade. Rylee rested her hand on her growing belly while Tiffany's rested lightly over hers. Larry remained close, never far from Tiffany's side, his eyes always drifting toward her. This was his favorite version of her, the one fully present, surrounded by family, relaxed, the breeze teasing her ponytail, and sunlight brushing across her cheeks.

When Patrick and Landon climbed back aboard, cheeks flushed and energy high, the boat shifted course once again, setting its sights on Isla Mujeres. They cruised toward the west side of the island, where the beach was soft and white, the waves gentle, and the palm trees swayed like dancers.

Anchoring to a large dock, the family stepped into a postcard-perfect scene of paradise. Lunch was served beachside—a feast of fresh tortillas, grilled seafood, guacamole, and ice-cold drinks under the shade of a palapa roof. The flavors of Mexico blended with laughter and storytelling, creating a meal they would remember forever.

After lunch, they strolled to a tucked-away spa hut built right on the edge of the water, where the sound of waves rolling onto shore became a lullaby. There, under the soft rustle of palm fronds, Tiffany, Rylee, and Patrick each lay back for a massage— the three connected by love, by time, by this moment.

Tiffany lay on her massage table, eyes closed, ocean air filling her lungs. She could hear the faint hum of Brennan laughing in the distance and feel the warmth of the sun filtering through the open slats of the hut. It was perfect. Not because everything in life was perfect, but because in that moment, she had everything that mattered.

Larry stood nearby, snapping a few quiet photos—none posed, all natural. Just the people he loved most, suspended in time, wrapped in peace.

It wasn't just a day on the water. It was a memory stamped on their souls.

It was freedom, it was healing, it was love.

It was Tiffany's kind of day.

The late afternoon sun blazed high above the island as the family climbed into their golf carts for the next part of their adventure—an open-air tour of Isla Mujeres. They had explored the east end of the

FOREVER TIFFANY

island many times before, zipping past cliffs and scenic overlooks in the breeze, but this time they took a different path, setting their sights on the quieter west end. It was less traveled, more rustic, and promised little shops, shaded corners, and the laid-back charm of island life.

At first, it was everything they hoped for. They stopped at a few roadside vendors—colorful stalls packed with handwoven bags, handmade jewelry, wooden carvings, and local trinkets. They took turns picking out souvenirs, sipping from icy bottles of Coke and tamarind-flavored drinks, smiling as they bartered playfully with friendly shopkeepers. Tiffany, never one to pass up a fun moment, slipped a woven bracelet on Brennan's wrist and laughed as he rolled his eyes in mock embarrassment.

But as the sun rose higher and the breeze faded, Tiffany's energy began to dim. Her face, always fair, was turning a deep shade of red. Larry noticed first—he knew that look. It wasn't the typical sunburn creeping up from too much exposure. Her shoulders were sagging, her movements slower, more labored. Sweat dotted her forehead. There was a tension in her jaw, a distant look in her eyes. Something wasn't right.

Concern became obvious on Larry's face. His protective instincts kicked in. "Let's head back to the boat," he said, his voice calm but urgent. The rest of the family followed, unaware at first of the rising panic quietly brewing inside him.

The ride back was silent except for the hum of the engine and the occasional bump of tires hitting uneven cobblestone streets. Tiffany wasn't speaking anymore. She leaned back against the seat, eyes fluttering closed, her breath shallow. Larry kept glancing sideways, gripping the steering wheel tighter. His mind raced—heat exhaustion. Maybe worse. He remembered Dr. Mantle's words: Stay in the U.S., stay near major hospitals. And here they were, far from both.

As they docked at the next stop on the island, Larry didn't hesitate. He rushed to the boat captain and asked with urgency, "Where's the nearest air conditioning?" The captain, clearly concerned, pointed to a small building just beyond the dock. "There," he said, "only one place sells tequila and shirts. Go now."

Larry wrapped his arm around Tiffany and led her, practically carrying her, toward the little shop. A modest, white-washed building with faded signs and sun-bleached posters. Inside, the air was still and heavy, but a small AC unit whirred behind the counter. Tiffany didn't speak. She simply walked straight to the back of the shop, behind a glass case filled with bottles of local liquor, and without saying a word, collapsed gently to the white stone floor.

Larry's heart stopped.

Tiffany—his Tiffany—would never do something like that unless something was seriously wrong. She was the woman who never showed weakness, never asked for help, never wanted to be the center of concern. And now she lay stretched on the cool tile floor, pale and silent.

The shopkeeper, an older man with soft, worried eyes, rushed over. He didn't hesitate. "She okay?" he asked, his accent heavy, but his tone kind. Larry knelt beside Tiffany, gently cradling her head, his voice cracking. "She just needs to cool down, just needs some time."

The shopkeeper disappeared and returned moments later with a large, whirring fan. He plugged it in and aimed it directly at her, then brought a few rolled beach towels for her to rest on. Rylee sat nearby, her eyes wide with concern, whispering quiet reassurances. Brennan stood frozen, helpless, while Patrick darted from the shop to find drinks—anything cold, anything with electrolytes.

Minutes dragged. Larry wiped Tiffany's forehead with a towel, whispering to her, holding her hand, watching her chest rise and fall with shallow, uneven breaths. Time slowed, warped, became impossible to track. Thirty minutes passed. Then sixty. Then ninety. Still she lay there, too weak to rise, too quiet for comfort.

The shopkeeper returned once more and knelt beside Larry. "I call doctor now," he said gently.

FOREVER TIFFANY

Larry felt the world incline. His stomach twisted. That scared Tiffany enough to open her eyes.

"No," she whispered. "No doctor. I'm okay." She sat up slowly, face flushed, hair stuck to her temples, and reached for the bottles of Gatorade Patrick had returned with. One. Two. She drank them down without pause, her body desperate for something, anything to bring her back.

Gradually, her color returned. Her breath steadied. Her legs, though shaky, began to work again.

With Larry and Patrick's help, she stood, leaning heavily into Larry's arms. The shopkeeper watched them go with a kind smile and a wave, as if he too had just witnessed a small miracle.

Back on the catamaran, Tiffany curled up near the shaded edge of the deck, her face hidden beneath her hat, her hand tightly gripping Larry's. The wind blew through her hair, the water slapped against the hull, and the rest of the family sat quietly, understanding that this wasn't just a scare—this was a warning.

When they finally returned to the resort, Larry helped Tiffany inside their room and straight into a cold shower. She stood there, quiet, letting the water run over her skin, trying to rinse off the weight of what had just happened.

Later, she climbed into bed, eyes barely open, body limp.

Larry ordered food and sat beside her, watching her sleep, listening to her breathing. He had never felt so terrified, so helpless, so close to a line he never wanted to see. And yet, she was here. She had come back.

But the fear dawdled.

It haunted him through the night.

Because for the first time, the thought he had pushed down, locked away, and buried under faith and hope was now louder than ever.

He might really lose her.

And he didn't know how he'd survive if he did.

The flight home from Mexico was layered in emotion—a delicate blend of comfort, exhaustion, gratitude, and an ache that neither Larry nor Tiffany could quite shake. As the wheels lifted off the tarmac and the shimmering coastline fell away beneath them, Larry held Tiffany's hand in silence, watching the tropical blues dissolve into the white clouds above.

He felt relief that Tiffany was returning to Colorado, back to Dr. Mantle, back to the comfort of the routine they had carved out in this battle. But he also felt the slow sting of sadness settle into his chest. Leaving Mexico always brought that twinge; it was their consecrated place, their escape, the land of frozen daiquiris and sunset dances. But this time, it felt heftier. There had been moments during the trip when he wasn't sure they'd all make it home together. And yet they had. By the grace of God, they had.

Patrick flew out from Cancun to Houston separately. Larry watched his son board the plane, tall and confident, headed back to the life he was building on his own. There was pride in his chest but also a familiar ache—the one that comes when your child leaves the nest for good. That's the cruel duality of parenting: you work tirelessly to prepare them for independence, and when they finally spread their wings, your heart breaks.

When the rest of the family landed in Denver, it was as if a page had turned. Tiffany, almost miraculously, seemed revitalized. Mexico, despite the scare, had not drained her—it had refueled her soul. She bounced back into the rhythm of life as if she'd never missed a beat. Within days, she was back in her upstairs office, headset on, leading Zoom meetings with the composure of an executive and the warmth of a mother hen. Her team depended on her, and she showed up every day, even when her body begged her to rest.

FOREVER TIFFANY

She dove straight into her mom duties with just as much fervor. Brennan was about to start his sophomore year, and Tiffany wasn't going to let anything slip through the cracks. She made sure he finished his driver's education classes, scheduling the final test and coaching him through every detail. Larry laughed, watching them go over parallel parking techniques in the driveway, Tiffany calling out instructions like a seasoned DMV official.

And then, with Brennan set, she turned her attention to Rylee and Landon.

Their new apartment in Boulder was the next big step. Like she had done for Patrick, Tiffany became the visionary designer and personal shopper for their first real home together. A trip to American Furniture Warehouse turned into a full-blown Tiffany-led adventure. She guided the young couple to a modern sectional sofa—something big enough for late-night baby feedings and lazy weekend naps. They picked out a sleek bedroom set, bar stools for the kitchen counter, and the perfect mix of decorative touches to make the space feel warm and welcoming. Tiffany's eye for aesthetics never failed her.

But the pièce de résistance was the nursery.

Tiffany's friend Jenna, a talented furniture restorer, had taken two old dressers and turned them into heirloom-quality pieces for the baby's room. They chose warm colors, gentle whites and greyish blue tones, accented with brushed gold handles. Tiffany helped Rylee pick out crib bedding, a glider chair, and framed art prints with watercolor animals and sweet quotes.

The nursery was going to be perfect—a combination of Rylee's youthful energy and Tiffany's timeless style. And though they were just two young college students preparing for a massive life shift, they had a secret weapon in their corner: a mother who loved with fierce intention and poured every bit of herself into making sure they were ready.

Whatever had shaken Tiffany in Mexico—whatever weakness or fear had briefly crept into her—felt like a distant memory now. It was a moment, a fluke, a passing shadow that couldn't dim her light.

She was back.

And with her back, the world felt steady again. Hope had returned to the house. Willpower echoed in every room. And if there was one unspoken truth that Larry could feel in every heartbeat, it was this: Tiffany was going to *beat* cancer.

And everyone around her believed it, because she believed it first.

Moving day for Rylee was, in Larry's mind, a necessary evil—the kind of day that tested patience, muscles, and marriage all at once. He groaned when he saw the size of the U-Haul truck he'd somehow managed to rent—an absolute beast, the largest they had on the lot. It looked like something fit for relocating a five-bedroom family home, not a two-bedroom Boulder apartment for a young couple just starting out. But as the garage door lifted and bin after bin was rolled out— clothes, shoes, bedding, dishes, monitors, computers, TVs, throw pillows, lamps, wall art, baby supplies—he realized, maybe it wasn't too big after all.

Tiffany, of course, was in her zone. She moved through the apartment with the calm intensity of a symphony conductor, directing the flow of bins and boxes, arranging furniture deliveries, and coordinating with the American Furniture Warehouse team, who were scheduled to arrive later that afternoon. Everything had its place—she saw it all in her mind before it was even unpacked. What Larry assumed would be a few hours of organizing stretched into an all-day marathon. After eight long hours of hauling, lifting, assembling, and answering Tiffany's "Could you run back to the truck and grab just one more thing?" requests, Larry hit a wall.

He kissed Tiffany on the cheek, handed her a coffee, and admitted defeat. "I love you," he said with a smile, "but I'm driving home before I lose all motor function." He knew she'd work through the night if needed—and she did. The place had to be perfect, and for Tiffany, exhaustion was just a speed bump on the road to a beautifully put-together home.

Just a few weeks had passed when another milestone arrived—September 11th. Brennan had just earned his learner's permit, and he couldn't have been more eager to hit the road. Larry and Tiffany knew exactly where to go: the quiet light industrial area on the edge of town, where traffic was scant, the roads wide, and nerves could settle without the pressure of impatient drivers honking behind a teen learning to navigate a turn.

They took Larry's new Land Rover Defender—the one Tiffany had insisted he trade his BMW for after she took it for a spin and announced, "This is more you." Larry had rolled his eyes at the time, but now, guiding Brennan behind the wheel, he had to admit—she was right. Again.

Brennan gripped the wheel tight at first, shoulders tense, face serious. Tiffany saw it in an instant. She always saw everything in Brennan—the smallest flicker of fear or joy in his eyes. He was still her baby, her youngest, the one she used to rock to sleep, the one who could make her laugh with a single look. She reached over, touched his shoulder gently, and said, "You've got this." With every block they drove, Brennan settled in, gaining confidence. Each stop and turn was smoother than the last. He was going to be just fine.

But even amidst all the movement and milestones, Tiffany's mind was occupied with something else—something she refused to let cancer or exhaustion take away from her: Rylee's baby shower.

She poured herself into it, the way she did everything that mattered to her, with intention, precision, and love. There would be no last-minute planning here. Every detail was accounted for. Guests were flying in from all over—family, friends, childhood neighbors. Hotels were booked, invites had gone out weeks earlier, and the cake was ordered from her favorite bakery. There were themed decorations, handmade centerpieces, and special gifts wrapped in soft blush and gold tones. The guest list had grown longer by the day, but Tiffany didn't flinch. If she had to host 100 people, she would make every single one of them feel like they were the only person in the room.

September 28th was circled, underlined, and highlighted on the calendar. It would be perfect. Because Tiffany was building a memory, not just for Rylee, but for herself. She was going to watch her daughter step into motherhood, and nothing—not even the growing pain in her arm or the tiredness that stayed a little longer each morning—was going to stop her from making this moment magical.

In her heart, she knew: life was a string of moments, and she was going to make this one shine.

The second week of September arrived with a crispness in the air, the kind that hinted at fall's approach—the leaves just beginning to turn, the mornings coming in cool. But for Larry and Tiffany, the change in season meant something more: another appointment with Dr. Luke Mantle, another moment where hope and fear would go to war inside their hearts.

They had walked into UCHealth with cautious optimism. Tiffany had been moving better, her spirits still high, her drive steady. Larry was holding onto the words from their last PET scan—the ones that suggested progress, or at least, no significant setbacks. But medicine, like life, doesn't always follow the script you write in your head.

Dr. Mantle's eyes said it before his words did. He greeted them warmly, but his usual lightness was shaded with something heavier—something that made Larry's stomach twist in quiet dread.

He pulled up the most recent scan, and as the images glowed softly across the screen, reality struck like a thunderclap.

"The lesions on your spine…" he began, "they're gone. The radiation worked. They're no longer active. That's a huge win."

Larry exhaled sharply, his hand instinctively reaching for Tiffany's. She gave his fingers a gentle squeeze—her silent way of saying, we're okay.

But then came the pause.

"However…" Dr. Mantle continued, his tone shifting. "We've discovered new growth. There's a lesion on your left upper humerus." He glanced at Tiffany and measured her reaction. "The bone is fractured."

Tiffany didn't cringe.

"There's also one on your right upper femur," he added. "It's also fractured. They're stable for now, but we'll need to bring in orthopedic surgeons. We need to evaluate the best way to support those bones, structurally, before anything gives."

Larry felt like the floor sloped beneath him. Two fractures. New growth. The weight of it was too much; his chest felt tight.

But Tiffany—she just looked at Dr. Mantle with that stanch stare, the same one she'd given since day one.

"Well," she said with the same boldness she brought to every battle in her life, "sounds good. I don't feel like I'm dying, so I'm not going to die. We're going to beat this."

Dr. Mantle gave a soft laugh, more exhale than amusement, and his expression softened. In that moment, it was as if her spirit pulled him back to hope, too. His eyes reflected something deeper—not just belief in medicine, but belief in her. It was rare, maybe even a first for him, to see someone fighting with so much light still burning inside them.

"I believe you," he said quietly.

Then, with a seriousness that returned the room to stillness, he leaned forward and said, "Tiffany, I need to ask again… I strongly recommend we do the brain MRI. Just to be thorough."

Tiffany's eyes dropped, her face unreadable for a moment, her eyes looking towards the door.

"I'll think about it," she replied, voice low but firm. "Maybe. Maybe for him." She nodded her head slightly toward Larry.

It wasn't a yes, but it wasn't a no either.

The drive home was quiet at first—just the sound of the tires on pavement and the occasional whistle of wind through the cracked windows. Larry finally broke the silence.

"You know I think you should get the scan," he said gently, his eyes fixed on the road ahead but his heart squarely in the passenger seat beside him.

"I know," Tiffany replied. "But if there's something there..." she paused. "What if knowing just makes it harder? What if not knowing lets me keep living like this—feeling strong, being present, pushing forward?"

Larry gripped the steering wheel tighter. He wanted to argue, wanted to plead, but he also understood. Deep down, he got it. He hated it, but he understood. It wasn't denial. It was a form of bravery he could only just comprehend.

"Just think about it," he said quietly.

"I will," she whispered. "For you."

And with that, they drove on, windows down, hearts heavy, but hands still holding onto each other and hope.

The end of September arrived quicker than anyone expected. It was the kind of busy, chaotic stretch that seemed to carry the days along like leaves caught in a swift river current. Between planning for the baby shower and managing her health, Tiffany was doing everything in her power to stay afloat—and make sure everything looked effortless while she did.

FOREVER TIFFANY

On the morning of Wednesday, September 25th, Larry boarded a flight to Baton Rouge, Louisiana. It wasn't just a trip—it was an industry golf event that had been scheduled for months, a networking opportunity he would normally enjoy. But leaving Tiffany, especially now, felt wrong. She insisted he go. "I'll be fine," she had said that morning, with her trademark strength tucked behind tired eyes.

She wasn't alone—Stacy was there, ever-present and reliable. And Tiffany's mother, Vicki, and her sister, Amanda, were flying in the very next day. The baby shower was just around the corner, and no matter what was going on beneath the surface, Tiffany was going to make sure it was perfect.

When Larry landed in Baton Rouge, the humidity hit him like a wave, but his thoughts weren't on the weather. They were on her. He called as soon as he was through the terminal.

"Hey, beautiful," he said.

"I'm okay," Tiffany replied softly.

But Larry heard something. It was in the way her voice glided, not quite anchored to its usual energy. There was a weight there. A distance. Something was off.

"You sound tired," he said gently. "If you need me to come home, I can catch the next flight out tonight."

She wouldn't hear of it.

"You're not coming home, Larry. You've been looking forward to this trip. Enjoy it, please."

He agreed, reluctantly. But something in his gut didn't settle.

He had already planned to leave Baton Rouge on Friday the 27th, flying directly to Houston to spend the weekend with Patrick. They had dinner reservations at Steak 48 with Nick, the president of a major firm in Houston, and Mike, a respected sales leader Larry had known for years. Then on Sunday, he and Patrick were heading to the Texans vs. Jaguars game. It was a much-needed father-son weekend, and Tiffany had pushed for it, knowing how important it was for Larry, but mostly, wanting reassurance that Patrick was doing well.

Still, Larry couldn't shake the feeling. On Friday, before boarding his flight to Houston, he called Amanda.

"She didn't sound right when I talked to her Wednesday," Larry said. "Something's wrong."

Amanda didn't disagree.

"She's weak," she admitted. "She's not really moving around much. Definitely not herself. But Larry… she wants you to be where you are."

The words were heavy, and they sat in Larry's chest like lead. He thought back to just a week earlier—Tiffany had bought new furniture for the formal living room. She wanted everything perfect for the baby shower, right down to the furniture layout and the way the light from the windows would catch the edge of the curtains.

It hadn't been that long since she and her close friends, Jessica and Stacy, had worked through a full redesign of the house. Every painting, every sculpture, every fresh coat of paint—handpicked. The guest bathroom had been completely remodeled. Gray and black floor tiles were laid down with precision, the walls redone in black mosaic stone, and gold accents that gave the space Tiffany's signature elegance. The whole home was her palette, and she had painted it with love, style, and intention.

She wasn't just decorating for a show. She was building warmth, creating a sanctuary for her family to hold onto, for whatever came next.

That night in Houston, Larry dressed for dinner, but his heart wasn't entirely in it. He stepped outside the restaurant before the reservation and called Tiffany. It was late, the baby shower would be winding down, and he wanted to check in.

FOREVER TIFFANY

Her voice came through the line.

"I'm good," she said softly, but the energy was gone. Larry heard it immediately. The weariness. The strain in her words. The exhaustion that wasn't just physical.

"You sound tired, babe," he said. "Was the party too much?"

"No," she whispered. "It was perfect."

But it wasn't her usual "perfect."

He called Amanda again—his voice more anxious this time.

Amanda didn't sugarcoat it.

"She didn't really get up today," she said. "She sat on the sofa and just watched. It was a big crowd. A lot of people. In the past, she would've been everywhere at once, running the show. Today, she handed it over to her girls. She was just... quiet."

Larry felt it in his bones. That ache of helplessness, that awful tug that comes when someone you love more than life itself is slipping into a harder part of their journey—and there's nothing you can do but hold on.

And he wanted nothing more than to be home.

But he stayed—for Patrick. For Tiffany. Because she asked him to.

He spent that night at dinner, sipping his cocktail, smiling when needed, but his thoughts never left her. As the evening pressed on, all he could picture was her, sitting on the couch at home, watching the baby shower unfold like a beautiful movie she'd once starred in, but now was quietly observing from the wings.

Tiffany had given her all. Her energy, her effort, her love. And now... she was tired. The kind of tired that went deeper than her bones.

And Larry knew. As much as he tried to stay strong, to hold it all together, he knew. Their war wasn't over. But a new, tougher chapter had just begun.

CHAPTER 24.
Forever Starts Now

Larry was home again. The baby shower was over, the rush of guests had come and gone, and for the first time in weeks, the house felt still. Not peaceful, not restful—just quiet in a way that felt frightening. It was just the three of them now: Larry, Tiffany, and Brennan.

They had grown used to a different rhythm, one filled with the buzz of excitement and the hopeful distractions of party planning and out-of-town visitors. But with the house quieted and the air settled, a heaviness came back. Their world, the one they once moved through with joyful ease, had become something altogether unfamiliar, like a dream that sometimes lifted them with beauty and wonder and other times dropped them into a nightmare they could not escape.

It was early October now. The golden leaves outside their windows rustled in the wind, and the evenings carried that familiar fall chill. Tiffany had been spending most of her time in bed, working when she could, resting when her body demanded it. One night, as she lay curled up under the blankets, she looked over at Larry and asked sweetly, "Can you get me a Sprite with ice?"

Larry jumped up, eager to do anything that brought her comfort. He grabbed a tall cup, filled it with cold soda, added the perfect amount of ice, and dropped in a straw—just the way she liked it. He handed it to her with a positive smile, and she took a long sip.

Then, she smiled and let out a small laugh. "It's dericious," she said through a giggle.

Larry raised an eyebrow and chuckled. "What did you just say?"

"Dericious," she repeated, her grin widening. "What is wrong with me? My tongue feels weird."

They both laughed, chalking it up to fatigue or maybe just a silly moment brought on by medication or exhaustion. She didn't seem concerned—just amused—and they let it go.

But in the days that followed, Larry began to notice more.

She couldn't swallow her chemo pills—those massive horse pills she once took without flinching. Now her tongue wouldn't cooperate. She looked frail. Her skin, though still radiant in its own right, lacked the vibrancy she always carried. He asked her if she was hungry, and she shook her head. "No," she whispered.

Larry's mind began to churn.

When was the last time she ate?

He couldn't remember. In fact, he realized that since he had returned from Houston, he hadn't seen her eat a single thing.

He called Amanda.

"Did she eat while you were here?" he asked, already knowing the answer.

Amanda paused. "No," she said. "Now that you mention it, I don't think she did."

He called Vicki and Holly next. Same answer. None of them could recall her eating anything beyond a spoonful of applesauce, a few sips of Sprite, or a couple of swallows of Gatorade.

It wasn't just that she wasn't eating—it was that she couldn't. Her body had crossed a line. One Larry feared she wouldn't come back from.

What Larry and Tiffany shared was a beautiful, passionate, out-of-this-world love—bond that transcended time and only deepened with each passing year. Their intimate moments were sacred, hugged by laughter, whispers, and the kind of closeness only true soulmates ever know. But as Larry looked back, it wasn't those candlelit nights or quiet mornings tangled in bedsheets that defined their intimacy. No, the most intimate moments of all came much later, when Tiffany's body began to fail her.

It was in those quiet, fragile hours that love revealed its truest form.

Helping her from bed, guiding her trembling frame into the warmth of the shower, Larry would wrap his arms around her—not just to steady her, but to shield her. He would gently wash her hair, careful not to let the water sting her skin. Her eyes often closed, her breath soft. She was in pain, and he hated that. God, how he hated it. But in the same breath, he was grateful. Grateful that he was the one there, the one holding her, the one she trusted to see her in her most vulnerable state.

That was intimacy—the quiet, unspoken kind. The kind born not of desire, but of devotion.

In those moments, he wasn't just her husband.

He was her caretaker, her protector, her safe place.

And that, he would carry with him forever.

When they met, all those years ago, Tiffany was barely 98 pounds. Petite, graceful, always strong in her own soft way. Over time, she had settled into a healthy, radiant 125-pound frame—a weight that suited her and matched her vitality. But now, Larry could see it in her face, her arms, the way her clothes hung on her. She was losing weight. Fast.

The second week of October rolled in, and things weren't getting better.

Nearly two weeks had passed since Larry had seen her eat anything nourishing. Apple sauce, yes. A few sips of soda or electrolyte drinks, yes. But food? Real food? No. She would whisper that she wasn't hungry. That it didn't taste good. That she would try later. But "later" never came.

And then came the vomiting.

Not much, because there wasn't much in her. But enough to terrify Larry. It was as if her body was giving up on the idea of nourishment altogether.

Midweek, the concern turned into action. Stacy came over and helped Larry drive Tiffany up to the UCHealth Anschutz campus. They checked her in and explained what had been going on.

The medical team ran fluids. Her electrolytes were low. They were worried about dehydration.

Larry was done waiting. He called Vicki and told her he needed her now, and without hesitation, she was on the next flight out.

Because something was happening, Tiffany, always the fighter, always the one to hold the family together, was slipping. And none of them could ignore it anymore.

This wasn't just a rough week.

This was a turning point.

And Larry, with a heart heavy and eyes wide with fear, clung to the only thing he could in that moment: hope.

Hope that this was just another valley they had to cross.

Hope that Tiffany, in all her beauty and grit, would rise again.

Hope that somehow, some way, they'd find their way back to the life they loved.

Together.

Monday, October 14th, arrived under a gray, cloud-stained sky, the kind of morning that felt heavy before the day had even begun. Tiffany wasn't well—Larry could see it, feel it, sense it in the air between them. She hadn't eaten. Not really. She still wasn't taking her chemo pills, and now the vomiting was back, more frequent than before. They were long past the stage of hoping this was a side effect or a passing spell. Larry had stocked the house with medical-grade blue vomit bags, trying to bring some small level of dignity and comfort to a situation that felt anything but.

That morning, Tiffany had a scheduled radiation appointment at the UCHealth Highlands Ranch facility. Larry helped her into the backseat of their SUV. She moved like a ghost of herself, so fragile, so slow. Her body was growing weaker by the hour, her limbs thin and delicate. When they pulled up to the hospital doors, Larry hit the suspension control to lower the SUV closer to the ground, then jumped out and retrieved a wheelchair from the entrance. He wheeled it to her side and gently helped her in. She was grateful. Too tired to pretend otherwise.

As they made their way through the sliding glass doors into the cancer center, everything felt muted—the lights, the sounds, the people around them. The only sharp thing in the room was Larry's worry, cutting through him like a blade.

Nurse Sharon, a woman with kind eyes and a motherly warmth, spotted them from across the floor and came rushing over. Her expression shifted the second she laid eyes on Tiffany. Without hesitation, she wrapped a blood pressure cuff around Tiffany's arm and read the numbers: 85/60.

Sharon didn't even blink. "We need to admit her immediately."

Larry's heart clenched.

The moment he'd been fearing was suddenly happening—not slowly, not gradually, but like a wave crashing through their lives without warning.

He stood frozen for a moment outside the room they wheeled her into, wondering—*Is this the moment? Is this when I start making the calls?*

When do you call her sister? Her mom? Her friends? When do you admit out loud that the fight has shifted? That the ground beneath you is starting to buckle?

But then—something changed.

Tiffany responded to being admitted with a sort of surprising strength. Within hours, her color returned, her cheeks pinked just slightly, and that signature smile of hers emerged once again. Somehow, someway, the hospital environment gave her a spark. Her phone was back in her hand, Teams meetings resumed, and she was managing her team from the hospital bed as if she were back in her office chair. There she was—Tiffany again.

But Larry noticed something.

Her right eye was mostly closed. She said it felt dry, like something was stuck in it. She couldn't fully open it. It was subtle, but unmistakable. Something was wrong.

Later that night, for the first time, Tiffany gave in. "Let's do the brain MRI."

Larry's breath caught in his throat. Finally. But even as he nodded and called for the order, his gut twisted with dread.

The scan came back quickly. Too quickly.

The news was devastating. A large mass had formed at the base of Tiffany's brain. It was not only embedded deep—it had connected itself to her skull and had already started to fracture it. As if that weren't enough, the PET scan revealed a massive growth in her chest as well. This one had wormed its way through her sternum, curling itself from the front side of her body to the back. Her sternum, like her skull, was fractured.

Larry sat there in the sterile hospital room, feeling the floor fall away beneath him.

Tiffany, ever resolute, took the news like a warrior.

"No," she told him plainly. "Do not call people. Do not bring everyone in here. I'm not dying. I'm still kicking. And I need people to treat me like I'm living, not like I'm already gone."

Larry nodded slowly. He knew better than to argue. That was Tiffany—strong, protective, and in absolute control of her story. She allowed Vicki to stay, of course—her mother, who had become Larry's strongest teammate in this battle. Vicki helped with Brennan's school runs, cared for the dogs, and kept the house running while Larry focused all his energy on Tiffany. Together, they made a good team, bonded by love for the same woman.

Twelve days passed in the hospital. Tiffany stayed strong through every one of them.

When she finally came home during the third week of October, she was thin, tired, and still unable to eat much, but she was alive. And more than that, she was still her. She resumed her radiation treatments immediately, never once backing down from the schedule, never once surrendering to the pain.

Cancer had the ball, sure.

First and goal, maybe from the five-yard line.

But in Tiffany's mind, she was still the defense, and she was about to make the biggest stop of her life.

"I'm not done," she said. "They haven't seen my fourth quarter yet."

Larry believed her. Because to him, there was no greater force in the world than the woman he loved.

The third week of October had arrived, and with it came a moment Larry wouldn't soon forget. His phone rang late that afternoon, and the caller ID displayed the name Jorge. Jorge, the CEO of Larry's company, wasn't just a boss—he was a leader in the truest sense of the word. From the very beginning of Tiffany's diagnosis, Jorge, Bruce, and everyone else on Larry's team had been solid in their support. There were no side-eyes about time off, no raised eyebrows at missed meetings or skipped travel. The only question they ever asked was simple, sincere, and constant: "What can we do?"

Larry stepped out onto the back patio and answered the call. The sun was dipping behind the mountains, forming warm gold streaks across the yard. With a sigh, he greeted Jorge, not entirely sure what to expect.

What followed was more than a business call—it was a lifeline.

For over an hour, Jorge spoke with empathy, grace, and genuine concern. "Larry," he said softly, "Tiffany sounds like an incredibly strong woman. I've been praying for her. I've been praying for you all. I can't pretend to know what this feels like, but I want you to know—I'm here."

Larry swallowed hard, trying to hold his composure. It wasn't easy. The world had been moving so fast, with so much uncertainty, but this moment grounded him.

And then came the gesture.

"As soon as she's able," Jorge said, "I want you to take her to Costa Rica. Take her to our home in Los Sueños. Stay as long as you need. Just be together. Rest. Heal."

The offer wasn't just generous—it was extraordinary. Jorge's home overlooked Herradura Bay and the marina, perched high above the coast with views that made the soul quiet. It was paradise, pure and simple. And now it was being offered not as a vacation, but as a sanctuary. A sacred space to breathe, to reflect, to try and reclaim something the cancer had tried so desperately to steal—peace.

Larry thanked him, his voice thick with emotion. "Jorge… I don't even know what to say. Just… thank you. From the bottom of my heart."

But Jorge, humble and grounded, simply replied, "Don't thank me. Just take care of her. That's all I ask."

FOREVER TIFFANY

Tiffany had that same kind of support in her corner, too. Her best friend Holly, who just so happened to also be her CEO, had been a rock through every twist and turn. And then there was Stacy—Tiffany's other ride-or-die—working right beside her, never letting her fall, never letting her fight alone.

It was divine, really.

The way their lives had been sewn together, not just by fate, but by faith. Because in a time when so many things were broken, what held them together was the strength of people. People who didn't just say they cared—they showed it. With time. With grace. With wide-open hearts.

Fighting cancer was never going to be easy.

But having the kind of support that Larry and Tiffany had? From bosses, from best friends, from colleagues who had become family. That made all the difference in the world.

They were blessed. Truly, unmistakably, blessed.

And both of them knew it.

The next night, as Halloween brought giggles and costumes to neighborhoods around them, Tiffany had one request. "Can you call Bishop Shane?" she asked Larry quietly. "I want a blessing."

Without hesitation, Larry made the call.

By 7 p.m., their living room—now converted into Tiffany's sanctuary—filled with the warm, calming presence of three men of faith: Bishop Shane, their dear friend Paul, and President Chris, the Stake President. Tiffany sat upright in the new leather recliner Vicki had purchased just weeks earlier. It was soft, supportive—exactly what she needed—and had become her favorite place to rest.

The conversation before the blessing was light with laughter and faith-driven energy. Tiffany, ever the one to lead with hope, smiled wide. "I'm gonna win," she said with conviction, "but we need a miracle."

Larry nodded, kneeling beside her. "We do," he said quietly, his voice cracking ever so slightly. "We need a blessing for a miracle... and we have huge faith."

President Chris looked at Tiffany with warmth and humility. "This is God's blessing," he reminded her gently. "These are just my words. But His hands... they are already here."

The room grew still as Chris placed his hands on Tiffany's head, his voice steady, soft, and full of spiritual gravity. The blessing poured out like a balm, like oil on wounds that no medicine could reach. They prayed for healing. For comfort. For peace. For a miracle, whatever form it may take.

Tears fell freely.

And again, Larry felt it.

God.

In the quiet stillness, in the flickering candles, in the courage of Tiffany's eyes. He was there. Not with thunder, not with fanfare—but with love. Gentle, holy love.

After the blessing, Larry leaned in and asked her once more, as he had so many times before, "Should I call everyone in? Patrick? Amanda? My mom and dad? Should I call them now?"

Tiffany looked at him with the same fire that had burned in her since the day he met her. "No," she whispered, shaking her head slightly. "Not yet. I'm still not giving up. We'll celebrate when I do."

It wasn't denial.

It was hope.

It was Tiffany.

And Larry believed her.

FOREVER TIFFANY

Because she had always given him a reason to.

Monday, November 4th, 2024—

A date Larry knew would be etched into his soul for the rest of his life. The kind of date you don't mark on calendars, yet one you never forget. The kind that whittles itself into your bones, into your breath, into the quiet pauses when your heart aches and your mind drifts.

He had just picked Brennan up from school for his lunch break and off-hours, a routine that had become comforting in its simplicity. As soon as they pulled into the driveway, Larry moved quickly. He wasn't hungry, not really. He was only thinking of her—his wife, his love, the light of his life.

He took the stairs, two at a time, and found her resting in bed, where she had been the night before. It had taken her over an hour just to make it up those same stairs the night before—every step agonizing, every breath heavy with implicit pain. Her body had betrayed her, bones weakened and broken by the silent, ruthless march of cancer, the only uninvited guest they had to cater to. Her left leg was fractured. Her left arm was fractured. Her sternum was fractured. Her skull was fractured. But not a single tear had fallen from her eyes. Not once. She was strength wrapped in fragility.

As he entered the room, she stirred, her voice small and tired.

"Can you help me get to the bathroom?"

"Of course," he said, instantly at her side.

He slid his arm gently around her waist, wrapped his other hand around hers, and together they moved. Her body, now barely a hundred pounds, felt impossibly light—but it was not the weight that Larry noticed. It was the weakness. Her fire was still there, but her body… her body was giving out.

They didn't make it far.

Seven or eight steps, maybe. And then, without warning, her knees buckled and she collapsed like gravity had suddenly decided to double its pull on her. Larry caught her instantly, refusing to let her fall. He held her close, supported her weight, but as he clutched her arm, he heard it. Snap.

He felt it break.

He looked down in horror. "I broke your arm," he whispered, the words cutting through his own heart.

Tiffany, ever his protector even now, shook her head. "No, you didn't," she said, barely above a whisper. "You didn't do anything."

Larry's chest compressed. He didn't care what she said—he had felt it. And now, for the first time in their twenty-four years together, he felt real panic take over.

"I need to call 911," he said, already reaching for his phone.

"No," she said softly, her eyes tired, distant. "Please don't. I can't do this anymore... I want to go home."

Larry froze.

"You are home," he said, gently, kneeling beside her.

She looked at him, her eyes holding something he hadn't seen before. Something infinite. Something surrendering.

"No," she whispered again. "I just want to go home."

And in that moment, Larry knew exactly what she meant.

She didn't mean their Colorado home, their sanctuary filled with memories and love. She meant the home beyond this one—the place where her dad was waiting, where her Uncle Dan was surely standing with open arms, where pain no longer existed, and peace flowed like a gentle river. She was tired. She had fought with everything she had. But now... she was ready.

His heart shattered in silence.

Still, he did what he had to do. He called 911.

The Castle Rock EMTs and fire department arrived within minutes, a full team entering the home with swift precision and gentle empathy. Larry met them at the front door, his voice calm but full of emotion.

"She's upstairs," he said. "She's only in a sweater and underwear—please, can someone help her with pants? She'd hate for anyone to see her that way."

One EMT nodded with compassion. "We've got it, sir."

Another had already slipped through the garage, placing the transport stretcher inside and closing the door again to keep the warmth in. These were the small things Larry would remember—the kindness in the chaos, the dignity preserved in the moments that threatened to undo everything.

They worked together to safely stabilize Tiffany, sliding her gently onto a portable lift bag to avoid any more pressure on her fractured body. When she was ready, they carried her carefully down the stairs and into the cold, late-autumn air.

Larry followed close behind. The wind bit at his skin, but he didn't feel it.

He rode the ambulance in spirit. As they sped toward UCHealth Anschutz, he and Vicki gathered her things—the essentials: a change of clothes, a toothbrush, her laptop, her hairbrush. He packed them like they were armor. Like they could somehow help her fight just a little bit harder.

They knew this could be a long stay.

But Larry had no idea just how long this chapter would linger in his heart. Or how deeply those words *I just want to go home* would echo through every room of their house for the rest of his life.

Even as Tiffany settled back into her hospital room, hooked up to machines and IV drips and surrounded by the sterile hum of medical equipment, she remained unshakably in control, at least in the ways that mattered most to her. Yes, she had agreed to be admitted again, but that didn't mean she was surrendering to anything. Her body might be weak, but her will was still granite.

She had one request—no flood of visitors.

She wasn't ready to be "said goodbye to." This wasn't that kind of hospital stay. Larry's mom, Diana, and his Aunt Karen had visited the week before, flying in with hugs and stories and hope. But in Tiffany's mind, that was just a social visit. A check-in. A loving gesture. Not a farewell tour.

Still, as the days unfolded and the people who mattered most to her began flying in—Amanda, Sandy, Holly—Tiffany orchestrated the week like it was a leadership summit. Every moment was scheduled. Every visit, intentionally crafted. This was her version of a boardroom, her final masterclass in love and purpose.

She declared it early: "Monday and Tuesday nights—Vicki. Wednesday—Larry. Thursday and Friday—Vicki again. Saturday night is for me, Amanda, and Sandy. A girls' slumber party."

And Sunday?

"That's Yellowstone night," she told Larry, "and I don't care what's going on—you're staying."

No one questioned her.

She was directing the play now, and everyone followed her lead. Each day, familiar faces filled her room. Rylee and Landon made near-daily appearances. Holly brought laughter. Vicki brought warmth. Amanda, her sister, and her heart brought calm. Sandy brought history, memories, and strength. And Larry—he was always close, never far from her side, even when others were staying overnight.

FOREVER TIFFANY

Still, there was one goal above all others that Tiffany held onto, like a sacred vow:

"I want to be in the birthing room when Rylee has her baby."

She repeated it often to Dr. Mantle.

"You get me there," she said.

And he, who had grown to admire her soul, simply nodded and replied, "We're going to do everything we can."

She loved the hospital staff at UCHealth Anschutz, and they loved her right back. She had Larry bring in cake—her favorite kind, Chantilly—and breakfast bagels for the nurses and doctors. It was her way of saying thank you, her way of reminding everyone that she was still her, still gracious, still thinking of others, even as her body fought harder than ever before.

By Wednesday, she was still running company meetings from her bed. At one point, she was sketching out a reorganization plan. Who does that from a hospital room while battling Stage IV melanoma? Tiffany does. Not because she was obsessed with work, but because when Tiffany gave her word, she followed through. Because having a purpose meant having a reason to keep moving forward.

Saturday night came, and so did the girls' slumber party. The hospital made an exception and allowed both Amanda and Sandy to stay. They brought in snacks, played music low, and shared stories deep into the night. They laughed until they cried. Then, when the laughter settled into soft silence, they just... cried.

For the first time since her diagnosis, someone truly saw Tiffany break.

She had shared that she'd had two private meltdowns before—but never in front of anyone. Not even Larry. But on this night, with her sister and her dearest aunt lying beside her, Tiffany's tears came freely. They were not tears of surrender; they were tears of being seen, of knowing she was deeply loved and held in the arms of people who had known her for decades.

It was a night that would live in Amanda and Sandy's hearts for the rest of their lives.

The next morning, Larry arrived early. The girls kissed Tiffany goodbye and headed to the airport, tears in their eyes, hearts heavy and full at the same time.

Sunday was quiet. Cozy. Normal, even.

The Broncos lost a heartbreaker to the Chiefs, 16-14, on a blocked field goal. NASCAR played in the background, followed by Christmas movies—a new obsession of Tiffany's in recent months. She'd never been one to binge movies, but now, she couldn't stop. Maybe it was comfort. Maybe it was nostalgia. Maybe it was hope.

When Rylee and Landon came by, the four of them lounged in the room, half-watching, half-talking. As they prepared to head back to Boulder, Tiffany told them to wait.

"I want to get you dinner."

She ordered PF Chang's to-go, timing it so it would be ready right when they got home. When Rylee began reading off the credit card numbers, Larry noticed something strange—Tiffany was struggling to repeat more than three or four digits at a time. A small hiccup. But it didn't sit right.

Later that evening, Larry dragged the recliner closer to Tiffany's bed. The lights were dim. Yellowstone was finally back—the second half of Season 5, long-awaited. Tiffany had been talking about this premiere for months.

Larry laid back in the chair, reached out his hand, and she met it with hers.

They watched in silence, her fingers laced through his.

And then she fell asleep.

FOREVER TIFFANY

Larry watched her for a few moments, then turned off the television. No skipping ahead. No spoilers. If they were going to watch Yellowstone, they were going to watch it together.

At midnight, the nurse came in to take vitals.

Larry stood quickly, ready to help. But something was off.

Tiffany was unresponsive.

Her arm, when lifted, dropped like dead weight. Her eyes didn't follow the nurse's movements. The nurse calmly but urgently called for the team and administered Narcan into her IV.

Tiffany's eyes shot open—but something was wrong.

She couldn't move her limbs. Her arms, her legs—paralyzed.

The neurosurgeon rushed in, immediately assessing her condition.

"What's your name?" she asked.

"Tiffany," she whispered.

"Do you know where you are?"

"The hospital."

She held up a pen. "Do you know what this is?"

Tiffany's eyes darted to Larry's. *Help me.*

She looked back at the pen.

"A fan," she said.

The surgeon held up two thumbs. "And what are these?"

"Fans," she said again.

Panic. It gripped Larry by the throat. This wasn't confusion from pain meds. This was something else. Something worse.

They rushed Tiffany out for a brain scan.

Larry stood frozen.

Minutes later, she was wheeled back into the room.

He stepped close, knelt beside her bed, and gently whispered,

"Do you know who I am? Blink once for yes, twice for no."

One blink.

"Do you know how much I love you?"

A faint smile.

One blink.

"I love you so much," he said, holding her hand against his chest.

"You're going to be okay."

And then, just like that...

She closed her eyes.

And the room, once filled with so much laughter, was now heavy with stillness. With uncertainty. With love so deep, it refused to let go.

The lights in the hospital hallway blurred into one another as Larry followed the nurse through a maze of sterile white walls and silent elevators. Tiffany had been rushed to the neurosurgical ICU—an emergency transfer after the terrifying episode in the middle of the night. Larry moved on instinct now. The floor felt uneven beneath him, the air thick and dry. He clutched her belongings in his arms, her favorite hoodie and water bottle clinking softly against the overnight bag he had hastily packed.

The ICU room was stark, humming with the dull buzz of medical monitors and machines. Within seconds of their arrival, two techs entered briskly, their expressions tight with focus. They began placing small round stickers across Tiffany's scalp, connecting thin wires to each one, creating a tangled network across her head like a crown of

FOREVER TIFFANY

confusion. The gel they used smelled faintly of menthol and antiseptic and quickly matted her golden hair into damp tufts.

Larry stood off to the side, unable to move, unable to breathe, caught in the most unreal moment of his life. His wife—his partner, his anchor, his everything—lay still in a hospital bed while strangers worked quietly around her, wires snaking from her head, blinking machines logging every heartbeat and flicker of brain activity.

He felt useless.

He felt like he was watching a scene from a movie he didn't want to be part of—a dream he couldn't wake up from.

His hands trembled as he reached for his phone. It was just after 1:00 a.m.

First, he called Patrick.

His son answered groggily but alert, and as soon as Larry told him what had happened, Patrick didn't hesitate. Within minutes, he was packed and heading to the airport. There was a red-eye flight that would land him in Denver just after sunrise.

Next, Larry called Vicki.

Then Rylee.

The time had come. The time he had prayed would never arrive. It wasn't the moment to say goodbye—not in the way people imagine—but it was time to say everything that ever needed saying. I love you. Thank you. I will carry you with me always. Until we meet again.

Larry sat in the corner of the room, silent now, watching the rise and fall of Tiffany's chest beneath a soft red Christmas blanket he had covered with. The soft beeping of the heart monitor kept time in the background like a solemn metronome. He couldn't cry. Not yet. The tears were there—burning behind his eyes—but for now, he had to stay still. Stay strong.

He thought back over the last week. How Tiffany had orchestrated her visits like a maestro guiding a symphony. The slumber party with Amanda and Sandy. Her insistence on Sunday night with Larry to watch Yellowstone. How she had called out dinner orders and remembered birthdays and checked in on coworkers, even while she was cradled by tubes and needles.

Larry's heart ached as he realized something he hadn't let himself consider until now.

She knew.

Somewhere deep down, Tiffany had known her time was near.

Maybe it was her dad. Maybe Dan had whispered in her ear from beyond. Maybe it was God giving her just enough time to tie her final ribbons, speak her final words, and smile those final, unforgettable smiles. Maybe the reason she'd looked so peaceful that week—so content even as her body was failing—was because her soul had already made peace.

For Larry, the pain of watching her body fail was a weight he couldn't describe. But that moment with her—their moment, her last true moment of clarity—would be something he'd treasure forever.

It had been her gift.

A kiss on the soul.

A final "I love you" wrapped in a blink, a smile, and the silence of a shared room where two people once lived as one.

It was too soon. It would always be too soon.

But in that strange, tragic, beautiful way...

It was perfect.

As loved ones began arriving at the hospital, the emotions hit with a force that shattered every defense. Tears poured like swollen rivers after a storm, overflowing the edges of every soul in that room. Larry stood at the center of it all, trying desperately to find the words that could soothe the hearts of his children. But he knew. He knew that no matter how comforting his voice tried to sound, no matter how strong he stood for them... they couldn't hear him. Not in this moment. Not now. It was too much. Too real. Too raw.

Brennan was still at home, curled up in bed, unable to face what waited for him at the hospital. He couldn't bear to see his mother like that. His mom—the vibrant, beautiful force of nature who wore her blonde hair like a crown and made every car ride to school feel like a celebration. The mom who let him pick the music and laughed at all his jokes. The mom every kid in town quietly wished was theirs.

Larry understood. Completely.

He called Brennan and held the phone gently to Tiffany's ear, watching the soft rise and fall of her chest. Brennan's voice was almost a whisper, but Larry heard every word.

"Mom... I love you so much."

Larry's hand shook as he held the phone. He tried not to listen, but his heart absorbed every syllable. Simple. Pure. Devastating.

The neurosurgery team pulled Larry aside. They explained, in careful, clinical language, that one of the tumors in Tiffany's brain had begun to bleed. There was a possible solution, they said—an emergency surgery that might stop the hemorrhage, that might wake her. But the words that followed were heavier than anything Larry had ever heard: minimal brain function... full paralysis.

They didn't need to say it outright. The prognosis was not life—it was existence. It was time measured in pain and wires and uncertainty. And Larry knew. He knew his wife, his angel, better than anyone. Tiffany would never want that. Not even for another month. Not even for another day. Her spirit—the very essence of who she was—could never survive in a body trapped and broken.

The choice was unbearable.

But the answer was clear.

He looked at them, eyes swollen and voice steady, and said, "Let her rest."

Larry turned back toward her room, the door still open, the hallway now filling with more of their people. People who loved her. People who had felt the warmth of her presence and couldn't imagine a world without it.

He stepped into the family lobby, just needing a moment. A breath.

And there, sitting quietly with tears in his eyes, was George.

He had flown in from Chicago the moment he heard.

For over twenty years, they had been more than colleagues. More than friends. In an industry built on competition and deals, their bond stood as something rare—something sacred. Everyone knew it: they were brothers in spirit.

George stood as Larry entered, towering and steady—six foot four, two seventy-five, a mountain of a man who'd never been anything but strength. He didn't say a word. He didn't need to. He wrapped Larry in a hug that said it all. A hug that held twenty years of friendship, of loyalty, of shared laughs, and now, shared grief.

Brian was there too, tall and silent, his arms wrapping around Larry with equal force. Larry could feel the pain in him, could sense the ghost of Brian's own father in the moment. Another life lost to melanoma. Another hole left in a family.

Patrick and Rylee… their heartbreak was visible. It lived in their eyes, in the trembling of their hands, in the vacant look that followed their every step. This woman—their mother—had been their compass, their comfort, their greatest advocate. She taught them to drive, to speak with confidence, to love deeply, and to fight hard. She was their lighthouse in every storm.

Now… they stood in the dark.

FOREVER TIFFANY

Rylee clutched her belly, feeling the soft, rolling kicks of her unborn daughter. Tiffany had fought like a warrior to see this through—to hold on long enough to see the next generation enter this world. That thought was both beautiful and cruel. She had fought so hard. She was so close.

The day outside was strangely calm. Blue skies stretched endlessly across the horizon. In the distance, the snowcapped peaks of the Rocky Mountains glistened like a painting come to life, standing tall and sacred, as if nature itself had paused to honor her. It didn't feel like the kind of day someone should die. And yet... here they were.

Larry made the most difficult decision of his life.

He asked that Tiffany be transferred to hospice care, right there in the hospital. She was too weak to make the short journey to the standalone facility. Moving her would be too much. He couldn't risk it. Every second mattered now.

And so, the transition began.

The monitors grew fewer.

The beeping slowed.

The room softened, quieted.

They weren't saying goodbye—not yet—but they were letting go.

Letting go of the fight. Of the battle. Of the hope that Tiffany had carried so fiercely for so long.

They were placing her gently into God's hands now.

And trusting, somehow, that her love—the kind of love that doesn't die—would carry them through the storm ahead.

Tiffany's will remained unbreakable, her body fragile, but her soul still reaching, still holding on. There was something unspoken she needed, something beyond the beeping machines and sterile hospital walls. Larry could feel it. He always could. He watched her lie still, her chest rising and falling with the rhythm of a fighter who had already gone twelve rounds and was gearing up for another.

He sat down with the hospice team and discussed the possibility of transferring Tiffany to their dedicated facility in Denver. The team was gentle and honest. They couldn't guarantee she would survive the ride—every mile was a risk. But they had a room ready. It was peaceful. Quiet. It looked more like a home than a hospital.

Larry said yes.

On the afternoon of Wednesday, November 13th, the EMTs arrived, moving with a grace that went beyond professionalism. They handled her with reverence, as if they knew—somehow—that they were transporting more than a patient. They were carrying someone extraordinary. Tiffany was not just a woman fighting cancer. She was a mother, a friend, a wife, a leader… a light. They gave her as much dignity as possible, wrapping her in warmth and gentleness.

Larry followed behind in his car, his heart thrashing in his chest. Somewhere on that drive, his phone rang. It was Alexis, the young pro golfer from the Epson Tour, who had stayed with them the previous summer. She'd needed a place to stay during a Denver tournament, and Tiffany—without hesitation—opened their home, gave her a room, full use of a car, and warm meals at night. She treated Alexis like family because, to Tiffany, kindness was never something you earned—it was something you gave freely.

"Your wife… she's such an amazing woman," Alexis said, her voice trembling. "She made me feel so welcomed, I will never forget that."

Larry choked on his response, tears pooling behind his eyes. Another soul touched by Tiffany.

When Larry pulled into the hospice center, he was greeted by an older gentleman, one of those men whose eyes speak before his mouth does. He offered Larry a soft smile and a knowing nod—the kind of look shared only by those who've walked the same path. Larry nodded

FOREVER TIFFANY

back, grateful for the silent solidarity of someone who understood that today was sacred.

The room was warm and bright, unlike the cold hospital suite she had left. Large windows framed the Colorado sky, and a gentle breeze slipped through the slightly cracked glass, carrying the scent of the outdoors Tiffany always loved. A small patio lay just beyond the doors, a quiet place for reflection. The room didn't feel like the end—it felt like a pause. Like the world itself had taken a breath to hold space for what was coming.

They had dressed her in a simple brown dress—not her usual style, but still soft and sweet. Larry whispered a silent thanks to the staff for their care. He had spent so many hours at her bedside in recent weeks, brushing her hair, untangling it after all the wires and hospital routines. He had gently wiped her face and sat singing to her the same song, over and over—Chris Stapleton's "Joy of My Life."

He sang it again now, his voice low and cracking:

I tiptoed in the room

I know you got to have your rest

She says, 'Come lay beside me...'

I've been waitin' since you left...

She's sweet to me

Must be the luckiest man alive

Did I tell you, baby—

You are the joy of my life.

He'd sung it countless times, but every word still hit like the first. Because every word was true. From the first time he saw her sitting in that church pew, from the moment she stepped over him on the living room floor, Tiffany had been his angel, his muse, the joy of his life.

That night, Vicki insisted on staying. She curled up in a chair next to Tiffany, refusing to let her daughter be alone. Larry, exhausted and knowing Brennan needed him, went home. He needed to be a father now, too. He needed to steady the ship for the children Tiffany had loved into life.

Rylee stayed at the house with him, and Brennan and Patrick, a family clinging to each other in the storm. Larry told them he would return to the hospice in the morning. Patrick said he would follow around lunchtime and maybe stay the night. The house was quiet, too quiet.

At 5:30 a.m., Larry shot out of bed, his breath caught in his chest.

"I have to go," he said aloud, startling Rylee.

"Now?" she asked, groggy.

"Right now. I feel her calling me."

By 7:30 a.m., Larry and Rylee were walking into Tiffany's room. Nurses were gathered around her, their eyes gentle but urgent. One took Larry aside and said, "She's close now... It's time to call anyone who may want to be here."

Larry called Patrick.

Patrick didn't hesitate—he jumped into his car and raced up I-25, speeding north with tears in his eyes and prayers in his heart.

At 8:35 a.m., Larry was on his knees beside Tiffany's bed. One arm cradling her delicate shoulders, his other hand softly stroking her face. He kissed her cheeks, her forehead, her lips—each kiss a memory, each kiss a goodbye.

She took one final breath. And then, she was gone.

Just like that, Tiffany Lynn Blake returned home. Not to the house in Castle Rock, not to the room she had decorated with such precision, but to Heaven. To her father. To her Uncle Dan. To God, whom she had spoken to so often in private prayers.

FOREVER TIFFANY

Patrick arrived minutes later. He had driven as fast as he could, praying for one last moment, one last hand squeeze. He walked into the room and fell into silence. The grief wrapped around him like a tidal wave, crashing into his chest. Larry caught him, held him. There were no words. Only pain.

George walked in twenty minutes after that, not to say goodbye—he had done that in his own way—but to stand by Larry. To be his anchor. To make sure his brother could keep breathing.

Vicki was shattered. She had buried her husband far too young, and now... her daughter.

Larry stood at the edge of the room and looked at the people around him. People who loved Tiffany. People who were trying to be strong. And he thought about her final week. The way she had organized it like a conference, assigning time to the people she loved most, like she was saying goodbye... but in her way. Quiet. Intentional. Strong.

He realized she knew.

She'd known.

And she'd faced it with grace.

With power.

With love.

Tiffany Blake didn't just die—she left a legacy. She left a story.

And for the rest of their lives, Larry and the kids would carry that story with them. In their smiles. In their laughter. In their strength.

In the way they lived.

Because that's what Tiffany would have wanted. Not for them to dwell in sorrow, but to live.

Fully.

With love.

With light.

Just like she did.

Family came in from every direction—Florida, Indiana, Ohio, Arizona, Colorado—drawn like a constellation of love to the place where Tiffany's light had last shone. Susan flew in from the coastlines of Florida. Charlene and Kim, with soft Midwest hearts, came from Indianapolis. Scott and Sandy arrived from their small Indiana town. Amanda and Bob made the trip with Jacob from Ohio. Holly and Steve came in with their children, Tyler and Dylan, and of course, Larry and Diana—her second parents, her constants. They all came. Because she mattered. Because Tiffany had been a beacon in all their lives.

In the quiet moments of stillness leading up to this day, Larry had played out this scenario in his mind—quietly, painfully—wondering what if it came to this. And now, here they were. It was real. The ache was real.

He had originally imagined that maybe, just maybe, if that time ever came, they'd gather somewhere upscale, refined. Flemings, perhaps. A private room, soft lighting, and a touch of elegance to match the grace she carried through her life. But then, the truth hit him—Tiffany would have never wanted that. She was elegant, yes, but not pretentious. Her place was The Office, the bar where she'd laughed with friends, celebrated birthdays, toasted holidays, and Friday nights, and laughed with friends just because the music was good and the company was better.

He called Pablo.

Pablo, the owner, didn't hesitate. "The whole place is hers."

And just like that, Tiffany had one more reservation at her favorite place.

The Celebration of Life was nothing short of spectacular—Tiffany Style from the very first step inside. The venue was transformed into

FOREVER TIFFANY

a vibrant shrine of her world. Centerpieces adorned with Minnie Mouse ears sat on each table, some pink, some glittered, some Disney vintage, each with a single word floating beside them: Love. Family. Friendship. Forever. Her favorite words.

A long table stretched across the front, draped in soft white linens and tiny sparkling lights. At the center of that table was Tiffany's urn—graceful and simple—flanked by photos of her life and surrounded by fresh flowers in shades of blush and lilac. Behind her, a massive screen descended, playing her favorite songs while photographs danced across the display: baby Tiffany in a swimsuit by the lake, teenage Tiffany with her bright blonde hair and wild eyes, young mom Tiffany holding Patrick, then Rylee, and finally Brennan. Trips to Disneyland. Mother's Day brunches. Tuesday night trivia. Laughter, joy, life.

These were the moments that made her.

Holly was the first to speak—poised, strong, the kind of strength that comes from years of knowing someone so deeply, it feels like a piece of your own soul. She spoke of their friendship, of working together, of raising kids side by side. Of sisterhood. And when she closed, she read the words of David Romano's "When Tomorrow Starts Without Me."

Each line cut through the room like a thread woven into every broken heart.

I had so much to live for,

So much left yet to do.

It seemed almost impossible,

That I was leaving you.

Rylee spoke next, holding herself with a quiet bravery that mirrored her mother's. Larry Sr. stepped up, voice cracking but strong, the weight of two generations of grief folded into every syllable. Dylan followed, steady, heartfelt—her words painting Tiffany not just as an aunt, but as someone who made her feel seen and loved in all the little ways that matter most.

And then came Brennan.

He walked up with no paper. No phone. No cue cards. Just Brennan. Just the boy who had always had his mother's spark. He looked out at the hundreds of faces, took a breath, and then began to speak straight from the marrow of his heart.

He talked about how his mom always told him to find great friends. Not good ones. Great ones. Because one day, she wouldn't be there to hold his hand. And so he did. His best friend Piper was sitting right there, her hand gripped tightly in his, her face streaked with tears—and he thanked her out loud, right there in front of everyone.

His voice cracked as he said his only real regret: "I didn't say 'I love you' enough."

He said it now, again and again.

And somewhere, somehow—Tiffany heard him.

Finally, Larry stood. His legs numb, his hands trembling. For a moment, he looked up at the screen where Tiffany's face—beautiful, joyful, infinite—lit up the room. His mouth opened, and the words came, not from his lips, but from his soul.

"Tiffany was my everything. She was a shooting star racing across the solar system, and I was lucky enough to have spent just shy of twenty-five years with her. She changed not only me—she changed the world.

She was fire when we needed warmth.

She was a cold drink on a summer day.

She was my soft place to fall when life got hard.

She was my lover. My best friend. My angel.

FOREVER TIFFANY

And I know—without a doubt—that she's waiting for me on the other side.

And I will see her again.

She will always be... Forever Tiffany."

He stepped down, hands still trembling. Somewhere in the crowd, someone whispered, Amen.

Tears flowed.

At The Office, laughter rang through the room as stories were told, clinking glasses of champagne and raised beers in her honor. Tiffany would've loved it. In fact, she did love it. She loved this—the people she touched, the legacy she left behind. This wasn't a goodbye.

This was a promise.

A promise to live like she did.

With fire, with love, and with grace.

Forever Tiffany.

Forever in their hearts. Forever in their lives. Forever.

Made in the USA
Columbia, SC
22 June 2025

89032955-17e2-4058-8daa-d8c7119d8cd1R01